The 100
Most
Influential
Women
of All Time

The 100 Most Influential Women of All Time

A Ranking Past and Present

Deborah G. Felder

A Citadel Press Book
Published by Carol Publishing Group

For the girls: Heather and Elizabeth Baker; Colleen, Katie, Molly, and Elizabeth Burt; Katie Monopoli; Katy and Elissa Verrilli; and darling Abigail Zocco.

A Citadel Press Book
Published by Carol Publishing Group
Citadel Press is a registered trademark of Carol Communications, Inc.
Editorial Offices: 600 Madison Avenue, New York, N.Y. 10022
Sales and Distribution Offices: 120 Enterprise Avenue, Secaucus, N.J. 07094
In Canada: Canadian Manda Group, One Atlantic Avenue, Suite 105, Toronto, Ontario M6K 3E7
Queries regarding rights and permissions should be addressed to Carol Publishing Group, 600 Madison Avenue, New York, N.Y. 10022

Carol Publishing Group books are available at special discounts for bulk purchases, sales promotion, fund-raising, or educational purposes. Special editions can be created to specifications. For details, contact: Special Sales Department, Carol Publishing Group, 120 Enterprise Avenue, Secaucus, N.J. 07094

Design by Arthur Hamparian

Manufactured in the United States of America

10 9 8 7 6 5 4 3 2 1

Library of Congress Cataloging-in-Publication Data

Felder, Deborah G.
  The 100 most influential women of all time: a ranking past and present / Deborah G. Felder.
      p.   cm.
  Includes index.
  ISBN 0-8065-1976-2 (sc)
  1. Women—Biography. 2. Women—History. I. Title.
CT3202.F395   1995
920.72—dc20
  [B]   95-19222
                                          CIP

CONTENTS

INTRODUCTION

This book generated controversy right from the start. When I began the project, I sent out questionnaires containing a list of 150 influential women to the women's studies chairs and professors of American colleges and universities. I asked the professors to choose from the list their top ten most influential women and to add any women they felt had been left out and should be included in the book. Using their input together with my original list, I planned to compile a final list of one hundred women. Only three of the professors who responded to the survey felt they could not supply me with the information I had requested. One of the three wrote, "Frankly, I think your project is misguided and will lead to more criticism than you can imagine." Fair enough. *The 100 Most Influential Women* is the kind of book that begs readers to differ.

It was admittedly a difficult undertaking to choose who I considered to be the one hundred most influential women from past and current history's vast pool of extraordinary women. I decided that the most objective method was to select women from a variety of professions; hence the inclusion of such divergent talents as Marie Curie and Lucille Ball. Some professions yielded more influential women than others. There are more writers and social reformers, for example, than there are scientists. This is because the former professions have, in my view, produced women with wider and more singular spheres of influence. Many of the women in this book are so famous, it will come as no surprise to readers to see them here; others, while equally significant, are less well known. The mission, as I saw it, was to choose the women who have had the greatest and longest-lasting historical and cultural impact, have inspired us, and whose lives and work have much to teach us about past and present culture, society, and selfhood. When it came time to prepare the ranking of "my" women, I split the list into thirds according to the various criteria of influence mentioned above.

A few of the women's studies professors expressed the opinion that my list was too Western and too white. However, the additional choices these particular professors offered me for inclusion were either all Western and white or were of such limited influence I strongly felt I could not use them. It is right and proper that women of color should be represented here, and I have tried to ensure that this is the case, but I did not believe it would be productive to base my list primarily on a concept of equal diversity and alter the book's theme in order to please all—an impossible task in any case.

Another writer would probably have selected other women of influence and ranked them differently. I have offered readers my choices. If these choices lead to criticism, I hope positive discourse on the indisputable significance of women's past, present, and future contributions to the world will follow.

The 100
Most
Influential
Women
of All Time

1

Eleanor Roosevelt

1884–1962

> Her liberation was not an uncovenanted gift. She
> attained it only through a terrifying exertion of self-
> discipline....If her mastery of herself was never
> complete, if to the end of her life she could still
> succumb to private melancholy while calmly
> meeting public obligation, this makes her
> achievement and character all the more formidable.
>
> —ARTHUR SCHLESINGER
> From the Foreword to
> Joseph P. Lash's
> *Eleanor and Franklin*

Eleanor Roosevelt was my choice for number one from the
beginning. It seemed fitting that this gently stubborn woman,
who endured such emotional pain, worked so hard to achieve
liberation and to come to terms with the loss of illusion, and
whose infinitely wise statement, "No one can make you feel
inferior without your consent" speaks to all women, should
preside over the rest of the women in this book.

Historians and columnists have called Eleanor Roosevelt
"the most liberated American woman of this century" and "the
most influential woman of our times." To her husband, Franklin
Delano Roosevelt, she was "the most extraordinarily interesting
woman" he had ever known. She did not claim to be a feminist,
yet she was the personification of the strong, independent,
liberated woman. She used her influence as first lady and private
citizen to advance the cause of human rights, and in doing so,

became the conscience of the country and the most important public woman of the twentieth century.

Descended on both sides from distinguished colonial Roosevelts, Eleanor was a child of wealth and privilege, destined to enjoy all the perquisites of her class. But wealth and privilege could not make up for a grim childhood. Born in New York City, Anna Eleanor Roosevelt was the eldest of Elliott and Anna Hall Roosevelt's three children. Eleanor later characterized herself as a "solemn child, without beauty" and as having been "like a little old woman." Her beautiful, self-absorbed mother called Eleanor "Granny" and kept her reserves of affection for her sons. Most of the family thought young Eleanor "very plain" and "old-fashioned." Her only emotional refuge was her father. Elliott Roosevelt, the younger brother of Theodore, was a handsome, warm, generous man of humanitarian principles and weak character. An alcoholic, unreliable and self-destructive, he nevertheless adored "his own little Nell" and, writes Roosevelt biographer and friend Joseph Lash, "gave her the ideals that she tried to live up to all her life." She later wrote that her father was "the one great love of my life as a child."

By the time Eleanor was ten, both her parents and a younger brother had died, and for the next five years she endured the austere, emotionally cold household of her maternal grandmother. At fifteen, she was enrolled in Allenswood, a girls' school outside London that catered to a wealthy international clientele. The school was presided over by seventy-year-old Marie Souvestre, an inspired teacher and outspoken champion of liberal and unpopular causes. It was Souvestre who provided Eleanor with the maternal affection she had been denied, and under her mentorship, the young woman blossomed, gradually gaining self-confidence and excelling at everything she did. Roosevelt looked upon her three years at Allenswood as the happiest years of her life and later credited Souvestre with planting in her the seeds of social and political activism.

After Roosevelt returned to New York in 1902, she dutifully made her debut in society, but kept her focus on social service. She worked at settlement houses and visited factories and sweatshops as a member of the National Consumer's League, an organization committed to bettering conditions for workers, especially women. At the same time, she became secretly engaged organization committed to bettering conditions for workers, especially women. At the same time, she became secretly engaged to her fifth cousin, Franklin. They married on March 17, 1905, with Uncle Teddy, then president, giving the bride away. Between 1906 and 1916, Eleanor bore six children, one of whom died in infancy. Her joy in motherhood was suppressed by the continual presence of her domineering, indomitable mother-in-law, Sara, who ruled the Roosevelt household and looked upon the children as her own. Eleanor also faced the task of battling her shyness so that she could successfully host the many social events associated with her husband's rising political career.

In 1918, while living in Washington, where Franklin was serving as Assistant Secretary of the Navy, Eleanor discovered her husband's affair with her social secretary, Lucy Mercer. As Eleanor later wrote, "the bottom dropped out of my own particular world." The discovery shattered her ideal of marriage, but it also enabled her to explore the possibilities of independence and, according to historian Doris Kearns Goodwin, left her "free to define a new and different partnership with her husband." She became active in the League of Women Voters and the Women's Trade Union League and worked to obtain maximum-hour and minimum-wage laws for women.

Eleanor Roosevelt's public life and political activism expanded still further after her husband was stricken with polio in 1921. During FDR's 1932 presidential campaign and throughout his presidency, she traveled extensively, lecturing, observing conditions, and then reporting the needs and concerns of the Americans she saw and met to her husband. She worked to bring more women into government, to secure day care and national health care, and was active in encouraging youth groups, in combating poor housing and unemployment, and in working for civil rights.

In 1933 Eleanor Roosevelt became the first presidential wife to host a press conference. She continued to hold regular sessions with a press corps composed of women reporters. Beginning in 1935, she wrote a syndicated newspaper column, "My Day," and for a time hosted a radio program. It was in "My Day" that Roosevelt announced her resignation from the Daughters of the American Revolution (D.A.R.) because that organization had refused to allow African-American singer Marian Anderson to

Basis of Democracy (1940), *This I Remember* (1949), *On My Own* (1956), and *The Autobiography of Eleanor Roosevelt* (1961).

After Franklin Roosevelt's death in 1945, Eleanor Roosevelt continued her social activism. She served as United States delegate to the United Nations, chaired the United Nations Commission on Human Rights in 1946, and played a key role in drafting the Universal Declaration of Human Rights that was adopted by the United Nations in 1948. During the 1950s, she traveled abroad, spoke out against McCarthyism, continued to argue vigorously for civil rights, and was a staunch supporter of Israel. Her last major official position was as chair for President John F. Kennedy's Commission on the Status of Women, to which she was appointed in 1961. The following year she died of tuberculosis at the age of seventy-eight.

The disappointments and shocks of Eleanor Roosevelt's life might have made her bitter and cynical; instead they made her caring and compassionate. She reached out to the poor and disenfranchised and became their champion, and they loved her for it. In the end, her greatest influence may lie less in her achievements than in the quiet force of her remarkable character. She gave herself the gift of liberation and used that gift to give others a new sense of possibility. She was, writes Arthur Schlesinger, "a great and gallant—and above all, a profoundly good—lady."

2

Marie Curie

1867–1934

I am among those who think that science has great
beauty. A scientist in his laboratory is not only a
technician: he is also a child placed before natural
phenomena which impress him like a fairy tale.

> —MARIE CURIE
> Remarks given during a debate
> on "The Future of Culture," 1933

The only woman to win two Nobel Prizes—in physics and in
chemistry—Marie Curie is celebrated for her work on radioactivity and radium, an element she discovered. Her research, begun

with her husband, Pierre, and continued after his death in 1906, opened a new field in physics and developed the primary technique for exploring the interior of the atom, that tiny unit of matter that came to dominate twentieth-century science. Marie Curie became the world's most famous scientist, yet as her friend Albert Einstein once said of her, "[She] is, of all celebrated beings, the only one whom fame has not corrupted." For Curie, the work came first; her husband and two daughters second. Fame simply did not enter into the equation.

Marie Curie was born Marya Sklodowska in Warsaw, Poland, the youngest in a family of four girls and a boy. Her childhood was difficult, given the harsh rule of the Russians who occupied the country. Her father, Vladislav, a physics professor, lost his job when Russians took over teaching positions, and the family was forced to live in her mother's boarding school; later her father took in student boarders for tutoring. The Sklodowskas were very supportive of the educational aims of their daughters, and despite the enormous strain of attending school under the Russian regime, Marie excelled at her studies. Since the Russian government prohibited women from attending university and the Sklodowska family was not wealthy, Marie agreed to help support her sister Bronya through medical school in Paris, with the understanding that Bronya would in turn support her. Marie spent the next six years as a governess to a wealthy but intellectually small-minded family, whom she described to her cousin as "sunk in the darkest stupidity."

In 1891 Marie finally reached Paris, where she entered the Sorbonne, one of the few European universities that admitted women science students. She lived alone, subsisting on bread, fruit, and hot chocolate. As she later recalled, "This life, painful from certain points of view, had, for all that, a real charm for me. It gave me a very precious sense of liberty and independence." By 1894 she had earned the equivalent of a master's degree in both physics and mathematics. The same year, she met Pierre Curie, a professor and director of laboratories at the Municipal School of Physics and Chemistry. After their marriage in 1895, Marie Curie began independent research in her husband's laboratory on her dissertation topic, the new subject of radioactivity (a word she coined).

Curie's study of radioactivity had been inspired by the work of A. H. Becquerel, who had discovered radiation in uranium. Curie first attempted to measure radiation in all of the known elements. Next, she measured the strength of radiation in compounds with uranium and thorium and deduced that radioactivity originates within the atoms themselves. This discovery would revolutionize modern physics and turn attention toward the interior of the atom. In 1898 she reported a probable new element in uranium, and Pierre Curie joined her in her work. Together they discovered two new radioactive elements—polonium and radium. Polonium, named for Marie Curie's native country, has been used in small portable radiation sources, such as those used to run heart pacemakers and those used in the control of static electricity. Radium, a small particle of which can emit heat and light for many years, was said to have been the most important element discovered since oxygen. In order to isolate both elements, the Curies worked in an abandoned shed on the grounds of the School of Physics to purify large amounts of pitchblende, a mineral in which radioactive uranium is found. The work was painfully slow in the ramshackle facility, and Marie Curie later estimated it took them four years to accomplish what could have been done in one year if they had been able to work in a modern laboratory. In addition, their exposure to radiation was debilitating and was likely the cause of the frequent exhaustion and illnesses experienced by both Curies. In 1900 Marie Curie suggested that the alpha rays emitted from uranium might consist of particles ejected from the radioactive substance, a hypothesis that was later proved to be true.

In 1903 Curie submitted her research on radioactivity for her doctoral degree. It was judged to be the greatest scientific contribution ever made by a doctoral candidate. The same year, the Curies received the Nobel Prize for physics, which they shared with Becquerel. The prize made Marie Curie a celebrity and brought the Nobel Prizes in science and medicine to the attention of a world audience for the first time. Three years later, Pierre Curie was run over by a wagon while crossing a busy street and was killed almost instantly. Marie Curie continued her research alone and accepted Pierre's vacant chair at the Sorbonne, becoming the first woman professor in the college's 650-year history. In 1910 she succeeded in isolating pure radium metal, and the following year was awarded a second Nobel Prize, this one in chemistry. That year she also endured an explosive scandal over a love affair with married scientist Paul Longevin. The right-wing press, perpetrators of the scandal, cited Curie's Polish background and status as a woman scientist as strikes against her. "There is nothing in my acts," Curie wrote of the scandal, "which obliges me to feel diminished."

During the First World War, Curie and her older daughter, Irène, organized a mobile radiology service in the war zone. By the end of the war, the Curies' X-ray stations had treated more than a million patients. After the war, Marie served as director of the laboratory of radioactivity at the Curie Institute of Radium and, on the institute's behalf, made a successful fundraising tour to the United States. She was a member of the International Committee on Intellectual Cooperation for the League of Nations and the recipient of more than 125 awards and honorary titles. During the 1920s, despite failing eyesight, she continued to apply herself with characteristically singular dedication to her research. As she wrote to her sister Bronya in 1927, "I don't know whether I could live without the laboratory." It is almost certain that her constant exposure to radiation caused her health problems and hastened her death from leukemia at the age of sixty-seven. However, she lived to see her daughter, Irène Joliot-Curie, and her daughter's husband, Frédéric Joliot-Curie, discover artificial radioactivity, which would earn them a Nobel Prize in 1935.

As a pioneer who established atomic physics for study, Marie Curie's achievements unquestionably rival those of her male colleagues. As a woman in the field, her contribution is unprecedented. Other great women scientists had preceded Marie Curie and would follow her, but Curie was the first to gain the world's approbation. As her biographer, Robert Reid, observed, "Her uniqueness during her creative years lay in the simple fact of her sex. Until the name Marie Curie reached the headlines of popular newspapers there had been no woman who made a significant contribution to science....She had tackled her profession's problems as an equal to all the rest involved; and all the rest happened to be men. She had expected no concessions and none had been made. She had survived because she had made men believe that they were not just dealing with an equal, but with an intensive equal."

3

Margaret Sanger

1879–1966

For more than half a century, Sanger dedicated herself to the deceptively simple proposition that access to a safe and reliable means of preventing pregnancy is a necessary condition of women's liberation and, in turn, of human progress.

> —ELLEN CHESLER
> *Woman of Valor: Margaret Sanger and*
> *the Birth Control Movement in America*

In 1965, the year before Margaret Sanger's death, the United States Supreme Court struck down the one remaining state law prohibiting the private use of contraceptives. For Sanger, the leader of the birth-control movement in America, this constitutional protection of the right to practice contraception was the final triumph of her long crusade to emancipate women's bodies. Obdurate, uncompromising, and unapologetic, Margaret Sanger was an idealist who mastered practical politics during her hard-fought struggle against the ignorance, prejudice, religious tenets, and law that prevented this liberation.

Like many visionary iconoclasts, Sanger's particular mission had its roots in personal experience. She was born Margaret Higgins in Corning, New York, the sixth of eleven children born to Anne and Michael Higgins. Michael, a stone mason and a supporter of radical social causes, was an indifferent provider for his large family. Margaret was encouraged to be independent and self-reliant, and her childhood was characterized by rebellious clashes against authority. After an eighth-grade teacher made fun of a new pair of elegant gloves, a gift from her oldest sister, Margaret refused to return to the Corning school. Her two older sisters paid her tuition at Claverack College, a private coeducational preparatory school in the Catskills. After graduation, Margaret worked for a time as a teacher but felt herself temperamentally unsuited for the work. Summoned by her father, she returned home to nurse her mother, who was dying of tuberculosis. She would later attribute her mother's death at the young age of forty-nine to the strain of enduring eighteen pregnancies and raising eleven children. Although Margaret's father expected her to manage his household after her mother's death, she instead entered the nursing school of White Plains Hospital in White Plains, New York.

In 1902, just before she had completed two years of practical nursing and was about to begin a three-year degree program, she married architect William Sanger. She became pregnant six months later. After a difficult pregnancy, Sanger delivered a son, but her compromised physical condition forced her to return to the sanitarium where she had spent most of her confinement. It was expected that she would always be an invalid, but she rejected the prescribed treatment and left the sanitarium determined to regain a normal life. Her health improved and two more children followed. After eight years of marriage, Sanger became dissatisfied with her lot as a housewife and began working as a midwife and home nurse on the Lower East Side of New York City. In this neighborhood, she daily confronted the sickness, misery, helplessness, and death that came to the poverty-stricken young mothers, whose "weary misshapen bodies," Sanger later wrote, "were destined to be thrown on the scrap heap before they were thirty-five." Sanger was also involved in the radical labor movement in 1911. She joined the Industrial Workers of the World (the Wobblies) and participated in several strikes they organized in Pennsylvania, Massachusetts, and New Jersey. Increasingly, Sanger came to associate economic issues with women's demands for equal rights and, because of the suffering she had witnessed while nursing, with their need to obtain sexual and reproductive autonomy. For Sanger sexual reform became the primary feminist issue.

In 1912 Sanger began publishing a series of articles on female sexuality and contraception in the socialist weekly *The Call*. It was a risky undertaking since the dissemination of information on venereal disease, contraception, and abortion was prohibited by censorship laws that judged such subjects obscene. Even doctors could not give out birth control information. Sanger set out to remove the stigma of obscenity from contraception and to provide women with the birth control information they needed. In 1914 she traveled to Europe to investigate birth control technology and returned to New York determined to publicize her findings and push for the legalization of contraception. She founded the National Birth Control League and, under the slogan "No gods; no masters!", published a monthly magazine, *Woman Rebel*, which was designed to challenge the prohibition of information on sexuality and contraception. The magazine lasted for seven months until it was declared unmailable by the U.S. Post Office. Sanger was indicted for attempting to mail the magazine but managed to avoid imprisonment. She then published and distributed a how-to pamphlet of contraceptive advice, *Family Limitation*.

In 1916 Sanger opened the first U.S. birth control clinic, in Brooklyn, New York. The staff, consisting of Sanger, her sister, and a friend who spoke Yiddish, dispensed birth control advice and sold contraceptives and copies of an article titled "What Every Girl Should Know." After only ten days of operation, the clinic, already visited by five hundred women, was closed by the police, and Sanger was jailed.

Her trial made her a national figure and resulted in a small triumph for the movement: The court's judgment was worded in such a way that it allowed doctors to provide birth control advice under the guise of preventing venereal disease. After her release from prison, Sanger campaigned for doctor-staffed birth-control clinics and began publishing *The Birth Control Review.*

In 1921 Sanger organized the American Birth Control League, which later became the Planned Parenthood Federation of America. She also opened the Birth Control Clinical Research Bureau in New York City, the first doctor-staffed birth-control clinic in the United States. It became the model for over three hundred clinics established by Sanger throughout the country. She was tireless in fundraising efforts and in initiating legal suits designed to legitimize the teaching of birth control information in medical schools. In 1937 the American Medical Association finally recognized contraception as a subject that should be taught in medical school.

Sanger, who had divorced William Sanger in 1920 and married millionaire oil manufacturer J. Noah Slee in 1922, moved from New York to Tucson, Arizona, where the couple had built a retirement home. Her repeated call to slow population growth was opposed until after World War II when the awareness of the population explosion legitimized and accelerated the urgency of Sanger's appeals. In 1952 she became the first president of the International Planned Parenthood Federation. She campaigned actively for a safe female-controlled contraceptive device, and her effort led to the development of the first birth control pill in 1960. During the final year of her life, family planning was incorporated into the foreign policy and domestic public health and social welfare programs of the Johnson administration.

Birth control has continued to face opposition from religious organizations, and the institutionalization of family planning has been criticized by those who view it as a form of social engineering. The legalization of abortion in 1973 further complicated the issue of reproductive rights. But few women would wish to return to the days before Margaret Sanger began her crusade, when these rights did not exist. As her biographer Ellen Chesler has observed: "Every woman in the world today who takes her sexual and reproductive autonomy for granted should venerate Margaret Sanger."

4

Margaret Mead

1901–1978

As the traveler who has once been from home is wiser than he who has never left his own doorstep, so a knowledge of one other culture should sharpen our ability to scrutinize more steadily, to appreciate more lovingly, our own.

—MARGARET MEAD
Coming of Age in Samoa

15

In 1925, twenty-three-year-old Margaret Mead, armed with a camera, a typewriter, and a newly acquired Ph.D. in anthropology, embarked upon her first field trip to the Samoan Islands. There she studied Samoan culture, with a particular emphasis on adolescent girls. Mead's aim was to contrast the maturation of Samoan young people with that of their Western counterparts and to question whether the upheavals suffered by Western adolescents were the result of biology or of Western culture. After living and working alongside Samoan villagers for several months, Mead concluded that culture was the primary determining factor in adolescent behavior. In 1928 she published *Coming of Age in Samoa: A Psychological Study of Primitive Youth for Western Civilization.* Mead's controversial landmark study became a bestseller that influenced many young people to become anthropologists and is still the most widely read book in the field of anthropology. It made Margaret Mead famous and launched a career that would firmly establish her as a pioneer and research innovator in social anthropology.

Margaret Mead was born into a progressive and unconventional Philadelphia family on December 16, 1901. She was the oldest of the five children of Edward Mead, an economist and professor of finance at the Wharton School, and Emily Fogg Mead, a sociologist, teacher, feminist, and suffragist. Margaret was chiefly educated at home by her grandmother, Martha Ramsey Mead, a qualified teacher and principal. "My family," Mead later wrote, "deeply disapproved of any school that kept children chained to their desks, indoors, for long hours every day." Of her grandmother, she wrote: "She thought that memorizing mere facts was not very important.... The result was that I was not well drilled in geography or spelling. But I learned to observe the world around me and to note what I saw."

In 1919 Mead entered De Pauw University, where she quickly became disillusioned with the snobbish fraternity- and sorority-driven social life on campus. Mead and four friends formed "The Minority," a diverse group that included an African American, a Catholic, and the only Jew at De Pauw. Seeking a more academically stimulating atmosphere, Mead transferred to Barnard College in her sophomore year. In her senior year, she began studying with Franz Boas, one of the world's ranking anthropologists and a strong opponent of the theory of racial determinism. Mead, raised to believe in racial equality, was receptive to Boas's refutation of the then-popular theory that race and character were closely connected. She was also intrigued by Boas's belief that the comprehensive study of other societies could help people to better understand their own culture. Mead's growing interest in anthropology was further strengthened by her close friendship with Ruth Benedict, Boas's teaching assistant.

After graduation from Barnard and marriage to seminarian Luther Cressman, Mead became one of Boas's four graduate students at Columbia University and completed her M.A. in psychology. Boas wanted Mead to do her field work among Native Americans, his own area of interest, but Mead insisted on investigating the less assimilated cultures of Polynesia. Boas gave in, and the result was *Coming of Age in Samoa*.

From 1926 to 1928 Mead worked as an assistant curator at the American Museum of Natural History. She divorced Cressman and undertook her second field trip to study Manus children in the Admiralty Islands of New Guinea. She was accompanied by New Zealand anthropologist Reo Fortune, whom she had met on her journey home from Samoa, and married en route to New Guinea. The outcome of Mead's field work with the Manus was *Growing Up in New Guinea*, another commercial and critical success. Mead's findings suggested that the impact of new and positive influences on children was ultimately limited by adult attitudes. In order for children to grow up free from prejudice and other undesirable traits, she argued, parents and educators would first need to focus on changing their own values.

Mead's subsequent studies of gender roles among three disparate cultures of New Guinea (1930–1933) yielded what she would consider to be the most important work of her career, *Sex and Temperament in Three Primitive Societies* (1935). By documenting the variations in social position of men and women in all three cultures, Mead found evidence to support her belief that gender roles were not universal and that temperament was determined by culture, not biology. Both men and women developed the personalities their society considered acceptable for their sex. As a woman who did not conform to the "acceptable" image of the American wife and mother and who had pursued a career in what was traditionally a man's field, Mead's findings held great personal significance for her. "It was exciting," Mead wrote in her autobiography, *Blackberry Winter*, "to strip off the layers of culturally attributed expected behavior and to feel that one knew at last who one was."

Mead divorced Fortune in 1935. The following year she married English biologist and anthropologist Gregory Bateson and set off with him on a third field trip, this one to Bali. During their two years in Bali, Mead and Bateson took and annotated twenty-five thousand photographs, many of which appeared in their joint book, *Balinese Character: A Photographic Analysis*. Mead and Bateson's unique study of Balinese life had a large impact on other anthropologists.

After the birth of her daughter, Mary Catherine Bateson, in 1939, Mead began work on *And Keep Your Powder Dry* (1942), an analysis of contemporary American character outlined against the primitive cultures she had studied. In 1944, Mead founded the Institute for Intercultural Studies, a nonprofit corporation, which, through grants, helped to finance work by young anthropologists. In *Male and Female: A Study of Sexes in a Changing World*, published in 1949, Mead explored male-female relationships, balancing an examination of biological differences with the cultural factors that determine gender roles. In the 1950s she documented the postwar changes taking place in the rapidly disappearing primitive cultures of New Guinea.

Margaret Mead became an adjunct professor in anthropology at Columbia in 1954, lectured at a number of other colleges, and was made curator emeritus of ethnology at the American Museum of Natural History in 1965. She dealt with the rift between generations in *Culture and Commitment* (1970), was an outspoken leader of the feminist movement of the 1970s, and lent support to such diverse causes as environmentalism, mental health, scientific freedom, improving race relations, and strengthening the family. She died of cancer in 1978, at age seventy-six.

Margaret Mead wrote over forty books and over a thousand monographs and articles. Her influence in her field was enormous, and she helped social anthropology to come of age as a science. But possibly her greatest contribution was that she made anthropology accessible to the nonscientist. She invited millions of people to look with her at other cultures and, as she wrote, "to cherish the life of the world."

5

Jane Addams

1860–1935

She had compassion without condescension. She had
pity without retreat into vulgarity. She had infinite
sympathy for common things without forgetfulness of
those that are uncommon.

    That, I think, is why those who have known her say
she was not only good, but great.

                —WALTER LIPPMANN
                  Quoted in Allan F. Davis, *American Heroine,*
                  The Life and Legend of Jane Addams

Jane Addams was described in polls during her lifetime as
America's "most useful citizen" and "the world's greatest woman."
Addams is best known as the founder and mainstay of Chicago's

Hull House, the first major social settlement house in the United States. What is less well known is that she was also a founder of the American Civil Liberties Union, the organizer and chair of the Women's Peace Party, and cofounder of the Women's International League for Peace and Freedom. In 1912 she became the first woman to make a nominating speech at a national political convention when she seconded the nomination of Progressive Party presidential candidate Theodore Roosevelt. She was also the first American woman to receive the Nobel Peace Prize (1931).

Born in Cedarville, Illinois, Jane Addams was the eighth child of John and Sarah Addams. Jenny, as she was called, was two when her mother died; five years later, John Addams married Anna Haldeman, a widow with two sons. Although Jane developed an affection for her stern but kindly stepmother, and was especially close to her stepbrother George, her primary relationship as a child and young adult was with her father. A Quaker known as "the king gentleman of the district," John Addams was a wealthy businessman, state senator, abolitionist, and friend of Abraham Lincoln. He was highly regarded by his neighbors and constituents for his moral integrity, honesty, generosity, sound judgment, and unswerving commitment to his convictions. These qualities, plus an belief in the simple life and the importance of civic responsibility, were inculcated into Jane Addams from an early age.

After graduating from high school, Jane followed the example of her older sisters and enrolled in the Rockford Female Seminary in Rockford, Illinois. An outstanding student, she designed her courses to meet the qualifications for a B.A. degree at nearby Beloit College for men and decided, with her father's approval, to study medicine with the intention of working and living with the poor. Soon after her graduation from Rockford in 1881, John Addams died of a ruptured appendix. His death was, Addams later said, "the greatest sorrow that can ever come to me." She felt "purposeless" and "without ambition," but continued with her plans to attend the Women's Medical College of Philadelphia. However, she soon discovered that medicine was not the right vocation for her. Depressed and suffering from severe back pain, she dropped out of school and underwent an operation to remedy a congenital curvature of the spine. In 1883, after a long convalescence, she wrote to her close friend, Ellen

Gates Starr, that she had "accepted the advice given to every exhausted American, 'Go abroad.'"

The poverty Addams witnessed in London's East End seemed to restore her determination to help the poor. During a second European trip in 1887, Addams, accompanied by Ellen Starr, visited Toynbee Hall, a London settlement house founded by social reformer Arnold Toynbee, the uncle of historian Arnold Joseph Toynbee. Addams was impressed by the British concept of aiding the poor, which rejected the traditional charity approach of sending servants to poor families with baskets of provisions in favor of enlisting volunteers who actually lived among the people they hoped to help. It was a concept Addams embraced as she began to formulate and then realize her plans for a settlement house in the United States.

In 1889 Addams and Starr moved to Chicago and began seeking financial support for their settlement house from church groups, civic organizations, and philanthropists. Addams was, for the most part, successful in mustering support for "a house, easily accessible, ample in space, hospitable and tolerant in spirit, situated in the midst of the large foreign colonies which so easily isolate themselves in American cities. " While visiting Chicago's Nineteenth Ward, a once-prosperous area then inhabited by European immigrants, Addams and Starr found a rundown but structurally sound two-story mansion that had been built by real estate developer Charles Hull in 1856. Addams and Starr secured a lease and, after several months of renovation and refurnishing, moved into Hull House.

By the end of the year, twenty volunteers lived at Hull House, and others worked there on a daily or weekly basis. The services Addams and her staff provided proved invaluable to the struggling immigrant community. Hull House offered day care; a kindergarten; a music school; vocational, recreational, and cultural programs; and classes in sewing, cooking, dressmaking, and millinery. "It was obvious," writes Addams's nephew and biographer, James Linn, "that if you went to the House you were welcome...if you let the young women know there was anything they could do for you, they did it if they could."

Addams's commitment to social reform extended beyond the programs of Hull House. In 1891 she started the Jane Club, a successful experiment in cooperative housing for young women factory workers who had lost their homes while on strike. She worked to obtain the first Factory Inspection Act, which regulated the sanitary conditions of sweatshops; published a report on child labor, which led to passage of a law raising the working age to fourteen; served on arbitration committees during labor disputes; and successfully campaigned for better sanitation, public baths, and municipal playgrounds. Sensitive to the hardships of Chicago's African Americans, Addams founded the Wendell Phillips Settlement to provide community services for black residents in a nearby racially mixed neighborhood, attended meetings of the National Association of Colored Women, spoke out forcefully against lynchings, and frequently invited eminent black leaders, such as Booker T. Washington, to speak at Hull House. When the NAACP was formed in 1909, Addams was a member of its executive committee.

Once dubbed by the press as "the only American saint," Addams's reputation was nearly shattered by her outspoken pacifist stance during World War I. She regained a measure of public respect when she toured the United States lecturing on food conservation and preservation for Food Administration director Herbert Hoover. However, she was again cast in the role of national villain after she pleaded for food relief for German children and defended the rights of those arrested during the postwar Red Scare. Emotionally bloodied but not defeated, Addams spent much of the 1920s in Europe and Asia working on behalf of the Women's International League for Peace and Freedom. By the 1930s, with the arrival of the Great Depression and the threat of a new war in Europe, Addams's pacifism seemed reasonable rather than revolutionary, and her achievements in social reform were once again viewed as invaluable contributions to American society.

In the early 1930s Addams served with the Public Works Administration under President Franklin D. Roosevelt and continued to manage Hull House. After her death in 1935, her body lay in state at Hull House for two days while thousands of mourners filed past her coffin. The work of this intrepid crusader for social justice continues to inspire and instruct us. As Allan F. Davis observes in *American Heroine*, "Those seeking to improve life in the cities and to promote peace in the world have to build on what Jane Addams and her co-workers constructed."

6

Mary Wollstonecraft

1759–1797

Many millions have died and been forgotten in the hundred and thirty years that have passed since she was buried; and yet we read her letters and listen to her arguments and consider her experiments...and realize the high-handed and hot-blooded manner in which she cut her way to the quick of life....We hear her voice and trace her influence even now among the living.

—Virginia Woolf
Essays: "Mary Wollstonecraft Godwin"

Mary Wollstonecraft deserves her ranking among the top ten most influential women. To her goes the honor of being the first great feminist writer. Her seminal work, *A Vindication of the Rights of Women*, has been widely held to be the cornerstone document of the women's rights movement. Writing in an age of revolution that championed equality and the rights of men, Mary Wollstonecraft broadened the argument to include women. Because she was a woman who dared to advance such radical notions, she was branded by her opponents "a philosophizing serpent...that hyena in petticoats." To scores of women, she became, and remains, a feminist saint.

Wollstonecraft's theories on women's education and status were based mainly on her own experiences. Her father, Edward, gave up his trade as a silk weaver and moved his wife and six children from London to Yorkshire, where he tried his hand at farming. Mary received some formal schooling and shared in the lessons of a close friend whose father was a schoolmaster. Edward Wollstonecraft's failure as a farmer caused him to become increasingly bitter and violent, and he began to drink and to abuse his family. As Wollstonecraft's husband and first biographer, William Godwin, writes, "She would often throw herself between the despot and his victim, with the purpose to receive upon her own person the blows that might be directed against her mother." It became clear to Mary that she would have to earn a living to support herself and her family. At the time, options for respectable women were few: They could work as a companion, a teacher, or a governess. Wollstonecraft tried all three. At nineteen, she left home to become the live-in companion of a Mrs. Dawson and accompanied her to the resort town of Bath, where she was exposed to the superficial high life of fashionable families of leisure. In 1783 Wollstonecraft interceded on behalf of her younger sister, Eliza, whose marriage was duplicating the pattern of domestic violence of their own family. With the aid of her close friend Fanny Blood, Wollstonecraft took Eliza away from her husband, and the three opened a school in Newington Green. There she wrote *Thoughts on the Education of Daughters*, in which she argued that a girl's intellect should be developed. In an age that reserved the intellect for men and emotions for women, such a philosophy was viewed as radical.

The school eventually foundered, and Wollstonecraft next accepted a position in Ireland as governess to the children of Lord and Lady Kingsborough. She entered service at the great Kingsborough mansion "with the same kind of feeling as I should have if I was going to the Bastille." Her independence and rebelliousness made her service as a governess intolerable, and she eventually left for London, where her publisher, Joseph Johnson, gave her lodging and sufficient editorial work to support herself. Johnson was at the center of intellectual London life, and his circle included the Anglo-American political theorist and writer Thomas Paine, the philosopher William Godwin, and the poet William Blake. Most were free-thinking liberals, and Mary shared their interests as she supported herself writing articles for Johnson's *Analytical Review* and preparing English adaptations of continental works.

The central event that absorbed Mary and her circle was the French Revolution. In general, the English greeted the overthrow of an outdated despotism with enthusiasm. However, Edmund Burke's 1790 conservative treatise, *Reflections on the Revolution in France*, which argued in favor of the English monarchical status quo over the upheavals in France, helped turn English opinion against the Revolution. Wollstonecraft's *Vindication of the Rights of Men* was among the first rebuttals of Burke's position. In it, she challenged Burke's complacence, focusing less on France and more on the injustices at home. It was Wollstonecraft's first popular success, and it was also one of the earliest political essays by a woman.

In 1792 Wollstonecraft turned to the issue of women in *A Vindication of the Rights of Women*, an unprecedented work in the history of social change. Wollstonecraft's unique contribution was to include the condition and the status of women in the debate over social reform. Her intention was to remove the stigma attached to being a woman, and she also argued that women must cease to be trivial-minded, defined solely by society in a subservient and dependent role, in order to become rational and useful citizens. She wrote: "It is time to effect a revolution in female manners—time to restore them their lost dignity—and make them, as part of the human species, labour by reforming themselves, to reform the world." Her proposals for educational equality of girls were equally radical. *Vindication* is a classic that has long been cited by feminist leaders as the central work in their decision to struggle for social and political freedom for women.

In 1793 Wollstonecraft visited Paris to observe firsthand the Reign of Terror. There she met a number of the revolution's leading political figures. She also began an affair with American adventurer Gilbert Imlay, who deserted her after she gave birth to their daughter, Fanny. Despondent, Wollstonecraft attempted to commit suicide by jumping off Putney Bridge into the Thames. She was rescued, and in 1796 married William Godwin. One year later, Mary Wollstonecraft Godwin died within days of giving birth to a second daughter, Mary, who would later marry the poet Percy Bysshe Shelley and create a classic of her own, the ever-popular *Frankenstein*.

Wollstonecraft's achievement, purchased by a hard-fought struggle for independence and security, was to begin the debate to reclaim from men the equality, freedom of choice, and opportunity women deserved and were denied. The debate would not lead to battle until the middle of the next century when feminists would rediscover and embrace the work of a woman ahead of her time.

Susan B. Anthony

1820–1906

Elizabeth Cady Stanton

1815–1902

In writing we did better work together than either could do alone. While she is slow and analytical in composition, I am rapid and synthetic. I am the better writer, she the better critic. She supplied the facts and statistics, I the philosophy and rhetoric, and together we made arguments which have stood unshaken by the storms of thirty long years; arguments that no man has answered.

—ELIZABETH CADY STANTON
On her partnership with Susan B. Anthony,
History of Woman Suffrage, Vol. 1

One of the most effective political teams in history, Elizabeth Cady Stanton and Susan B. Anthony are renowned for spearheading the suffragist movement in nineteenth-century America. Together they waged an unceasing battle for women's rights, withstanding virulent attacks from both men and women, and created a movement that would represent the critical first wave of American feminism.

Born in Adams, Massachusetts, Susan Brownell Anthony was the second of Daniel and Lucy Anthony's six children. Daniel was a Quaker abolitionist who ran a cotton mill. Sent to a Quaker school in Philadelphia, Susan began her career as a teacher, eventually becoming headmistress of Canajoharie Academy in New York. In 1849 she rejoined her family, which had moved to a farm in Rochester, New York, and became active in both the antislavery and temperance movements.

Elizabeth Cady was born in Johnstown, New York, where her father was a judge and a state legislator. After graduating from the Troy Female Seminary, she read law with her father and became involved with the abolitionist movement. She met and married Henry Stanton, an antislavery activist, in 1840. In 1848 Stanton and Lucretia Mott, a Quaker minister and social reformer, organized the first women's rights convention, held in Seneca Falls, New York. A highlight of the convention was Stanton and Mott's Declaration of Sentiments, a paraphrased version of the Declaration of Independence, which called for property rights for women, equal pay for equal work, and, despite Mott's objections, women's suffrage. Of the 260 women and 40 men who attended the convention, only one, Charlotte Woodward, lived to see women win the right to vote.

In 1851 Stanton met Susan B. Anthony in Seneca Falls, after a lecture given by celebrated abolitionist William Lloyd Garrison. Anthony was thirty-one, reserved and single; Stanton was thirty-six, outgoing and the mother of three boys. They complemented each other perfectly: Anthony became the movement's logician and organizer; Stanton its theorist and emotional center. In 1852 Anthony broke with the Sons of Temperance for its refusal to grant equal rights to women in the movement and established the Women's New York State Temperance Society, the first such society formed by and for women. With Stanton, the society's first president, she organized a statewide temperance meeting for women, where Stanton shocked the five hundred present with her demand that drunkenness become legal grounds for divorce. Thereafter, Stanton pushed the women's movement with ever more radical notions, while Anthony mobilized and consolidated support. Eventually both realized that it would be necessary to establish women's legal rights before equality could be gained, and they shifted their emphasis from temperance to winning property rights for women. Petition drives followed and persistent appeals to the New York State legislature met with repeated failures until 1860, when the Married Women's Property Act was passed and became the model for similar laws in other states.

During the Civil War, Anthony became increasingly involved in the antislavery movement, and she and Stanton led petition drives for full emancipation. After the Fourteenth Amendment extended equal rights to African Americans and the Fifteenth Amendment guaranteed the right to vote to all citizens, Anthony and Stanton argued that since women were also citizens, they too should be allowed to vote. They formed the National Women's Suffrage Association in 1869 and broadcast their views in *The Revolution*, a feminist newspaper published by Anthony and coedited by Stanton. In 1872 Anthony and twelve other suffragists were arrested for voting in the presidential election. Anthony was convicted and fined, but her plan to contest her conviction in court was thwarted when she was released and her fine canceled. Both Anthony and Stanton began to realize that only the passage of a separate constitutional amendment would secure the vote for women.

During the 1870s and 1880s suffrage became Anthony's single-minded cause, while Stanton expanded her activism to include campaigns for broader women's rights reforms. Despite their diverging interests, Anthony and Stanton collaborated on a three-volume work, *History of Woman Suffrage*, published one volume at a time between 1881 and 1886. Each year, beginning in 1878, a constitutional amendment extending voting rights to women was presented to Congress; each year it was ignored or rejected. Neither Anthony nor Stanton lived to see women given the vote nationally; that battle would be won in 1920 by the next generation of activists trained and inspired by them.

Late in life, Anthony wrote: "We little dreamed when we began this contest that half a century later we would be compelled to leave the finish of the battle to another generation of women. But our hearts are filled with joy to know that they enter this task equipped with a college education, with business experience, with the freely admitted right to speak in public—all of which were denied to women fifty years ago." Succeeding generations of women would not have been so well equipped to carry on the struggle without Anthony's and Stanton's untiring efforts on their behalf.

9

Harriet Tubman

1820(?)–1913

Well has she been called "Moses," for she has been a
leader and deliverer unto hundreds of her people.

—SARAH H. BRADFORD
Scenes in the Life of Harriet Tubman, 1869

Harriet Tubman's remarkable exploits and extraordinary
courage as the first woman "conductor" on the Underground
Railroad are legendary. But General Tubman, as fiery abolitionist
John Brown called her, did not end her career with the rescue of

some three hundred slaves. She went on to serve as a nurse and spy during the Civil War and to work on behalf of former slaves in the South. Tubman's achievements and inspirational leadership justify her high ranking here.

Harriet Tubman was born into slavery on the eastern shore of Maryland. She was the daughter of Benjamin Ross and Harriet Green, whose parents had been brought from Africa in chains. Originally named Araminta, Tubman later adopted her mother's first name. She was put to work when she was five, first as a domestic servant and maid, and then as a field hand. She was a slightly built woman, barely five feet tall, but had great strength and withstood many physical adversities, such as a fractured skull she sustained when she was struck on the head by a two-pound weight thrown at another slave by the overseer. For the rest of her life Tubman suffered from seizures as a result of this near-fatal blow.

In 1844, while still a slave, she married John Tubman, a former slave. Five years later, her master died, sparking rumors that his slaves were to be sold out of state. Tubman, guided by the North Star, escaped to Philadelphia, and then went further north, to Saint Catharines, Ontario. She recalled to her biographer, Sarah H. Bradford, her first reaction when she realized that she had reached freedom and safety in the North: "When I found I had crossed that line, I looked at my hands to see if I was the same person. There was such a glory over everything." However, Tubman's heart was still "down in the old cabin quarters, with the old folk and my brothers and sisters." Over a ten-year period, she made approximately nineteen trips to the South to lead slaves through the Underground Railroad to safety in Canada. She eluded the slave-catchers and their bloodhounds, and endured attacks and beatings, persisting in her mission despite a $40,000 reward offered by slaveholders for her capture, dead or alive. By 1857 Tubman had managed to free her entire family, including her parents, then over seventy years old. Once her "passengers" were underway Tubman insisted there was no turning back. Carrying a loaded rifle, she would convince the fainthearted at gunpoint to "live North or die here."

Tubman spoke at numerous meetings and conventions, winning the admiration and respect of prominent abolitionists, including Frederick Douglass, who wrote to her, "Excepting John

Brown—of sacred memory—I know of no one who has willingly encountered more perils and hardships to serve our enslaved people than you have." She lived in Saint Catharines until about 1858, when Republican senator William H. Seward, an antislavery advocate, sold her a small farm in Auburn, New York. During the Civil War she enlisted for war work and was sent to Beaufort, South Carolina, where she nursed wounded soldiers and helped educate newly freed slaves. She spied for the Union Army by going behind Confederate lines to gather information from slaves and facilitated Union raids by organizing a group of African-American men to scout the inland waterways of South Carolina.

After the war Tubman labored for the welfare of the emancipated slaves, establishing schools for freedmen in North Carolina. She worked with black women's organizations and was a delegate to the first convention of the National Federation of Afro-American Women, in 1896. Her talk at that first meeting was "More Homes for Our Aged." The same year, she purchased twenty-five acres of land adjoining her home in Auburn. There she established the Harriet Tubman Home for Indigent Aged Negroes, supported after her death by friends, former slaves, and Auburn citizens. Tubman's final years were spent in poverty. Thirty years after the end of the Civil War she was finally granted a government pension of twenty dollars a month in recognition of her war service. Harriet Tubman died of pneumonia in her ninety-third year. She remains today an enduring and inspirational figure in the history of human liberation.

10

The Virgin Mary

c. 1st century B.C.—1st century A.D.

A myth of such dimension is not a simple story, or a collection of stories, but a magic mirror like the Lady of Shalott's, reflecting a people and the beliefs they produce, recount, and hold....For the Virgin is a protagonist in the drama of the Incarnation and the Redemption of Christ, and consequently is the personal salvation of each individual who feels himself to belong to Christian history and professes Christian beliefs.

—MARINA WARNER
*Alone of All Her Sex: The Myth
and the Cult of the Virgin Mary*

Mary, the mother of Jesus, is undoubtedly the most famous woman of all time. Yet her fame and influence does not stem from her life and work (we know little of either) but rather from the purposes she has served for Christians over the centuries. More a myth and an article of faith than a flesh-and-blood woman, Mary reflects the times and culture of those who view her as an embodiment of their faith, hopes, and desires. She also reveals much about how women have been seen over time, becoming for each age a guide to the ideal and the perfect.

The Bible gives little information concerning the historical Mary. Tradition has it that she was the daughter of Joachim and Anne, and that she was presented and dedicated at the temple as a virgin. The Gospel writers—Matthew, Mark, Luke, and John— differ in the details of her life and the importance of her role. Mark mentions her only once by name as the mother of Jesus, and in chapter 3:31–35, she makes a brief appearance, which only serves to provide Jesus with another teaching lesson for the multitude ("For whosoever shall do the will of God, the same is my brother, and my sister, and my mother"). John, the last of the Gospel writers, shows Mary twice: at the feast of Cana with Jesus and at the foot of the Cross during Jesus' crucifixion. Our knowledge of Mary is largely derived from the stories of Jesus' infancy told by Matthew and Luke, written, it is thought, more than eighty years after the events described. Both agree that Jesus was of the house of David and was born in Bethlehem; his father was Joseph, and his mother was named Mary. In other details the stories are different.

According to Matthew, after Mary is "found with child by the Holy Ghost," an angel announces to Joseph that the child will be the savior and that Joseph should not condemn his wife. When the child is born in Bethlehem, an angel warns Joseph to flee with his family to Egypt to avoid Herod's wrath. After Herod's death, the family returns to Nazareth. It is Luke who puts Mary at the center of the Christian drama. He tells of the angel Gabriel's visit and his announcement of Mary's destiny: "Blessed art thou among women." Mary visits her cousin Elisabeth, herself pregnant with the child who will become John the Baptist, and is again made aware of her blessed status. Luke then tells the nativity story of Jesus' birth. We next see the twelve-year-old Jesus and his parents in Jerusalem for Passover. As Mary and Joseph set out for Nazareth, they discover their child is missing. They find him three days later in discussion with the elders in the temple. While Mary does not understand Jesus' response to his parents' anxiety—"Wist ye not that I must be about my Father's business?"—she nevertheless keeps this and other sayings of her son "in her heart."

From these sketchy and contradictory details, the myth and legend of Mary has been created over time in support of the divinity of Jesus. Each Marian aspect becomes important as an article of faith but also reflects attitudes about women, who have been judged in her image. At the center of the Mary story is her Immaculate Conception. Mary's virginity establishes her in Christian dogma as pure, innocent, and free from sin, and establishes sex as a barrier to spiritual purity. Although Matthew writes that Joseph "took unto him Mary his wife and knew her not till she had brought forth her first born son," and other sources suggest that Jesus had brothers, the Catholic Church has insisted on Mary's perpetual virginity and purity. As Jesus' mother, Mary is also the Madonna, the emblem of motherhood, and has been associated with the Church itself as mother. Finally, in the stories concerning her direct Assumption, a doctrine that did not appear until the fifth century A.D., Mary is celebrated as the crowned Queen of Heaven, which establishes her nobility and is very much a reflection of the feudal hierarchy of the Middle Ages. Both human and divine, Mary has, therefore, served as an intermediary between God and mortal, and devotion to her as spiritual intercessor has dominated Catholic worship and has been criticized by Protestants as Mariolatry, the Catholic Church's cult of Mary.

As a symbol, Mary has, from medieval times, inspired architects, poets, and painters as the exemplum of perfection, of goodness, purity, and motherhood. Yet the "Madonna and Child" divinity depicted in art separates these ideals from humanity, and Mary's reputation as a virgin mother provides a contradiction only resolved by faith. In Jungian terms, Mary represents a man's need for the virgin mother, a symbol "so powerful," writes Marina Warner, "that it has a dynamic and irrepressible life of its own." Women have been reflected through the "magic mirror" of the myth of Mary, and have been measured by the lofty standard of perfection encased and codified in the dogma and ritual that has turned Jesus' mother into an obscure object of desire, as well as a sustaining source of inspiration and redemption.

11

Georgia O'Keeffe
1887–1986

Her story was not only that of a gifted artist, but also of a forceful American woman with extraordinary qualities of intellect and character....Georgia O'Keeffe has given us great gifts not only in her paintings but also in the very way she has lived her life.

—LAURIE LISLE
Portrait of an Artist:
A Biography of Georgia O'Keeffe

Artist Georgia O'Keeffe's influence in her field lies with her innovative technique of magnifying and framing parts of familiar objects found in nature so that they take on new and startling shapes and colors. O'Keeffe is known as an abstract painter, but during her lifetime she was also labeled a "precisionist," because she used a smooth, precise, hard-edged way of simplifying forms, and a "surrealist," because of her unusual combinations of images, such as skulls and flowers. Her work has been variously interpreted as transcendental, mystical, minimal, and fraught with female sexual imagery (an interpretation O'Keeffe found ludicrous and vehemently denied throughout her career). What is incontrovertible is the unique essence of the artist herself—original, individualistic, independent, and innately private. She has been greatly admired by women for her work and for the uncompromising way in which she led her life, hence her high ranking here.

Georgia O'Keeffe grew up on a farm in Sun Prairie, Wisconsin, the second of seven children. She was gifted in music and showed early signs of artistic talent and interest, later claiming to have known by the age of ten that she would be an artist. She attended a convent school in Madison until 1902, when her family moved to Williamsburg, Virginia. O'Keeffe continued her education at Chatham, a girls' boarding school, where her talent was recognized and encouraged by art teacher and Chatham principal Elizabeth May Willis. O'Keeffe was awarded a special art diploma at her graduation. From 1905 to 1906 O'Keeffe studied cast-and-figure drawing at the Art Institute of Chicago, and then enrolled at the Art Students League in New York, where she won a prize for a still-life painting of a dead rabbit and a copper pot. Despite her success, O'Keeffe felt that she was merely imitating her teachers and using tired, traditional techniques in her work. Discouraged, she stopped painting entirely for several years.

O'Keeffe's father was suffering financially at this time, and her mother was dying of tuberculosis. Georgia needed to support herself, and in 1909 took a job in Chicago drawing lace and embroidery advertisements. The following year, after a bout with measles weakened her eyes, she returned to her family at their new home in Charlottesville, Virginia. At her sisters' urging, she took a class at the University of Virginia with Alon Bement, who introduced her to oriental principles of design and to modern art, especially the work of Vasily Kandinsky, one of the founders of Abstract Art.

Beginning in 1913 O'Keeffe embarked on a series of teaching jobs. One job she particularly enjoyed was teaching art to Mexican children in Amarillo, Texas. However, she quit at the end of the year after the school board insisted she use dull, stale copybooks, which she felt would stifle her students' creativity. She then decided to enter Columbia University's Teachers College to study abstract design with Arthur Wesley Dow. At Columbia she became excited by Dow's method of having his students draw abstract lines and shapes to music. She tried this technique on her own during time spent teaching at a small college in South Carolina. She first worked in charcoal, and then progressed to watercolor. Her goal was to develop a style that would express her own ideas and private vision.

In 1915 O'Keeffe sent some of her charcoal drawings to her close friend and Columbia college mate, Anita Pollitzer, with the proviso that Pollitzer not show them to anyone else. Pollitzer immediately took the drawings to Alfred Stieglitz, the celebrated photographer and owner of the avant-garde New York gallery 291. Stieglitz, impressed with the drawings and the fact that they were done by a woman artist, exhibited them in a show in 1916, along with two other artists. When O'Keeffe discovered this, she went to New York, stormed into the gallery, and demanded that Stieglitz remove her work. He convinced her to leave it up. The result of that meeting was a long professional and personal relationship between O'Keeffe and the fifty-one-year-old Stieglitz. In 1917 Stieglitz sponsored the first of twenty one-woman shows for O'Keeffe. In 1919 she moved to New York to live with him; five years later, they were married. O'Keeffe became the only woman member of a group of modern artists known as the Stieglitz Circle. She was also a willing subject for Stieglitz, who took about five hundred photographs of her from 1917 to 1937. The couple divided their time between New York City and a farmhouse on the Stieglitz family estate on Lake George.

During the 1920s O'Keeffe began to paint simplified, abstract, and magnified representations of flowers, city scenes, and farmhouses. Her "blown-up" images of flowers, sometimes said to have been the result of Stieglitz's influence, are particular favorites among many O'Keeffe aficionados. An example is *Black Iris*, painted in 1926. By 1928 O'Keeffe felt she needed to find new sources of inspiration. At the invitation of two women friends, she spent the summer of 1929 in Taos, New Mexico. O'Keeffe loved the wide, color-rich expanses of land and sky in New Mexico and thereafter spent every summer there, returning to Stieglitz each winter. The aging Stieglitz initially felt threatened by these separations, but he finally came to accept the arrangement. During their separations, the two wrote constantly to each other, sharing their thoughts and feelings.

In 1946 O'Keeffe was given the first retrospective of a woman artist ever held at the Museum of Modern Art in New York. That same year Stieglitz died, and O'Keeffe moved to New Mexico permanently. She divided her time between a house she had bought in Abiquiu in 1945 and her ranch outside the village, purchased five years earlier. She painted prolifically and lived simply, growing her own vegetables and grinding wheat flour by hand for bread. Her years in New Mexico yielded such notable paintings as *Cow's Skull* (1931) and *Pelvis With Blue* (1944), as well as several studies of Taos Pueblo. O'Keeffe's journeys abroad in her later years inspired her to paint clouds seen from the perspective of her airplane window. In these paintings, the clouds appear to move swiftly backward toward an infinite horizon. This suggestion of infinity, present in many of the artist's later works, led to their description by art critics as mystical or transcendental. Perhaps the later paintings represent the vision of an artist who was growing older or were simply a new way for O'Keeffe to interpret what she saw in the vistas of Abiquiu and beyond.

In the 1960s O'Keeffe had several major retrospective exhibitions in cities throughout the United States. She was elected to the American Academy of Arts and Letters and the American Academy of Arts and Sciences. In 1968 a collection of her drawings was published.

A 1994 exhibit titled "Of, For, and By Georgia O'Keeffe" at the Whitney Museum in Stamford, Connecticut, featured photographs of her taken by Stieglitz and others, among them Todd Webb, who documented the artist's daily life from 1955 until shortly before her death at the age of ninety-eight. Exhibit organizer Kathleen Monaghan feels O'Keeffe emerges in these photos "as a calm, unperturbed, and contented subject." This description suggests the inner peace of a woman and an artist who sought and succeeded in achieving life and work completely on her own terms.

12

Frances Perkins

1880–1965

Americans who have learned so much out of these four years of depression often say with a great soberness that what we all need and want is a sense of security—the ability to make a plan that can look at least a year or two years ahead with some reliance that we can carry through that plan and that life will not be pulled out from under us by some inexplicable situation. In other words, we are all tired of living in a cyclone area and would like to live in a serene, sunny belt where peace of mind could have an opportunity to flower.

—FRANCES PERKINS
People at Work

Caught in the grip of the Great Depression, Americans were indeed existing on either side of a cyclonic maelstrom when President Franklin Roosevelt appointed Frances Perkins to be his secretary of labor in 1933. Perkins was the first woman to hold a cabinet post in the United States and the second-longest-serving cabinet member in U.S. history. Her tenure lasted the length of the Roosevelt administration. During the course of her remarkable career as a committed social reformer, Perkins fought to improve the lives of working people and to diminish the massive ranks of the unemployed by creating jobs and training programs and by establishing maximum work hours, minimum wage standards, unemployment insurance, and Social Security. She oversaw a social revolution in the United States that helped repair the lot of workers during the 1930s and continued in influence long afterward.

Perkins was born Fannie Caroline Perkins in Boston, Massachusetts, and grew up in Worcester, where her father ran a stationery store. After attending the Worcester Classical High School, a predominently male institution, she went on to Mount Holyoke College where, as she later recalled, "I discovered for the first time...that I had a mind." She excelled in acting and debate, and in her senior year was elected class president. Perkins was also encouraged by one of her professors, historian Annah May Soule, to investigate working conditions in the nearby factory town of Holyoke. There she observed men, women, and children laboring under harsh and grinding conditions for long hours at low wages and using unsafe machinery. In her senior year, Perkins attended a talk given by Florence Kelley, general secretary of the National Consumer's League, on efforts to prohibit child labor and to limit working hours for women. According to Perkins, Kelley's speech "first opened my mind to the necessity for and the possibility of the work which became my vocation."

After her graduation in 1902 Perkins worked as a teacher in Chicago and spent her free time volunteering at settlement houses, including Hull House. One of her jobs was to collect wages for workers who had been cheated by their employers. While making her rounds, she visited the homes of the poor and received her first exposure to labor unions. Deciding that she "had to do something about unnecessary hazards to life, unnecessary poverty," Perkins made up her mind to become a social worker and found a job with the Philadelphia Research and Protective Association investigating rumors about the mistreatment of immigrants and black women in that city. She uncovered abuses and lobbied for laws to correct them.

Perkins next moved to New York City to study at the New York School of Philanthropy. She earned her Master's degree in 1910 and was hired as the executive secretary of the New York City Consumers' League, where she worked for industrial reform and the improvement of sweatshop conditions. A turning point for Perkins came in 1911 when she witnessed the tragic Triangle Shirtwaist fire in which 146 women workers perished in their factory because of the lack of fire escapes. The scene of women who fell to their deaths to avoid the fire "struck at the pit of my stomach," Perkins recalled. "I felt I must sear it not only on my mind but on my heart as a never-to-be-forgotten reminder of why I had to spend my life fighting conditions that could permit such a tragedy."

In 1912 Perkins successfully fought to pass a fifty-hour maximum work week in the New York State legislature. While working for the New York Committee on Safety, from 1912 to 1917, she exposed employers who were jeopardizing the health and safety of their workers. After Al Smith was elected governor of New York in 1917, he asked Perkins to become the first woman member of the New York State Industrial Commission, a post that made her the highest-paid state employee in the nation. Perkins took charge of the Bureau of Mediation and Arbitration, reorganized the Factory Inspection Division, and went into the field to settle strikes. At Smith's urging, Perkins, a longtime Republican, also joined the Democratic party. Having firmly established a reputation as one of the foremost experts in labor relations, she went on to serve as chair of the New York State Industrial Board and of the Industrial Commission under governors Smith and Roosevelt.

When a newly elected President Roosevelt chose Perkins as his secretary of labor, she wavered, suggesting that a woman from the ranks of organized labor should be named. Roosevelt, who had selected Perkins partly because she had "no axe...to grind," insisted that she accept. She relented, with the proviso that his administration would dedicate itself to liberal social policies. As secretary of labor, Perkins played a major role in drafting legislation and developing the programs that would become the cornerstone of Roosevelt's New Deal: the National Labor Relations Act; the Federal Emergency Relief Administration to help states assist the unemployed; the Civilian Conservation Corps to provide jobs and job training; the National Industrial Recovery Act and its Public Works Administration, which created jobs for the unemployed; and the Division of Labor Standards, which improved working conditions. Perkins also promoted passage of the Social Security Act, a comprehensive program that included unemployment and old-age insurance. As Perkins told reporters, "It is a great satisfaction to see the foundation stone laid in a security structure which aims to protect our people against the major hazards of life."

The controversy caused by the fact that a woman was leading the nation through its most severe depression and that Perkins had, in defiance of convention, kept her name though married, did not disappear, but it eventually receded. However, Perkins' prolabor determinism earned her the emnity of the political right, which began a rumor that she was a "foreign-born Jew" and branded her a Communist for failing to deport a strike leader. Perkins was threatened with impeachment, but she managed to diffuse the opposition with an appearance before the Senate Judiciary Committee. The strain on Perkins was enormous, however, and in 1940 she pressed Roosevelt to accept her resignation. He wisely declined her offer.

During World War II, Perkins tried and failed to dissuade Roosevelt and FBI director J. Edgar Hoover from fingerprinting aliens and opposed the forced conscription of labor. She helped bring business and labor together in support of the war effort, creating the character Rosie the Riveter to represent women who went to work in war industries. Rosie became a national heroine and paved the way for the acceptance of women in an expanded workplace, at least for the course of the war. Yet Perkins was not an unconditional feminist: During the Depression she had stated that married working women should give up their jobs to provide more work for unemployed men, and she was an opponent of wartime day-care centers and the Equal Rights Amendment.

After Roosevelt's death, Perkins served briefly under Truman, stepping down as Secretary of Labor in 1945 after twelve years on the job. The following year she published a biography of FDR, *The Roosevelt I Knew*, which she acknowledged was completely "biased in his favor." From 1945 to 1953 she was a member of the Civil Service Commission, and from 1957 until her death she was a professor at Cornell University's School of Industrial and Labor Relations. She died in New York City at the age of eighty-five, the architect and engineer of some of the most profound social changes in U. S. history.

13

Jane Austen

1775–1817

I think I may boast myself to be, with all possible vanity,
the most unlearned and uninformed female who ever
dared to be an authoress.

—Jane Austen
In a letter to Rev. James Clarke, 1815

It would be interesting to know Jane Austen's reaction to
posterity's evaluation of this "unlearned and uninformed
female." She has been called the "prose Shakespeare," and her
contemporary, Sir Walter Scott, one of the age's greatest writers,

once lamented that her "exquisite touch, which renders ordinary commonplace things and characters interesting, from the truth of the description and the sentiment, is denied to me." Today Austen is regarded as one of the greatest novelists of all time; some critics have even claimed she is the first great novelist. There are Austen societies and circles, and the Regency Period of her novels (1811–1820) has become the preferred setting for countless historical romances—mostly overheated and sentimental imitations of Austen's work. So modest that her name never appeared on the title page of her books in her lifetime, Austen, despite her humility and sense of her limitations, has become the ideal example of the maxim that a writer should write about what he or she knows best, and that commonplace, everyday experience can be the source of great and enduring art.

Jane Austen was the youngest of seven children of George Austen, the rector of Steventon in Hampshire, England, and Cassandra Leigh Austen. Her father, who privately tutored sons of the gentry to prepare them for Oxford and Cambridge, felt ill-equipped to teach his daughters, but he nevertheless encouraged their education. Jane and her older sister, Cassandra, were educated privately and at schools in Oxford, Southampton, and Reading. Jane Austen grew up well read in English classics, prose, and poetry, was reasonably well versed in languages, and was also skilled in such traditional feminine pursuits as music and needlepoint. She began writing during her adolescence, composing plays, satires, and stories to amuse her family.

In 1801 George Austen, accompanied by his family, retired to Bath. After his death in 1805, the family moved to Southampton to live nearer to the two youngest of the five Austen sons, who were in the navy. The Austens returned to Hampshire in 1809, settling in the village of Chawton, where Jane remained until her death from Addison's disease at the age of forty-two.

Because Austen never married, the tendency is to see her as a wise, ironic spinster aunt, writing exclusively about courtship and marriage matters outside her own experience. But she was not a recluse: There were opportunities for marriage and proposals, and a woman who knew Jane from the Steventon days once characterized her as "the prettiest, silliest, most affected, husband-hunting butterfly she ever remembers." Eschewing marriage, Austen involved herself instead with her wide circle of friends and relatives while helping to run the household of her modest gentry family.

Austen's writing career is divided into two periods: her earliest work, written in Steventon, then a twelve-year lull, followed by the relocation to Chawton, where her early novels (*Pride and Prejudice*, *Sense and Sensibility*, and *Northanger Abbey*) were reworked and the later novels (*Mansfield Park*, *Emma*, and *Persuasion*) were written. She wrote between domestic and social duties at a tiny table in the drawing room. She chose for her subject the world she knew best, once explaining to a niece who was thinking of writing novels: "three or four families in a country village is the very thing to work on." Her novels, socially sophisticated, sharply rendered comedies of manners, were described by her as "the little bit (two inches wide) of Ivory on which I work with so fine a Brush, as produces little effect after much labour."

A miniaturist by design, Jane Austen recognized in the things closest to view—the ordinary experiences of country gentry families—the medium to explore human nature and English character and society in the opening years of the nineteenth century. The great events of those years—the war with Napoleon and the industrial revolution—were largely omitted from her books. At the center of each Austen novel is the central question of marriage and the intricate and difficult courtship negotiation that is required to reach that all-important goal. In an age when women had few professional options and were totally dependent on marriage for status and economic survival, a woman was forced to stake her all in the quest for the right husband. Beyond the practical drama of courtship and marriage, Jane Austen schooled her heroines in the unalterable laws of human nature, class, and custom. Willful and headstrong heroines like Elizabeth Bennet and Emma Woodhouse are shown going through a sobering process of maturation and gaining a deeper appreciation of the rules and elements that govern their lives. Austen's grasp of that world, and her eye for the nuance of behavior, was restricted by her unwillingness to imagine or explore beyond what she observed. For example, there is not a single scene in all of her novels of two men alone together simply because Austen could never have witnessed such a scene and was unwilling to create one from her imagination.

Jane Austen's truthfulness and restriction of subject matter have been charges against her. Emerson characterized her novels as "vulgar in tone, sterile in artistic invention, imprisoned in the wretched conventions of English society." Charlotte Brontë complained that Austen "ruffles her readers by nothing vehement, disturbs him by nothing profound." Despite these complaints about what Austen never professed to offer in her fiction, she is rightly seen as a true literary revolutionary who broke new fictional ground for later novelists to cultivate. She demanded that the reader accept the recognizable, unextraordinary, middle-class individual as the subject of the writer's most intense moral and psychological exploration and regarded the crises of everyday life as the best focus for insight, not only into character, but into higher moral meaning.

Jane Austen's perceptiveness has never become dated; women readers continue to identify with her heroines, and both men and women claim her as a favorite novelist. Her timeless capacity to delight readers was praised by Somerset Maugham, who said of her: "Nothing very much happens in her books, and yet, when you come to the bottom of the page, you eagerly turn it to learn what will happen next. The novelist who has the power to achieve this has the most precious gift a novelist can possess."

14

Mary Harris "Mother" Jones

1830–1930

Get it right. I'm not a humanitarian. I'm a hell-raiser.
—MOTHER JONES
In response to a college professor who
referred to her as "a great humanitarian"

She was a sweet-faced, white-haired woman, barely five-feet tall and sturdily built; the very picture of an amiable, doting mother or grandmother. If tragedy had not deprived her of her husband and four children, Mary Jones might very well have lived up to her affable appearance. Instead, she summoned up her considerable reserves of emotional strength, feistiness, fearlessness, and passion, and used them in tandem with a remarkable talent for rhetoric to agitate on behalf of the American laborer. Called "the miner's angel," Mother Jones was utterly dedicated, unrelentingly stubborn, and completely single-minded in her quest to better conditions for workers and make life hell for their overseers.

Despite her singleness of purpose, Mother Jones herself was a study in contrasts. She was, writes biographer Dale Fetherling, "an outrageously irreverent Catholic, a conservative radical, a gregarious individualist, and an ascetic who eschewed the very comforts she sought for her 'boys.'" Although a staunch advocate of social change, she was adamantly opposed to women's suffrage, which she viewed as a diversion from the class struggle. In her low and pleasant voice, she would call the workers to arms, scold them for their cowardice, or inform a prestigious corporation president that he was "a high class burglar." One friend commented that if she had stayed in Ireland, she "probably would have been hanged...or else, she would have been president of the Irish Republic." As it was, she did not return to the land of her birth but stayed in this country to become, in the words of a West Virginia prosecutor, "the most dangerous woman in America."

Mary Harris Jones was, by her own admission, "born in revolution." Her father and paternal grandfather had both been deeply involved in the struggle for Irish independence. Her grandfather was hanged as an agitator, and in 1835 her father, Richard Harris, was forced to flee Ireland to escape arrest. He went to the United States, established American citizenship, and worked first on a canal-building crew and then on a railroad gang. In 1838 his wife, and their three children joined him in Toronto, Canada.

Mary Harris attended one of that city's first free public schools and graduated from high school in 1847, having attained proficiency in the dissimilar skills of debating and dressmaking. She worked out of her home as a dressmaker, then left Toronto to work as a teacher and private tutor in New England and as a secular teacher at Saint Mary Convent in Monroe, Michigan. After a year at the convent she decided she "preferred sewing to bossing little children," and moved to Chicago, where she supported herself as a dressmaker. In 1860 she again returned to teaching and traveled to a job in Memphis, Tennessee. The following year she married ironworker George Jones, a staunch member of the Iron Molders' Union and an organizer for the Knights of Labor.

In the fall of 1867 a yellow fever epidemic swept through Memphis, claiming 236 lives, including Mary's husband and their four children. Mary Jones stayed on through the epidemic to nurse other victims, then left for Chicago to work as a dressmaker. While sewing for the wealthy who lived on Lake Shore Drive, she would look out her shop window and see the poor, "jobless and hungry, walking alongside the frozen lakefront. The contrast of their condition with that of the tropical comfort of the people for whom I sewed was painful to me. My employers seemed neither to notice nor care."

In 1871 disaster once again struck Jones when her home and dressmaking shop were destroyed during Chicago's Great Fire. Homeless and without any possessions other than the clothes she wore, she spent a night and a day on the lakefront without food and then sought refuge with other Chicagoans in the basement of a church. She eventually reestablished her business and began to attend Knights of Labor meetings, where her grasp of labor issues and debating skills attracted the notice of Terence V. Powderly, later the Grand Master Workman of the Knights. During the early years of her involvement in the labor movement, Jones urged the Knights to recruit more workers for the cause, spoke to working men around the city, and witnessed many of the labor upheavals that took place in the industrial states after the financial panic of 1873. For the rest of her life, Mother Jones had no fixed address. She lived wherever she found shelter, most often in workers' shanties or strikers' tent cities. Having no property or bank accounts, she sometimes derived income from union activities, but more often she relied upon friends to supply her with whatever necessities she lacked.

It was Jones's immersion in the struggles of the United Mine Workers that brought her to prominence as a labor leader.

Beginning in 1891, she participated in strikes in Virginia, West Virginia, Colorado, Kansas, and Pennsylvania; fighting for shorter hours, better pay, and the right of workers to unionize. Some strikes were won by the workers, others were lost. When one fight was over, Mother Jones moved on to the next. "With one speech," a worker recalled, "she often threw a whole community on strike, and she could keep the strikers loyal month after month, on empty stomachs and behind prison bars." Jones herself was frequently jailed, and in 1913 was accused of inciting violence during a West Virginia strike and convicted of conspiracy to commit murder. The sentence was commuted, and in 1914 her graphic account of the massacre of twenty people by machine-gun fire during a Ludlow, Colorado, miner's strike convinced President Wilson to try to mediate the dispute. Believing that "the militant, not the meek, shall inherit the earth," Mother Jones was unapologetic concerning any violence she incited or which erupted among the miners to counter the violence used by strikebreakers.

Mother Jones was a founding member of the Social Democratic Party and joined the Socialist Party of America as soon as it was formed. In 1905 she helped found the Industrial Workers of the World. She continued to agitate well into her nineties, rallying on behalf of garment, steel, and streetcar workers. She spent her last years in the home of a retired miner and his wife near Washington, D.C. On her one-hundredth birthday, Jones received greetings from prominent officials across the country, among them John D. Rockefeller Jr., whose father had owned some of the copper mines where she had led strikes. She died seven months later and was buried in a miners' cemetery in Illinois.

Although Mother Jones was an important labor leader who achieved significant gains for the movement, her greatest influence was inspirational. She was a true folk heroine, the "Jeanne d'Arc of the miners," who, writes Fetherling, "was a benevolent fanatic, a Celtic blend of sentiment and fire, of sweetness and fight. [She] captured the imagination of the American worker as no other woman—perhaps no other leader—ever has."

15

Simone de Beauvoir

1908–1986

One is not born, but rather becomes, a woman. No
biological, psychological, or economic fate determines
the figure that the human female presents in society; it
is civilization as a whole that produces this creature,
intermediate between male and eunuch, which is
described as feminine.

—SIMONE DE BEAUVOIR
The Second Sex

One of the most prominent literary figures and intellectuals of her generation, existentialist philosopher and author Simone de Beauvoir is primarily celebrated for *The Second Sex*, a comprehensive and controversial polemic on the inferior historical and contemporary status of women. First published in 1949 and partially translated into English in 1953, it remains one of the most influential works of the twentieth century and one that served as the sourcebook for the revived women's movement of the 1960s.

Simone de Beauvoir was born in Paris, the elder daughter of Françoise and Georges de Beauvoir. Early in life she rebelled against her middle-class Catholic upbringing and education, and the social restrictions imposed upon her by her gender, proclaiming at nineteen, "I don't want my life to obey any other will but my own." Happily freed from the prospect of a stultifying bourgeois marriage by her father's inability to provide dowries for either of his daughters, Beauvoir continued her studies, with the intention of pursuing a career. A brilliant student, she earned her degree at the Sorbonne in 1929.

While at the Sorbonne, Beauvoir met fellow student Jean-Paul Sartre, whom she later described in the first volume of her autobiography, *Memoirs of a Dutiful Daughter*, as "a soulmate in whom I found, heated to the point of incandescence, all of my passions. With him, I could always share everything." The couple shared their lives for fifty-one years, until Sartre's death in 1980. Except for a brief period during World War II and during an annual six-week vacation in Rome, Beauvoir and Sartre lived in separate apartments, coming together in the evenings to discuss their ideas and to read and criticize each other's work. Their liaison, which both viewed as essential and indestructible, precluded traditional notions of marriage and children, and included a mutually agreed upon concession for "contingent loves" of lesser importance. "We have," Beauvoir once said, "pioneered our own relationship—its freedom, intimacy, and frankness." As well known for their literary output and political commitment as they were for their unconventional relationship, Beauvoir and Sartre together formed the center of the postwar French left-wing intellectual and existentialist movements.

Beauvoir taught philosophy at several colleges until 1943,

after which she devoted herself to writing full time. Her first published novel, *She Came to Stay* (1943), examines a love triangle between a leftist intellectual, his longtime lover, and a younger lover, an emotionally painful situation experienced by Beauvoir in the early years of her relationship with Sartre. Beauvoir's other notable fiction includes *All Men Are Mortal* and *The Blood of Others*, which are both interpretations of the existential dilemma, and *The Mandarins*, a roman à clef based on Beauvoir's affair with American novelist Nelson Algren and featuring thinly disguised portraits of Sartre, Albert Camus, and other French intellectuals. *The Mandarins* won the prestigious Prix Goncourt in 1954. Beauvoir's *The Woman Destroyed*, a collection of three short stories, focuses on three women who are unable to control their fates. Among Beauvoir's nonfiction works are four highly acclaimed volumes of autobiography; *Ethics and Ambiguity*, an explanation of existentialism that offers an affirmative view of life based on commitment and freedom of choice and complements Sartre's great work, *Being and Nothingness; The Long March*, a study of the title event in China; and *The Coming of Age*, a monumental historical treatise on the social treatment of the aged in many cultures.

But it was with *The Second Sex* that Beauvoir first gained worldwide fame. Upon its publication, the book, like most singular and revolutionary works, was both praised and excoriated, provoking reactions that ranged from the horrified gasps of traditionalists to the impassioned gratitude of women who had finally found in Beauvoir the first true explicator of their condition. Critics have variously described *The Second Sex* as pretentious, inflated, implacably dogmatic, pessimistic, contradictory, and unjust to women in its assumptions of inherent male superiority and female inferiority, while at the same time acknowledging its greatness and influence. In *Simone de Beauvoir on Women*, Jean Leighton writes that Beauvoir's "analysis of the subtle and insinuating way women are molded by society to accept their inferior role is masterful and devastating. Her perception of how the male-dominated culture tries to transform women into an 'object' [what Beauvoir also termed the "other"] who exists primarily to please men has had profound reverberations." Despite the gains made by women in recent decades, the issues addressed by Beauvoir, who was herself profoundly influenced, not to say dominated, by a man, still reverberate.

With Sartre, Beauvoir edited several left-wing publications and participated in marches, demonstrations, and other anti-establishment political activities. She wrote manifestos, lectures, speeches, and articles championing such causes as Third World independence, safety for factory workers, and abortion reform. In 1981 she published an account of her final ten years with Sartre that was translated into English in 1984 as *Adieux: A Farewell to Sartre*. That their relationship was central to her life and work does not diminish Beauvoir's status as a singularly perceptive witness to the twentieth century and a feminist whom Betty Friedan called "an authentic heroine in the history of womanhood."

16

Queen Elizabeth I

1533–1603

Queen Elizabeth is the greatest of English, perhaps of all modern sovereigns. In a period remarkable for long and sanguinary wars, she made her name respected abroad without a waste of blood or treasure; and, in a time of a great political ferment, she maintained the most absolute authority at home, without any loss of the affections of her people. She obtained glory without conquest, and unlimited power without odium.

—LORD JOHN RUSSELL
The English Government and Constitution

Elizabeth I, the first ruler to appear here, deserves her ranking among the top twenty most influential women. She ruled England for nearly forty-five years, reigning with supreme authority in a world where power had been exercised exclusively by men. Pope Sixtus V, who sanctioned Philip II of Spain's holy war against England, an endeavor that ended with the defeat by the English of the Spanish Armada, said of her: "She is only a woman, only mistress of half an island, and yet she makes herself feared by Spain, by France...by all." Elizabeth may have been feared by the enemies of Protestant England, but at home she was the popular "Good Queen Bess," diplomatically astute and fiscally responsible, whose era saw such towering English Renaissance writers, statesmen, and adventurers as Walter Raleigh, Francis Drake, Lord Burghley, John Donne, Edmund Spenser, Christopher Marlowe, and, of course, William Shakespeare.

Elizabeth was the last of the Tudors, whose dynasty had begun with the usurpation of the crown by her grandfather, Henry VII. She was the daughter of Henry VIII and Anne Boleyn, whom Henry married after divorcing his first wife, Catherine of Aragon, an act which brought about his excommunication from the Roman Church and produced the English Protestant Reformation. After Anne failed to provide Henry with a male heir, she was beheaded, and her three-year-old daughter was declared illegitimate. Elizabeth grew up a motherless and, for all practical purposes, a fatherless royal princess, tainted by the calumny heaped upon the hapless Anne to justify her execution. She was provided with an estate and a governess, Katherine Ashley, and was well educated by a series of tutors. In 1544 Parliament reestablished her in the succession, after her half-brother Edward, son of Henry's third wife, Jane Seymour, and her half-sister Mary, daughter of Catherine of Aragon. When the fifteen-year-old Edward died in 1553, Elizabeth supported Mary's claim to the throne over that of the unfortunate Lady Jane Grey and was careful to avoid implication in Sir Thomas Wyatt's insurrection against the new Catholic queen. Still, as a Protestant, Elizabeth served as a rallying point for those discontented with Mary's attempts to restore Catholicism in England. Alternatively solicitous, jealous, and distrustful of Elizabeth, Mary had her imprisoned in the Tower of London for a time and kept her under virtual house arrest upon her release. Until Elizabeth's accession to the throne in 1558, she lived continually under the threat of execution.

Elizabeth's accession effectively brought to an end the long factional religious and political struggle that had been set into motion by her father and ushered in one of the greatest commercial, industrial, and literary periods in English history. During the Elizabethan Age, England united as a nation, became a major European power with a strong navy, and began to fashion an empire through the acceleration of exploration and colonization. Elizabeth ruled with an unmatched skill at diplomacy and statecraft, choosing her ministers wisely and giving Parliament the illusion of power while retaining her authority. She avoided marriage, once stating that she would "rather be a beggar and single than a queen and married." She used her unmarried state to her advantage in dealing with ministers at home and in diplomatic maneuverings with France and Spain, each of which nurtured the possibility of a royal alliance. Urged to marry, if only to mute court gossip surrounding her love affair with the married Lord Robert Dudley, Elizabeth resisted, no doubt because of a combination of childhood trauma and her desire to maintain her power unencumbered by a consort. As historian Elizabeth Longford observed, "The union of the Virgin Queen with her people was virtually an explicit substitute for the marriage she never made."

However, Elizabeth could not postpone naming a successor, and she finally fixed on her cousin, Mary, Queen of Scots, the chief claimant, with the additional plan of marrying her to Robert Dudley, now earl of Leicester. The marriage did not happen, and Mary was forced to abdicate her Scottish throne in 1568. Elizabeth gave the deposed queen refuge in England for nineteen years, despite numerous real and alleged Catholic plots to put Mary on the English throne sooner rather than later. In 1587, to put an end to Catholic rebellion, Elizabeth heeded the advice of her ministers and ordered Mary's execution. The following year, Philip II of Spain, Elizabeth's former brother-in-law and one-time suitor, launched his mighty naval Armada as a great Catholic crusade against Protestant England. At Tilbury, to embolden defense against the armies of the Duchy of Parma, which was allied with Spain, Elizabeth gave a stirring speech to her troops in which she reportedly offered "to lay down for my God, and for my people, my honor and my blood, even in the dust. I know I have the body of a weak and feeble woman, but I have the heart and stomach of a king." The Armada was destroyed by a combination of English guns, bad weather, and poor Spanish preparation.

England's victory over the so-called Invincible Armada was the crowning achievement of Elizabeth's reign. Afterward, the queen's popularity began to wane. She maintained less control over Parliament, which objected to the abuse of royally granted monopolies, and she showed poor judgment in the selection of her new favorite, the young, ambitious earl of Essex. Sent to Ireland in 1599 to put down a rebellion, Essex returned defeated and frustrated. He rashly planned a coup, intending to seize the court and the Tower of London but failed to rouse enough support against the queen. He was captured and executed. This would prove to be the final crisis of Elizabeth's long reign. She waited until she was on her deathbed to name her successor—the son of Mary, Queen of Scots, James VI of Scotland, who became the first of four Stuart kings.

Historians have characterized Elizabeth as vain, fickle, vacillating, prejudiced, and miserly. Her persecution of English Catholics grew harsh over the course of her reign, particularly after the rebellion of the Catholic earls of Northumberland and Westmoreland in 1569, the queen's excommunication by the pope in 1570, and the arrival of the Jesuit missionaries in 1580. However, Elizabeth has also been recognized as a woman of great personal courage, a ruler who was keenly aware of her responsibilities and who, throughout her reign, commanded the unswerving respect and loyalty of the vast majority of her subjects. The Elizabethan chronicler Raphael Holinshed offers an appropriate epitaph of the age over which Elizabeth ruled: "It pleased God to send England a calm and quiet season, a clear and lovely sunshine, a quittance from former broils of a turbulent estate, and a world of blessings by good Queen Elizabeth."

17

Rosa Parks
1913–2005

One evening in early December 1955 I was sitting in the front seat of the colored section of a bus in Montgomery, Alabama. The white people were sitting in the white section. More white people got on, and they filled up all the seats in the white section. When that happened, we black people were supposed to give up our seats to the whites. But I didn't move. The white driver said, "Let me have those front seats." I didn't get up. I was tired of giving in to white people.

—ROSA PARKS
My Story

62

It is no wonder that Rosa Parks has been called "the first lady of civil rights" and "the mother of the civil rights movement." Her quiet gesture of defiance on that December evening was the spark that ignited the demonstrations of the 1950s and 1960s. Because of her action, segregation laws were eventually struck down, Martin Luther King Jr. emerged as a national leader, and a long struggle for racial equality was engaged with renewed fervor.

Parks was born Rosa McCauley in Tuskegee, Alabama, in the segregated South of Jim Crow laws that guaranteed separate and unequal facilities and opportunities for African Americans. Her father was a carpenter, and her mother was a teacher in one-room, rural schoolhouses. When Parks was two years old, her parents separated, and her father moved North. Rosa and her younger brother moved with their mother to their grandparents' home in Pine Level, Alabama. After her grandfather's death, ten-year-old Rosa and her family went to live with an aunt in Montgomery. Parks attended the Montgomery Industrial School, where she was taught such vocational skills as cooking, sewing, basketry, and embroidery. After completing junior high school, she went on to Alabama State High School, but was frequently forced to interrupt her studies in order to nurse her ailing mother and grandmother.

In 1932 Rosa married Raymond Parks, a barber and civil rights activist. She sold insurance and mended clothing and in 1934 finally received her high school diploma. During the Depression, there were few job prospects for African Americans and racial abuse was a constant. In her autobiography Parks recalls that "whites would accuse you of causing trouble when all you were doing was acting like a normal human being, instead of cringing. You didn't have to wait for a lynching. You died a little each time you found yourself face to face with this kind of discrimination." Parks joined the NAACP, eventually becoming secretary of the Montgomery chapter from 1943 to 1956. She also started an NAACP youth council and became active in voter registration drives sponsored by the Montgomery Voters League.

Parks was returning home from her job as a seamstress at a Montgomery department store when she refused to give up her seat on the bus. The driver called the police. They arrested Parks for violating Montgomery's transportation laws and took her to jail. She was released on one hundred dollars bail, and her trial was scheduled for Monday, December 5. Over the weekend seven thousand members of the black community met to protest Parks's arrest. This meeting led to the creation of the Montgomery Improvement Association and the selection of twenty-six-year-old Reverend Martin Luther King Jr. as its president. King called for a one-day bus boycott, which was extended after Parks was found guilty and fined $10 and court costs of $4. She refused to pay and appealed her case before the Montgomery Circuit Court. As a result of these events, Rosa Parks and her husband both lost their jobs and were harassed and threatened. Finally, in 1956, the United States District Court declared that segregated buses were unconstitutional. The Supreme Court upheld the ruling and ordered the integration of Montgomery buses. After a boycott of 381 days during which African Americans rode black-owned cabs, car-pooled, or walked to work, segregation of the city's buses ended. The peaceful Montgomery bus boycott catalyzed the civil rights movement and served as the model for nonviolent campaigns throughout the South. These included sit-ins and other boycotts spearheaded by Martin Luther King Jr., who emerged from the Montgomery protest as a national figure.

Unable to find work in Montgomery, Rosa Parks and her husband moved to Detroit in 1957. There Parks worked as a seamstress and remained active in the movement. In 1965 she became a staff assistant to Representative John Conyers, for whom she worked until she retired in 1988. Honors have come to Parks from a variety of places, including the NAACP, which awarded her its Spingarn Medal in 1979. In 1980 she became the ninth person and the first woman to receive the Martin Luther King Jr. Nonviolent Peace Prize. The same year, she was honored by *Ebony* magazine as the living black woman who had done the most to advance the cause of civil rights. Few would disagree.

18/19

Helen Keller

1880–1968

Anne Sullivan

1866–1936

You are a wonderful creature, the most wonderful in the world—you and your other half together—Miss Sullivan, I mean, for it took the pair of you to make and create a perfect whole.

> —SAMUEL CLEMENS
> From a letter to Helen Keller after the publication of her first book, *The Story of My Life*.

The story of Helen Keller's triumph over disability is one of the best-known and most inspiring in the history of women. Left blind and deaf at nineteen months after an attack of scarlet fever, by the age of six, she was, as she later wrote, "a phantom living in a 'no world'...I had neither will nor intellect. I was carried along to objects by a certain blind animal impetus....I never viewed anything beforehand or chose it." She could not speak, and her parents, Arthur and Kate Keller, had no way of communicating with her. She was indulged, spoiled, undisciplined, and unrestrained. One of her uncles advised her mother, "You really ought to put that child away, Kate. She is mentally defective, and it is not pleasant to see her about."

The Kellers had no intention of abandoning their daughter to what they viewed as the dubious care of an institution. Instead, on the advice of family friend Alexander Graham Bell, they wrote to the Perkins Institute, a well-known training school for the blind in Boston, and asked the director to send them a teacher. In March 1887 twenty-year-old Anne Sullivan arrived at the Kellers' home in Tuscumbia, Alabama. The "creator of a soul," as educator Maria Montessori later called her, Sullivan had survived a sordid childhood as a half-blind orphan in a squalid Massachusetts almshouse, where the only playroom for herself and her brother had been the institution's deadhouse. She had come to the Perkins Institute alone at fourteen, illiterate and almost as unruly as Helen was when the two met, and was provided with an education and a series of operations that improved her eyesight. Sullivan, perhaps seeing herself reflected in Helen, was determined not to break the child's spirit as she took on the formidable task of trying to tame and teach her.

While Anne Sullivan worked to discipline Helen Keller and at the same time build a trusting relationship with her, she would spell out words with her fingers into the child's hands and then give her the objects to touch. The exercise made no impression on Helen until one day in April, when Sullivan took her to the water pump and let the cold water spill over one of the child's hands as she spelled "water" into the other. "Suddenly I felt a misty consciousness as of something forgotten," Keller later wrote, "and somehow the mystery of language was returned to me." She spelled out "water" several times and then started touching objects and indicating a desire to know their names. By the end of August, Helen had mastered 625 words. She went on to read braille, to write using thin rulers to keep her hand in alignment, and to eventually use a typewriter.

Another breakthrough came about when Sullivan taught Helen's parents and her younger sister, Mildred, the manual alphabet so that the family could talk to one another. In 1889 Sullivan's eyesight began to worsen, and she considered ending her tutorship. She was convinced otherwise by Bell and Samuel Clemens (Mark Twain), another Keller family friend, who felt that Helen, although becoming increasingly self-reliant, would continue to need her. Helen had grown deeply attached to "teacher," an attachment shared by Sullivan.

Sullivan accompanied Helen to the Horace Mann School in New York, where Helen took lessons in oral speech, and was with her when she attended the Wright-Humason School for the Deaf for advanced study in oral speech and lip reading. When Helen entered Radcliffe College, the result of a fundraising effort by Samuel Clemens, Sullivan sat beside her and spelled the lectures into her hand. In 1904 Keller graduated *cum laude*, and, at her request, Sullivan mounted the platform with her and stood beside her as she received her diploma.

After Helen's graduation, she and Sullivan settled in Wrentham, Massachusetts. A year later Anne married writer John Macy, who had edited Keller's first bestselling book, *The Story of My Life*. Keller continued to write and, with Sullivan, embarked on a series of lecture tours, where she spoke on the problems of the disabled, with a particular emphasis on the blind. In 1914 Polly Thomson joined the household as the pair's assistant and secretary; she remained with Keller for the next forty-five years. The same year, John Macy, who had been feeling increasingly left out of Sullivan's life, separated from his wife. The couple did not divorce, and Macy, Sullivan, and Keller remained friends until Macy's death from a stroke in 1932.

In 1917, Keller, Sullivan, and Thomson moved to Forest Hills, New York, where they lived until Sullivan's death in 1936. In addition to writing and lecturing, Keller appeared in a 1918 film, which portrayed highlights of her career, and, somewhat improbably, toured the vaudeville circuit for two years with Sullivan in an "act" that featured a twenty-minute demonstration of

Anne's teaching methods and Helen's means of communication.

Throughout their lives, Keller and Sullivan were frequently courted and feted by presidents, royalty, and other luminaries. Yet Keller's mission was not to become a celebrated oddity, albeit a heroic one. She dedicated herself to raising funds for the American Foundation for the Blind and to lobbying for legislation for talking books and pensions for the blind. She also lectured on behalf of the blind in a number of countries around the world. Her efforts led to better care, training, and employment for the visually impaired. Besides *The Story of My Life*, her other popular books include *The World I Live In, Out of the Dark, Midstream—My Later Life*, and *Helen Keller's Journal*.

Helen Keller's remarkable achievements are legendary, and her status as one of the most influential women of all time is undisputed. But with all her fame, she never forgot her first and greatest teacher, the other half who made her whole. Of Anne Sullivan, she wrote: "How much of my delight in all beautiful things is innate and how much is due to her influence, I can never tell. I feel that her being is inseparable from my own, and that the footsteps of my life are in hers.... There is not a talent, or an aspiration or a joy in me that has not been awakened by her loving touch."

20

Sojourner Truth

c. 1797–1883

I have ploughed, and planted, and gathered into barns, and no man could head me! And ain't I a woman? I could work as much and eat as much as a man—when I could get it—and bear the lash as well! And ain't I a woman? I have borne thirteen children, and seen 'em mos' all sold off to slavery, and when I cried out with my mother's grief, none but Jesus heard me! An ain't I a woman?

—SOJOURNER TRUTH
From a speech before a women's rights convention in Akron, Ohio, May 1851

Sojourner Truth, itinerant preacher, fiery orator, abolitionist, and women's rights activist, was, along with Harriet Tubman, the most widely known African-American woman of the nineteenth century. An illiterate former slave, she was an eloquent critic of slavery and sexism, particularly sexism toward black women. She became, as one of her biographers, Nell Irvin Painter, has observed, "the symbol of the conjunction of race and sex."

Sojourner Truth was born around 1797 in upstate New York, the ninth child of James and Betsey Bomefree, slaves on a farm near the Hudson River. She was named Isabella, and her first language was Dutch. She was sold as a child to several owners; the last being John Dumont, for whom she worked from 1810 to 1826. At fourteen she was married to an older slave named Thomas. The couple had five children, although Truth, with her remarkable talent for rhetorical elaboration, later claimed to have borne thirteen. In 1826, a year before she was to be legally freed by New York State law, Truth ran away from her master and found protection with a Quaker family, the Von Wageners, whose last name she took. While she was working for the Von Wageners, she learned that her son had been illegally sold into perpetual slavery in Alabama. Truth went to court in Kingston, New York, and successfully sued for his return. In the early 1830s she relocated to New York City where she worked as a domestic servant and joined the Magdelene Society, a Methodist mission dedicated to the reformation of prostitutes. Through the society she met the wealthy religious fanatic Elijah Pierson and the self-proclaimed prophet Robert Matthews, who called himself Matthias. Truth lived at Matthias's commune, Zion Hill, until 1835 when the commune collapsed after the mysterious death of Pierson; an event in which Truth was unjustly implicated.

In 1843 the deeply religious former slave experienced a calling to become a wandering evangelist. She then changed her name to Sojourner Truth and began to preach and sing at camp meetings, churches, and on the roadside, depending on the sufferance of her audience. Most were thrilled by the force and the simplicity of her message of Christian love and tolerance. Truth eventually found her way to Northampton, Massachusetts, where she became a member of the Northampton Association, a utopian community founded by George W. Benson. There Truth was exposed for the first time to liberal ideas such as abolitionism and feminism. Benson's brother-in-law, abolitionist leader William Lloyd Garrison, persuaded Truth to dictate her life story, and *The Narrative of Sojourner Truth*, one of the first accounts of a woman slave, became a powerful weapon in the abolitionist cause, exposing the evils of slavery. Published in 1850, *The Narrative of Sojourner Truth* was the first portrait of Truth; other profiles appeared during her lifetime. In 1863 "Sojourner Truth, the Libyan Sibyl," a profile written by Harriet Beecher Stowe, was published in the *Atlantic Monthly*, and recollections of Truth by Francis Dana Gage were included in his *History of Woman Suffrage* (1881).

In the late 1840s Truth traveled widely on the antislavery lecture circuit, where she uttered her famous phrase to Frederick Douglass when he doubted the possibility of a peaceable end to slavery: "Frederick, is God dead?"

By 1850, Sojourner Truth had made the connection between the deprivation of rights of the slave with those of women, and she began lecturing at women's suffrage gatherings. Her message was simple: "If women want any rights more than they's got, why don't they just take them, and not be talking about it?" Her famous "Ain't I a Woman" speech "demands," writes Nell Irvin Painter, "that definitions of female gender allow for women's strength as well as their suffering attendant upon poverty and enslavement." Many of Sojourner Truth's male audiences were not receptive to mixing what they considered to be the separate issues of abolitionism and women's rights; others were openly hostile to the presence of an uneducated black woman who spoke so powerfully and eloquently on the two issues that in her view were inextricably linked. "If colored men get their rights and not colored women," she declared, "colored men will be masters over the women, and it will be just as bad as before."

During the Civil War, Truth worked tirelessly on behalf of black soldiers and freed slaves, whose children were still being kidnapped and sent back to the slave state of Maryland, and in 1864 she was received by President Lincoln at the White House. After the war Truth worked for the Freedman's Relief Association, leading an unsuccessful petition drive to secure land grants for the resettlement of African Americans in the West. However, in 1879, a large number of black Southerners, called Exodusters, migrated to Kansas spontaneously, a venture Truth applauded. She died at her home in Battle Creek, Michigan, after a long life in which she fought with evangelical fervor for the rights of African Americans and women, "disrupting," writes Painter, "assumptions about race, class, and gender in American society."

21

Queen Isabella

1451–1504

...the trust she inspired among her subjects would become the cornerstone of a new national identity—one enabling her to consolidate royal power, codify the Castilian laws, administer justice, conquer the Moors, and support visionaries such as Christopher Columbus....Over time, Isabella's personal vision and political policies would spread far beyond Spain....

> —NANCY RUBIN
> *Isabella of Castille: The First Renaissance Queen*

Remembered today primarily for financing Columbus's voyage to what the Europeans described as the New World, Isabella is equally significant as the monarch who welded Spain into a unified and powerful nation of lasting influence. The reign of Isabella and Ferdinand, "the Catholic Kings," resulted in the centralization of power in the monarchy, produced the Spanish Inquisition, and marked the emergence of Spain as a colonial power in the Americas.

Isabella, the only daughter of King Juan II of Castile, was born into a Spain divided into Castile, Aragon, and a third kingdom, Granada, which had been a Moorish-held enclave since the thirteenth century. Since she had an older half brother, Enrique, and a brother, Alfonso, Isabella was not expected to rule. When she was three, her father died, and she was exiled from the court by Enrique and sent with her mother to live in a small castle in Arévalo. In 1468 Alfonso died, and Isabella became Enrique's heir. Although she was a desirable spouse for a political alliance, she resisted all arranged matches, having decided to marry Ferdinand, heir to the throne of Aragon. In 1469 Isabella and Ferdinand married secretly four days after meeting for the first time. The marriage was an important first step toward the unification of Spain and would prove to be an enduring personal as well as political union.

Enrique's response to news of the wedding was to disinherit Isabella, which split Castile into opposing camps and nearly brought on civil war. In 1474 Enrique died suddenly without designating an heir, and Isabella proclaimed herself queen of Castile. Her succession was contested by Enrique's daughter, Juana La Beltraneja, who received military support from Alfonso V of Portugal in the civil war that followed. The war ended with the defeat of the Portuguese at Toro in 1476. Three years later, Isabella was recognized as queen of Castile, and Ferdinand became king of Aragon. The consolidation of their joint reign was cemented by the birth of their son Juan, heir to both kingdoms.

Isabella's first priority was to break the power of the lawless Castilian nobility and assert royal authority over them. To accomplish this, she revived the Hernandad (Brotherhood), an armed peacekeeping association comprised of rural constabularies and judicial tribunals, each of which operated under royal jurisdiction. Isabella also took over the administration of the powerful religious military orders by making Ferdinand their grand master. The combination of royal, military, political, and economic strength allowed Isabella and Ferdinand to mount the long-awaited crusade to drive the Moors out of Spain by retaking the Moorish stronghold of Granada. In 1492, after an eleven-year campaign against the Moors, Granada fell, and for the first time in eight hundred years Spain was united.

The year 1492 saw two other major events in Spanish history: the first voyage of Christopher Columbus and the creation of the Spanish Inquisition. The latter event, prompted by Isabella's devotion to religious orthodoxy, was established under royal control. Torquemada, Isabella's own confessor, was named Grand Inquisitor, and the targets of his autos-da-fé were Moors, Moorish converts suspected of reverting to their original faith, and the Jews, who were forced either to convert or leave Spain. With the exquisite paranoia such institutions invariably develop, the Inquisition finally began to persecute any citizen even remotely suspected of heretical behavior. It is estimated that during Isabella's reign some two thousand people lost their lives at the hands of the Inquisition, and thousands more became displaced persons. The intention of the Inquisition was to help create social stability and religious purity. That goal was achieved, but at a considerable cost. While it established a Spanish cultural identity, the Inquisition also limited Spain's tolerance for new ideas and isolated the nation from the influence of European thinking that would create the modern world.

Isabella's vision for Spain included world expansion, which began with the voyages of Columbus. They opened up a new realm of Spanish influence, making that nation the undisputed leader in the exploration of the globe and a world power. Committed to conquest and conversion, Isabella forged both a nation and a national character, leaving behind a legacy for good and ill at home and especially in the Americas for centuries to come.

22

Florence Nightingale

1820–1910

Miss Nightingale did inspire awe, not because one felt afraid of her per se, but because the very essence of *Truth* seemed to emanate from her, and because of her perfect fearlessness in telling it.

—WILLIAM RICHMOND
The Richmond Papers

Florence Nightingale wrote in her seminal work, *Notes on Hospitals* (1859), "It seems a strange principle to enunciate as the very first requirement in a hospital that it should do the sick no harm." Her comment illustrates the state of medical care as she found it in the 1840s when she abandoned her expected role as a society wit and beauty to single-handedly raise the standard of hospital and nursing care in Great Britain, which was eventually modeled worldwide. As a pioneer in nursing, with a genius for organization and innovation, Nightingale completely changed the profession, which had been dominated by uninformed and socially disreputable women; bringing it into its modern respectable and valued position. Her courage and devotion were raised to the status of myth in which Nightingale became for all time the romantic healing heroine known as the Lady With the Lamp.

Florence Nightingale was born into a family and social set that made her eventual achievements seem unlikely if not impossible. Her father, William E. Nightingale, inherited a large fortune, and with his wife, Fanny, pursued an active life in society. Their two daughters, Parthenope and Florence, were born during the couple's extended honeymoon on the Continent. The girls were tutored by their father in languages, history, and mathematics, and they divided their lives between a country estate in Hampshire and a house in London during the social season. Like every wealthy girl of her class, Florence Nightingale dutifully made her debut and devoted herself to the social whirl of balls, dinners, and other entertainments. However, she felt that there might be a higher purpose to her life than an endless round of frivolity followed by marriage. At the age of seventeen, she wrote in her diary, "God spoke to me and called me to His service." When she announced to her family that she felt called upon to become a nurse, they were horrified, partly with good reason. Hospitals of the time were squalid and filthy, and it was not unusual for first-time visitors to the wards to become sick from the sights and smells. Nurses were often prostitutes, entirely untrained medically and with a reputation for drunkenness. In the view of Nightingale's family, no respectable lady could conceivably enter such a disreputable profession. Florence remained adamant, however, and in 1845 she began visiting hospitals and health facilities to collect information on them.

While visiting Germany with her family in 1851, Nightingale pursuaded her parents to allow her to train as a nurse at the Institute of Protestant Deaconnesses at Kaiserswerth. In 1853 she accepted a position as superintendent of the Institution for the

Care of Sick Gentlewomen in London and seized the opportunity to make it a model hospital of the time. She put in call bells so that patients could summon nurses, dumbwaiters to have food delivered quickly to the wards, and plumbing so that hot water would be readily available. She also undertook to train nurses, ensuring their professional competence as well as their moral habits to attract respectable women to the profession.

The following year saw the emergence of Nightingale as a nursing legend. With great enthusiasm the British Army embarked on military campaign against Russia in the Crimea for which it was ill prepared. Because of too few transports, medical supplies were left behind. There were no bandages, splints, or anesthesia, and the wounded lay on the ground on filthy straw, where many of them succumbed to cholera and dysentery. The major British hospital in Scutari, Turkey, had no beds, no kitchen, no cups or buckets for water, and insufficient doctors to treat the thousands of patients. This disaster became known in England from the reports of the war correspondent William Howard Russell of the *London Times*, who wondered, "Why have we no Sisters of Charity?" Secretary of War Sidney Herbert, one of Nightingale's many influential friends, responded by asking Nightingale to supervise a contingent of nurses to be sent to Scutari to assist doctors at the Barracks Hospital. Nightingale immediately agreed.

Hospital and army authorities in Scutari did not welcome the prospect of having the situation and their reputations saved by a socialite civilian with her brigade of volunteer nurses. The doctors refused to give Nightingale any assistance, though their need was great, and only relented when the crisis of so many casualties became overwhelming. Nightingale moved with astonishing speed and skill to improve conditions and to aid the sick and wounded, eventually making it possible for twelve thousand patients to be treated despite a deplorable lack of supplies and facilities. She essentially took over the running of the burgeoning medical complex, diplomatically balancing jealousies and infighting, and established discipline and order among her nurses. On call twenty-four hours a day, it was not unusual for her to be on her knees bandaging patients for eight hours at a time. She contracted almost every illness offered by the war, including dysentary, rheumatism, and a fever that nearly killed her and caused her to lose all her hair. Although weak and emaciated, she refused to leave Scutari until the British were evacuated from Turkey in July 1856. Nightingale sustained feelings of failure for not having achieved more in Scutari, but her accomplishments there made her the English national hero of the war. As her biographer, Cecil Woodham-Smith, observed: "Two figures emerged from the Crimea as heroic, the soldier and the nurse. In each case a transformation in public estimation took place and in each case the transformation was due to Miss Nightingale.... She taught officers and officials to treat soldiers as Christian men. Never again would the picture of a nurse be a tipsy, promiscuous harridan.... In the midst of the muddle and the filth, the agony and the defeats, she had brought about a revolution."

Nightingale returned to a nation prepared to lionize a saint. She made no public appearances, however, nor did she grant any interviews. Instead, for the next sixteen years she threw herself into medical and public health reform. In 1860 she established the Nightingale School and Home for training nurses at St. Thomas's Hospital in London. Over time her health and eyesight began to fail, and by 1896 she was completely bedridden. In 1907 she became the first woman to receive the British Order of Merit, and five years after her death, the Crimean War Monument was erected in her honor. Called the Lady With the Lamp because she believed a nurse's care never ceased, night or day, Florence Nightingale profoundly influenced the future of hospital care by transforming nursing into a noble profession.

23

Melanie Klein

1882–1960

Melanie Klein was a woman with a mission. From the moment she read Freud's paper *On Dreams* in 1914, she was enraptured, converted, and dedicated to psychoanalysis. Captivated by the concept of the unconscious, she followed its seductive lure into speculative depths from which even Freud had retreated. This was her offense: for daring to branch out on her own paths of investigation, she was branded, vilified, and mocked.

—PHYLLIS GROSSKURTH
Melanie Klein: Her World and Her Work

One of the first Freudian-trained psychoanalysts to work with children, Melanie Klein was an important and influential contributor to the field of early childhood development. She is especially recognized for her technique of play therapy, the first important therapeutic innovation designed to suit psychoanalytic methods to young children. Klein's technique remains a standard method used by child psychologists.

Melanie Klein was born in Vienna, the youngest child in a family of three girls and a boy. Her father, Moriz Reizes, was a doctor who had difficulty establishing a successful practice in Vienna because he was Jewish. He was forced to take up dentistry and supplement his income by serving as a medical consultant to a vaudeville theater. Klein's mother, Libussa, helped with the family finances by operating a plant shop. Klein decided early to study medicine and to specialize in psychiatry. She graduated from the local gymnasium but abandoned her plans for further study when she married her second cousin, Arthur Klein, a chemical engineering student, in 1903. Klein's marriage was an unhappy one, due to the continual interference of her overbearing, manipulative mother and her husband's frequent job transfers and business trips, as well as to his conjugal indifference. Cast in the emotionally draining role of wife, mother, and needy child, Klein grew increasingly depressed.

In 1914, while living in Budapest, Klein's interest in psychoanalysis was sparked after she read Freud's 1901 work *On Dreams*. That same year her mother died, which intensified her depression. She began undergoing analysis with Sandor Ferenczi, a close associate of Freud. Ferenczi urged her to study the psychoanalysis of young children. In 1919 Klein produced her first paper in the field, "The Development of a Child," which she presented to the Budapest Congress of Psychoanalysis. Soon afterward, she was given membership in the Hungarian Psychoanalytic Society. The disguised subject of Klein's paper was her son Erich, the youngest of her three children. Klein also analyzed her daughter, Melitta, and her older son, Hans. "Through her close observation of their behavior," writes her biographer Phyllis Grosskurth, "she learned much about the origins of anxiety and how it impeded development, knowledge that undoubtedly contributed to her understanding of other young patients...tormented children whom she undoubtedly helped." Nevertheless, all three children went on to other analysts.

At the invitation of Freudian Karl Abraham, Klein moved to Berlin in 1921. There she joined the Berlin Psychoanalytic Institute as its first child therapist. In Berlin, Klein elaborated her concepts and refined her technique. She evolved her system of play therapy to supplement the usual psychoanalytic procedure, believing that the young age of her patients indicated more appropriate methods than the exclusively verbal free-association technique then used with adults. By providing her small patients with toys representing father, mother, and siblings, observing how they played with the toys, and responding to their spontaneous communication during play, Klein was able to elicit the children's subconscious feelings. Klein's technique also resulted in her discoveries of what goes on in the subconscious of the two-year-old and of even younger children, ages which had been largely ignored by Freudians.

Klein divorced her husband in 1926, and moved to London. The following year at the invitation of Ernest Jones, Freud's biographer and friend, she became the first European analyst elected to the British Psychoanalytical Society. In 1932 she published *The Psychoanalysis of Children*, which presented her theories of child analysis. An important and enduring aspect of Klein's work is her object-relations theory, which links ego development during the early years of life to the experience of physical objects that are associated with psychic drives. The very young child first relates to parts rather than complete objects; the later capacity to relate to whole objects, such as the mother or father, is marked by the child's ambivalent, usually hostile, feelings toward objects and the anxiety produced by those feelings. Klein also developed the concepts of introjection, the process whereby an external object is internalized, and projection, in which internal objects are imagined to be located in an external object.

During the 1930s Klein began to analyze adults as well as children. She was castigated by many Freudians for indicating possible ways in which depressive and schizoid-paranoid states in young children relate to psychotic processes in adults. However, Klein's defection from Freudian orthodoxy led her to a greater understanding of severe mental disorders and ultimately extended the range of patients who can be psychoanalyzed. Klein stopped analyzing children in the late 1940s. She then treated adults, analyzed students of psychoanalysis, taught, and wrote. Her best-known books are *Envy and Gratitude* (1957) and *Narrative of a Child Analysis*, published posthumously in 1961. Klein died in London in 1960, leaving behind, writes Grosskurth, "a legacy of rich, provocative, and enduring ideas."

Angelina Grimké
1805–1879

Sarah Moore Grimké
1792–1873

I am confident not many years will roll by before the horrible traffic in human beings will be destroyed...my earnest prayers have been poured out that the Lord would be pleased to permit me to·be instrumental of good to these degraded, oppressed, and suffering fellow-creatures.

—ANGELINA GRIMKÉ
From her diary, 1835

The Grimké sisters, daughters of an aristocratic slaveholding family, became the first women to dare to speak out publicly against slavery and perhaps the first Americans to argue in print for the legal and social emancipation of women. Their efforts inspired such women as Lucy Stone, Lucretia Mott, Elizabeth Cady Stanton, and Susan B. Anthony to take up the dual cause of abolition and women's rights.

Born in Charleston, South Carolina, Sarah was the sixth and Angelina the youngest of the fourteen children of John Faucheraud Grimké and Mary Smith Grimké. Their father was a wealthy planter, and a lawyer and politician, who had served as a lieutenant colonel in the American Revolution and had later risen in the South Carolina judiciary to a position comparable to chief justice. The sisters were given a rudimentary education by private tutors, but Sarah protested the lack of Greek, Latin, philosophy, and law, and she eagerly learned these subjects from her father and brothers. Both sisters were deeply religious Episcopalians and became increasingly disturbed by the treatment of slaves. In 1819 Sarah accompanied her father on a trip to Philadelphia where she was impressed by the sincerity, simplicity, and piety of the Quakers she met. Their opposition to slavery had a major impact on her, and after returning to South Carolina, she taught in Sunday school for slaves and defied state law by teaching slaves to read. In 1821 she moved to Philadelphia to join the Society of Friends.

Angelina's opposition to slavery became even stronger than Sarah's. In 1829 she wrote in her diary, "That system must be radically wrong which can only be supported by transgressing the laws of God." Alienated from her family and unable to live any longer in a slave society, Angelina joined her sister in Philadelphia. There the sisters devoted themselves for a time to charity work and religious activities. Sarah hoped to enter the Friends ministry, and Angelina planned to train as a teacher, but neither goal was realized. Angelina was the first of the sisters to decide that she would devote herself to the antislavery cause. She joined the Philadelphia Female Anti-Slavery Society and wrote a letter of support to abolitionist leader William Lloyd Garrison. The unexpected publication of this letter in Garrison's *The Liberator* publicly identified Angelina Grimké with the abolitionist cause, to the great consternation of her family and friends in Charleston. In 1836 she published *An Appeal to the Christian Women of the South*. Copies of the pamphlet were destroyed by Southern postmasters, and Angelina was warned not to return home to Charleston. Shortly afterward, at the request of the American Anti-Slavery Society, Angelina moved to New York City, where she held meetings for women interested in the abolitionist movement.

Sarah Grimké's involvement in the abolitionist cause came about after she clashed with Quaker elders over their discriminatory treatment of blacks at meeting. Frustrated by the orthodox Quaker environment and furious at being denied the right to speak out on behalf of black members, she broke with the Quakers and enlisted full time in the antislavery crusade. In 1836 she wrote the *Epistle to Clergy of the Southern States*, a refutation of the Biblical justification for slavery.

During lecture tours of the North, the Grimkés drew mixed (male and female) audiences, which created a sensation and prompted the Congregational ministerial association of Massachusetts to issue a "Pastoral Letter" condemning the sisters' behavior as "unwomanly." This controversy, one of the earliest in the history of women's rights in America, turned the sisters' activism in a new direction. As Angelina wrote, "We are placed very unexpectedly in a very trying situation, in the forefront of an entirely new contest—a contest for the *rights of woman* as a moral, intelligent and responsible being." Abolitionists urged them not to distract themselves from the antislavery cause, but they would not be dissuaded. "We cannot push abolitionism forward," they argued, "*until* we take up the stumbling block out of the road." Both wrote strong pamphlets asserting women's rights to free speech and their right to participate in the creation of laws.

In 1838 Angelina married antislavery activist Theodore Weld. Two days later, she delivered an impassioned lecture at an antislavery convention in Philadelphia while an angry mob raged outside. The protestors later burned down the convention hall. That same year the sisters persuaded their mother, as their share of the family estate, to give them slaves, whom they immediately freed. The Welds and Sarah then settled in New Jersey where the sisters began to compile articles culled from Southern newspapers for a book entitled *American Slavery As It Is: Testimony of a Thousand Witnesses* (1839). The book was a major source for Harriet Beecher Stowe while writing *Uncle Tom's Cabin.*

After serving diligently at the center of the antislavery movement and the women's rights tumult, the sisters retired to the background. Their belief in the equality of black Americans was tested in 1868 when they discovered that their brother, Henry, had fathered two sons by a slave. They welcomed both young men into their home and gave them aid and encouragement. Archibald Henry Grimké eventually graduated from Harvard Law School and became an author and prominent civil rights leader. Freeman Jones Grimké graduated from the Princeton Theological Seminary and also achieved prominence as a spokesperson for African Americans. The sisters concluded their careers in Boston as teachers and enthusiastic supporters of progressive causes.

Popular history has tended to overlook the important contribution of the Grimkés in favor of the more organized and publicized battles for abolition and women's rights associated with Mott, Anthony, and Stanton. Yet Sarah and Angelina, as Southern women, risked far more censure because of their vocal opposition to slavery that did their Northern abolitionist counterparts. And as early supporters and articulators of women's emancipation, they fulfilled Angelina's hope that they would "be the means of making a break in that wall of public opinion which lies right in the way of woman's rights, true dignity, honor, and usefulness."

26

Elizabeth Blackwell

1821–1910

What special contribution can women make to medicine? Not blind imitation of men...for this would endorse the widespread error that the human race consists chiefly of men. Our duty is loyalty to right and opposition to wrong, in accordance with the essential principles of our own nature.

—ELIZABETH BLACKWELL

In 1847, after unsuccessfully applying to twenty-eight medical schools, Elizabeth Blackwell was accepted by Geneva (later Hobart) College in New York as a medical student. This might seem to have been the work of an unusually enlightened nineteenth-century college administration, but the reality, unknown to Blackwell, was quite different. Geneva's administrators were also opposed to admitting a woman but had been prodded into seriously considering Blackwell's application by the eminent Philadelphia physician Joseph Warrington, who had taken a professional interest in the young woman. Unwilling to offend Warrington, the administrators left the decision of whether or not to admit Blackwell up to the students, believing that they would vote against her. However, the students voted unanimously to accept Blackwell—as a joke. Their decision was final, and their hilarity was short-lived. Blackwell graduated in 1849 at the head of her class, becoming the first American woman to obtain a medical degree. She would go on to become the first woman doctor of modern times and to influence scores of other women to follow in her trailblazing footsteps.

Born in Bristol, England, to Hannah and Samuel Blackwell, Elizabeth was the third daughter in a family of five girls and four boys. Her father was a prosperous sugar refiner who could afford to have his children privately tutored. Blackwell and her sisters, regarded as "thinking creatures" by their parents, were taught the same academic subjects as their brothers. In 1831 the Blackwells emigrated to New York City, where Samuel Blackwell established a sugar refinery. Ardent abolitionists, the Blackwells also became involved in the American antislavery movement,

After fire destroyed the Blackwell refinery in 1835, the family relocated to Cincinnati, where Samuel Blackwell hoped to raise beets and refine their sugar, a form of sugar production that did not require the use of slaves. Unfortunately, he died of malaria a few months later, leaving his family nearly destitute. The older Blackwell children were forced to find work. Elizabeth taught music, then ran a boarding school in the Blackwell home with her two older sisters. When the school closed, Elizabeth accepted a teaching job in Kentucky, but her distress at living in a slave state caused her to resign from the school after one term.

Upon returning to Cincinnati, she joined the antislavery society and, at the invitation of family friend Harriet Beecher Stowe, became a member of the Semi-Colon Club, a literary association. Nevertheless, Blackwell was restless and, as she later wrote, longed for something more than "the ordinary interests that social life presented." She was also determined, despite her strong attraction to what she called "the other sex" and the presence of several suitors, to avoid marriage. She became inspired to study medicine after visiting a friend, Mary Donaldson, who was dying from what was probably uterine cancer. Donaldson had expressed her belief that she would have been treated earlier and with more care and concern if she had been able to consult a woman doctor, a belief Blackwell shared.

From 1845 until her admittance to Geneva College, Blackwell taught school in the Carolinas, applied to medical schools, and studied medicine privately, using the books of the few physicians who supported her ambition. During the summer following her first term at Geneva, Blackwell worked in the women's syphilis ward at Blockley Almshouse, a Philadelphia charity hospital. Although she was the only woman on staff and was bitterly resented by the young resident doctors, Blackwell valued her work at Blockley, which instilled in her an enduring compassion for poor women suffering from venereal disease.

Following her graduation from Geneva, Blackwell served an internship in midwifery at La Maternité hospital in Paris, which was the only hospital that would accept a woman doctor. While there, she contracted an eye disease, which resulted in the loss of her left eye and ended her hopes of becoming a surgeon. In 1850 she began a year of internship at St. Bartholomew's Hospital in London. During that time she met Florence Nightingale, who would become a lifelong friend.

In 1831 Blackwell returned to the United States, where hospitals refused to hire her because she was a woman. She set up a private medical practice in New York City and gave a series of lectures on female health. In 1853 she opened a tiny clinic, the New York Dispensary for Poor Women and Children, in the slums of lower Manhattan, where the poor could receive treatment and medicines at little or no cost. Two other women doctors later joined her at the clinic: her sister Emily, and Marie Zakrzewska, both of whom had gained admittance as medical students to Western Reserve College (now Case Western) with Blackwell's help.

Successful fundraising attempts and a thriving practice allowed Blackwell and her two associates to expand the clinic. The New York Infirmary for Women and Children (now New York Infirmary–Beekman Downtown Hospital) opened in Greenwich Village in 1857. In 1858 Blackwell and her adopted daughter, Kitty, traveled to England, where Blackwell revised her book, *The*

Laws of Life, for British publication, visited hospitals, and gave lectures on women's health and on the fitness of women for the medical profession. Her lectures were greeted with contempt by some but were enormously popular among young women eager to pursue careers in medicine.

During the 1860s Blackwell organized a Civil War nursing service and established the first visiting-nurse program in New York. She also began a health-inspection program, which by 1872 was headed by Dr. Rebecca Cole, the first African-American woman physician. In 1868 a longtime dream of Blackwell's was realized when the Women's Medical College, the first such institution in history, opened in New York City.

Blackwell returned to England in 1869, lecturing on such topics as sanitation, hygiene, and nutrition, as well as on the controversial subjects of family planning and sex education for children. She also helped found the British National Health Society, taught gynecology at the newly established London School of Medicine for Women, and published *The Moral Education of the Young*, a guide to sex education. She retired from medical practice in 1894, but continued to lecture and write pamphlets on social and medical issues. Her autobiography, *Pioneer Work in Opening the Medical Profession to Women*, was published in 1895. She died of a stroke in 1910 and was buried in the Scottish mountain village of Kilmun.

Blackwell's obituary in the London *Times* stated that she was "in the fullest sense of the word a pioneer." Thanks to that pioneering spirit, women have been able to echo Blackwell's assertion that "the practice of medicine by women is no longer a doubtful but a settled thing."

27

George Eliot

1819–1880

My artistic bent is not at all to the presentation of eminently irreproachable characters, but to the presentation of mixed human beings in such a way as to call forth tolerant judgment, pity, and sympathy. And I cannot stir a step aside from what I *feel* to be *true* in character.

—GEORGE ELIOT
From a letter to John Blackwood,
February 18, 1857

If the nineteenth century was the golden age of the English novel, George Eliot has only one serious challenger as the age's greatest novelist: Charles Dickens. Dickens's triumph as a novelist was the result of his unique powers of visualization and imagination; George Eliot's greatness derived from her power of intellect. More than any other Victorian novelist, Eliot succeeded in transforming the novel, previously regarded as lightweight and sensational entertainment, into an instrument for the most subtle and profound social and psychological inquiry. As D. H. Lawrence said of her, "It was really George Eliot who started it all.... It was she who started putting all the action inside."

George Eliot was born Mary Ann Evans in Warwickshire in the English midlands. The youngest of the five children of Robert Evans, an estate agent and a staunch political and Church of England conservative who was distrustful of change and innovation, Mary Ann was a serious and studious child who read widely. While attending boarding school, she came under the influence of the charismatic, evangelical clergyman John Edmund Jones. Evangelicalism was a reaction against the secular and complacent Anglicanism of the day and emphasized personal salvation by faith and the absolute divine authority of the Bible. To a precocious and thoughtful young girl like Mary Ann, Jones's dramatic preaching and message of religious self-sacrifice were major attractions. In 1841 she moved with her retired father to Coventry, where her family, worried about her religious zeal, encouraged her friendships with such local progressive freethinkers as Charles and Caroline Bray in the hope that she would moderate her pious views. Instead, the philosophical rationalism to which she was exposed caused her not only to renounce her evangelical faith but to lose all religious faith entirely. Thus disillusioned, she refused to attend church any longer, a development her family had not expected. A compromise was reached in which Mary Ann agreed to go to church but would not give up her newfound liberal opinions. She divided her time between her duties as the mistress of her father's household, reading, and translating David Strauss's iconoclastic *Lieben Jesus*, the story of Christ shorn of all supernatural elements, which was published in 1846.

After her father's death in 1849, Eliot was free to enter a

wider circle, better suited for her considerable intellectual gifts. She went to London where she was employed as an assistant editor of the progressively liberal *Westminster Review*. She reviewed a number of works of literature and criticism, and mingled with the literary, somewhat bohemian circle surrounding the magazine, which included critic and author George Henry Lewes. Eliot fell in love with Lewes, who, despite his estrangement from his wife, was unable to divorce her because of the laws of the day. However, Eliot and Lewes defied convention and established a home together, managing a happy if secluded life in London, ideal for their literary work. It was Lewes who encouraged Eliot to begin to write fiction. To avoid associating her work with other "lady novelists," whose sentimental and trivial fare ensured a lack of serious response, she chose the pseudonym George Eliot for her first book, *Scenes of Clerical Life*, three stories that first appeared in *Blackwood's Magazine*. In it she set the pattern for her subsequent novels: an insistence that the commonplace is the proper domain of fiction, tolerance and sympathy toward her characters, and dramatizations of lessons of human nature and behavior through what she called "aesthetic teaching." Eliot's first effort was well received by critics, particularly Dickens and Thackeray, although it was not a popular success.

If *Scenes of Clerical Life* established Eliot's characteristics as a writer, it was her first novel, *Adam Bede*, that brought her acclaim and success. Critic Gordon Haight has observed that "No book had made such an impression since *Uncle Tom's Cabin* swept the world." *Adam Bede* and her other early novels of provincial life, *Silas Marner* and *The Mill on the Floss*, owe much of their power and appeal to George Eliot's sympathetic reconstruction of her own life in Warwickshire. When these sources began to run thin, Eliot attempted a departure in *Romola*, a historical novel of fifteenth-century Italy. To research the novel, Eliot traveled to Italy and studied the customs and values of a different culture with the eye of the social scientist, achieving the needed distance from her material. With *Romola* Eliot learned to go beyond her own memories and see an entire society as a complex whole. This deepened and widened her scope as a novelist when she returned to more familiar English scenes for her last three novels. Each (*Felix Holt*, *Middlemarch*, and *Daniel Deronda*) is a masterpiece, created by a mature novelist at the height of her powers. In *Middlemarch* Eliot creates a detailed depiction of life in a provincial English town, with dozens of characters all carefully and completely rendered. Virginia Woolf, in a well-known appreciation of the novel, wrote that *Middlemarch* is "one of the few English novels written for adult people."

By the 1870s Eliot had largely won the battle for respectability caused by her life with Lewes and was recognized as the most eminent novelist of the day. Heralded now as a modern freethinker, she nevertheless shocked her supporters after Lewes's death in 1876 by marrying John Cross, a close friend of Lewes and herself. She died in 1880, the same year she married Cross.

George Eliot's influence, both as an intellectual and a novelist, is unrivaled. Insisting that the novel be the truthful examination of character, Eliot excluded from her fiction the idealization and exaggeration of other novelists. Her plots were generated by her characters, not imposed upon them. Instead of the ordinary fictional fare, Eliot offered an exhaustive, extensive study of society, bringing to this study the sensitivity and simultaneous skills of a sociologist, psychologist, and cultural historian. She set the course the novel would take into the twentieth century, defining for the future the essence of the novelist who insists that her readers rise to her standards and not the other way around.

28

Ida Bell Wells-Barnett

1862–1931

Not until the Negro rises in his might and takes a hand in resenting such cold-blooded murders, if he has to burn up whole towns, will a halt be called in wholesale lynching.

—IDA WELLS-BARNETT
From an editorial in the
Memphis Free Speech and Headlight, 1892

Born into slavery six months before the signing of the Emancipation Proclamation, Ida Wells-Barnett lived and worked during several epochs in African-American history. An influential journalist, lecturer, and social activist, Wells-Barnett was an ardent and outspoken advocate of black civil and economic rights as well as women's rights. Her fiery and fearless one-woman crusade to end the infamous practice of lynching makes her especially worthy of recognition.

Wells-Barnett was born in Holly Springs, Mississippi, the eldest in a family of four boys and four girls. Like many African Americans during the Reconstruction era, Wells-Barnett's parents, Lizzie and Jim Wells, believed in the importance of education and sent their children to school as early as possible. Wells-Barnett was educated at Rust University, a high school and industrial school for freed blacks established in Holly Springs in 1866. After the death of her parents and youngest brother in a yellow fever epidemic, sixteen-year-old Ida left school to assume responsibility for her brothers and sisters. She passed the teachers' examination and taught in a rural school, earning $25 a month.

In 1884 Wells-Barnett moved to Memphis, Tennessee, where she taught first at a rural school in Woodstock, outside Memphis, and then in the city's black schools. She also continued her own education by taking summer classes at Fisk University in Nashville. Her activism began when, commuting by railroad to her job in Woodstock, she refused to move to a seat in a Jim Crow car and was forcibly removed from the train. She sued the railroad and won her case in the circuit court, but the decision was overturned by the Tennessee supreme court in 1887. Shortly thereafter, Wells-Barnett began writing a weekly column for some of the small black-owned newspapers then springing up in the South and East. Using the pen name Iola, Wells-Barnett devoted her column to issues of concern to African Americans. Because she criticized the poor conditions of schools for black children, the all-white Memphis school board failed to renew her teaching contract in 1891. Wells-Barnett then became a full-time journalist, buying a one-third interest in the weekly newspaper *Memphis Free Speech and Headlight.* In 1894 she became half-owner of the newspaper.

In March 1892 Wells-Barnett wrote a column in the *Free Speech* denouncing the lynching of three of her friends who had been falsely accused of raping three white women. She charged that the lynching had been committed not on the familiar pretext of defending Southern white womanhood but because the victims, grocery store owners, had been successfully competing with white shopkeepers. Wells-Barnett urged Memphis African Americans to "leave a town which will neither protect our lives or our property, nor give us a fair trial in the courts" and to emigrate to the West. She also investigated other lynchings and reported her findings. In May 1892, while she was visiting Philadelphia and New York, a white mob destroyed the *Free Speech* offices. Wells-Barnett was warned by a group of white Memphis civic leaders not to return to the city or she would be hanged in front of the courthouse. Wells-Barnett took the warning seriously and remained in New York.

After a brief stint as a staff writer for the black-owned weekly newspaper *New York Age*, Wells-Barnett lectured and founded antilynching societies and black women's clubs. In 1893 she moved to Chicago where she wrote for the *Chicago Conservator*, founded by lawyer Ferdinand Barnett, whom Wells married in 1895. Wells-Barnett momentarily turned her attention away from the lynching issue, editing a pamphlet protesting the virtual exclusion of African Americans from the 1893 World's Columbian Exhibition in Chicago. She then took her antilynching crusade to Great Britain where she was instrumental in the founding of a British antilynching committee and a society to combat racial segregation. She continued her antilynching campaign by publishing *A Red Record*, a statistical survey of lynching.

Wells-Barnett's antilynching activities made her an active participant in the Niagara meeting in 1910 that led to the formation of the NAACP. She served on the NAACP's executive committee, but later broke with the organization because of its predominantly white board and its timidity in confronting racial issues. A firm believer in agitation, activism, and protest as the only means of change for African Americans, Wells-Barnett opposed the doctrine of compromise and accommodation advocated by Booker T. Washington and allied herself with more radical black leaders such as W. E. B. DuBois and Marcus Garvey.

Among Wells-Barnett's many efforts on behalf of the black community was the founding in 1910 of the Negro Fellowship League to provide lodging, recreational facilities, a reading room, and employment for African-American men who had migrated to Chicago from the South. In 1913 she formed the

Alpha Suffrage Club, said to be the first black women's suffrage organization. That same year, as a delegate to the National American Woman Suffrage Association's march in Washington, D.C., Wells-Barnett refused to march with the other African-American delegates at the back of the procession. Instead, she joined her white colleagues in the Illinois delegation, and by doing so integrated the U.S. suffrage movement. Following the 1918 race riots in East St. Louis, Missouri, Wells-Barnett visited the area to seek legal aid for black victims of mob assault. In a 1919 letter to the *Chicago Tribune*, Wells-Barnett warned that Chicago would face a similar racial upheaval unless it "set the wheels of justice in motion." A few weeks later nearly forty people were killed and hundreds were injured in a race riot.

Wells-Barnett also worked with Jane Addams in a successful attempt to block the setting up of segregated schools in Chicago and was a founder and president of the Cook County League of Women's Clubs. In 1930 she ran as an independent candidate for Illinois state senator and was defeated. She died of uremia in 1931 at the age of sixty-nine.

Through her lectures, articles, and activism, Ida Wells-Barnett raised crucial questions about the future of African Americans. Her courage and lifelong commitment to racial justice have made her one of the most preeminent black leaders of all time.

29

Betty Friedan

1921– 2006

Who knows what women can be when they are finally free to become themselves?...It has barely begun, the search of women for themselves. But the time is at hand when the voices of the feminine mystique can no longer drown out the inner voice that is driving women on to become complete.

—BETTY FRIEDAN
The Feminine Mystique

100

No written work in the history of feminist thought has sounded the clarion call for change in the status of women with as much reverberating success as Betty Friedan's 1963 book *The Feminine Mystique*. The women's movement of the 1960s and 1970s effectively began with this book's publication and ready absorption into the hearts and minds of American women. Friedan would go on to become one of the most influential leaders of the movement she helped to set in motion.

Born in Peoria, Illinois, Betty Goldstein Friedan was the oldest child in a family of two daughters and one son. Her father, Harry Goldstein, was a jeweler; her mother, Miriam, had been a writer and editor before her marriage. An academically gifted child, Betty founded a literary magazine in high school and graduated as class valedictorian. At Smith College she studied psychology and, after graduating summa cum laude in 1942, won two research fellowships to the University of California at Berkeley. Unwilling to commit to a doctorate and a career as a psychologist, Friedan left Berkeley to work as a journalist in New York. In 1947 she married Carl Friedan and a year later gave birth to the first of the couple's three children. The Friedans divorced in 1969.

In the 1950s, Betty Friedan lost her job as a newspaper reporter after requesting her second maternity leave. She continued to write, however, contributing articles to women's magazines. Deeply dissatisfied with her primary role as wife and mother, she began to wonder if other women shared her dissatisfaction. In 1957 she sent an intensive questionnaire to two hundred of her college classmates. The answers she received convinced her that her ailment, a psychic distress she would come to define as "the problem that has no name," was widespread. She began several years of research into the origins of, as she later wrote, "the strange discrepancy between the reality of our lives as women and the image to which we were trying to conform." Friedan analyzed the image and found it to be a fantasy of post–World War II happy suburban female domesticity created and reinforced by educators, sociologists, psychologists, and the media. She called the image and the book that resulted from her research *The Feminine Mystique*.

An immediate and controversial success, *The Feminine Mysti-*

que spoke to legions of women who had sacrificed their identities and sense of self-worth by succumbing to the gilded cage of the suburban home. Friedan wrote of these women, "Their only dream was to be perfect wives and mothers, their highest ambition to have five children and a perfect house, their only fight to get and keep their husbands." *The Feminine Mystique* helped women to understand that their existential unease with the narrow lives they were living was not the result of neurosis but the consequence of their status as second-class citizens. Friedan saw education and new opportunities for women outside the home as solutions to the problem, insisting that "Drastic steps must now be taken to re-educate the women who were deluded or cheated by the feminine mystique."

The Feminine Mystique was seen as a new unifying force in the second wave of twentieth-century feminism, and its now-famous author emerged as a leading figure in the women's liberation movement that followed. In 1966 Friedan cofounded the National Organization for Women and served as NOW's president until 1970. During the 1970s Friedan continued her activism while lecturing and teaching at various universities. She also wrote articles for a wide range of magazines as well as a column for *McCall's*, "Betty Friedan's Notebook." In 1976 she published *It Changed My Life*, in which she assessed the progress of the women's movement and her relationship with it. Concerned with the splintering of the movement into special-interest groups, Friedan called for an end to polarization and a new emphasis on "human liberation."

With *The Second Stage*, published in 1981, Friedan offered a reformist view of feminism based on the acceptance of men and the family in women's quest for equality. Partly influenced by the emergence of the superwoman myth—the image of the woman who effortlessly copes with a both a career and family—Friedan suggested that this "feminist mystique" was as much a fantasy as the feminine mystique was in an earlier era. Friedan's revisionism caused a backlash from more militant feminist critics, who felt that the author had strayed from the basic goals of the movement she had helped to establish. Other critics applauded Friedan's new thesis, seeing in it a new, more humanistic direction for feminism.

Friedan's activism shifted focus somewhat in the 1980s when

she began researching a book on age discrimination. Published in 1993, *The Fountain of Age* analyzes and deconstructs what Friedan terms "the mystique of aging," the negative image American society has created for men and women over sixty-five. Aging baby boomers, especially women well-schooled in *The Feminine Mystique* and the women's movement, may also find *The Fountain of Age* a useful revolutionary primer in the years to come.

30

Rachel Carson

1907–1964

It is not my contention that chemical insecticides must never be used. I do contend that we have put poisons and biologically potent chemicals into the hands of persons largely or wholly ignorant of their potentials for harm. We have subjected enormous numbers of people to contact with these poisons, without their consent and often without their knowledge....

I contend, furthermore, that we have allowed these chemicals to be used with little or no advance investigation of their effect on soil, water, wildlife, and man himself. Future generations are unlikely to condone our lack of prudent concern for the integrity of the natural world that supports all life.

—RACHEL CARSON
Silent Spring

It is generally acknowledged that the modern environmental movement began with the publication of Rachel Carson's *Silent Spring*, a provocative study of the harmful effects of chemical pesticides on the earth's air, water, and soil. Carson, a marine biologist who had first won recognition as the author of *The Sea Around Us*, diagnosed in *Silent Spring* one of the central ills of modern life with a moral force and urgency that continues to be felt today.

Rachel Louise Carson was the youngest child in a family of two girls and a boy. She grew up along the Allegheny River on sixty-five acres of dense woodland purchased by her father, an unsuccessful businessman, near Springdale, Pennsylvania. Carson early developed an interest in nature and later characterized herself as "rather a solitary child" who "spent a great deal of time in woods and beside streams, learning the birds and the insects and flowers." She was also an avid reader and an enthusiastic student, though illness kept her out of school for long stretches. At eighteen she entered the Pennsylvania College for Women (later Chatham College) in Pittsburgh and majored in English with the intention of becoming a writer. However, in her second year she took a required biology course given by a brilliant teacher, Mary Scott Skinker, that aroused in her a passion she had formerly felt only for literature and writing, and she changed her major to science.

After graduating magna cum laude in 1929, Carson obtained a summer study fellowship at the United States Marine Biological Laboratory in Woods Hole, Massachusetts—her first experience with the ocean. With Skinker's help, she won a scholarship to Johns Hopkins University in Baltimore. While attending graduate school, she worked as a laboratory assistant at Hopkins and as a teaching assistant in zoology at the University of Maryland. She received a master's degree in zoology in 1932.

In 1935 and 1936 the Carson family, which had moved to Baltimore at Rachel's urging, suffered two tragedies: the deaths of Rachel's father and sister. Her sister's death left two young daughters to be raised by Carson and her mother. To help support the family, Carson found a job with the United States Bureau of Fisheries in Washington, D.C., writing a series of short radio programs on marine life. At the end of the year, she passed the Civil Service examination with the highest score possible and was offered a full-time job as an aquatic biologist for the department. A writing assignment for the bureau on marine life was submitted to the *Atlantic Monthly*, where it was published as "Undersea." From this first article, Carson later recalled, "everything else followed." She expanded her article into a book titled *Under the Sea-Wind*, which was published in November 1941, but was largely ignored in the wake of the Japanese attack on Pearl Harbor and America's entry into the war. During the war, Carson wrote conservation bulletins for the government and continued her work for the reorganized Fish and Wildlife Service as editor in chief of the information division. In 1951 she published *The Sea Around Us*, which remained on the bestseller list for eighty-one weeks, won numerous awards, and was eventually translated into thirty-two languages. This book and its companion work, *The Edge of the Sea*, published in 1955, provide a vivid account of the physics, chemistry, and biology of the ocean and its shores, and combine keen scientific observation with rich, poetic description.

In 1958 Rachel Carson received a letter from a friend, Olga Huckins, describing the devastating effects on her private bird sanctuary in Massachusetts after it was sprayed with the pesticide DDT under the state's mosquito control program. Carson, who had long been aware of the dangers posed by chemical poisons, felt it was time for her to speak out or "there would be no peace for me." She knew the subject would cause considerable controversy, given industry's dependence on chemicals to increase crop yields and manufacturing's widespread indifference to the effects of chemical waste. Even the Department of Agriculture advocated the use of herbicides and pesticides. After several years of careful research throughout America and Europe, Carson produced *Silent Spring* in 1962. In it, with apocalyptic force, she demonstrated how the fragile existence of all creatures, humans included, could easily be imperiled by DDT and other, still more toxic, chemicals. She argued for the use of biological controls to fight insects "based on understanding of the living organisms they seek to control" and of "the whole fabric of life to which those organisms belong." As Carson had predicted, *Silent Spring* was violently attacked by the agricultural chemical industry, which mounted a massive but unsuccessful campaign to discredit the book and its author. President John F. Kennedy, who had been impressed by the book, ordered a reevaluation of Federal Pesticide Policy. In 1963 the president's Science Advisory Committee formed a subcommittee to study "Activities Related to the Use of Pesticides." The committee endorsed Carson's position, and its findings led to legislation banning the use of DDT.

Having won an important battle, Carson actually precipitated a much wider war that challenged the assumption that progress must come at the expense of the environment. Today, environmental awareness, first called for by Carson in 1962, is central to mainstream thinking though the larger issues of conservation and the protection of the environment continue to be debated with uncertain outcomes. Rachel Carson is principally responsible for influencing the debate on the environmental costs to the natural world she so lovingly depicted. As one editor observed: "A few thousand words from her, and the world took a new direction."

31

Dorothea Lynde Dix

1802–1887

Gentlemen of Massachusetts, I have come to present to you the strong claims of suffering humanity. I come as an advocate of the helpless, forgotten, insane men and women held in cages, closets, cellars, stalls, pens; chained, naked beasts, beaten with rods and lashed into obedience....

—DOROTHEA DIX
Upon presenting her findings on treatment of the insane to Massachusetts legislature, 1843

Dorothea Dix, American nurse and crusader for the mentally ill, led the way toward reform of the treatment of the insane and laid the foundation for later psychotherapeutic practice. When she began her work in 1841, there were thirteen mental asylums in the United States; by 1880 that number had increased to 123. Dix herself was directly involved in the founding of thirty-two state mental hospitals. Because of her tireless efforts to better conditions for the mentally ill, I have ranked her among the top third of history's most influential women.

Dix's childhood in Maine was an unhappy one. Her father was an itinerant preacher who had failed as a farmer and as a manager of her grandfather's land holdings. Dorothea cared for her invalid mother while also raising her two younger brothers. At twelve she was sent to Boston to live with her well-to-do grandmother, who found the headstrong child too great a responsibility and turned her over to her great-aunt in Worcester. There, Dix studied on her own and developed a considerable aptitude for teaching. At the age of fourteen she opened a school for small children. She continued to teach throughout her young adulthood and to further her own education via private study and public lecture courses. Between 1824 and 1832 she published an elementary science textbook, a hymnbook for children, and other devotional works that reflected her commitment to Unitarian principles. She drove herself until the onset of tuberculosis and exhaustion forced a rest. In 1836, on her doctor's orders, Dorothea Dix went to England, where she spent eighteen months at the Liverpool estate of William Rathbone, a wealthy Unitarian merchant and philanthropist. Through him, Dix met other illustrious British social reformers. She returned to Boston in 1837, but her health did not allow her to resume teaching, and she was left with few other options for her interests.

In 1841 Dix was asked to teach a Sunday school class for women in the East Cambridge jail. This would prove to be the turning point in her life. There, she was horrified to find mentally ill women jailed with criminals and living in squalid conditions. Appalled by their treatment and by a jailer's callous response that "lunatics" did not feel the cold, Dix began to lobby the local court for improvements. As a result, heat was provided for the women and their quarters were renovated. Having found a new vocation, Dix next began to investigate treatment of the insane in a month-long survey of every jail, prison, and almshouse in Massachusetts. She presented her findings to the Massachusetts legislature, emphasizing the need for patients to be freed from restraints such as ropes and chains, and to be housed in institutions separate from criminals. Her factual evidence of mistreatment and abuse shocked the legislature into appropriating funds to create state facilities for the proper care of the mentally ill.

Dix widened her crusade to neighboring states and succeeded in opening additional facilities, including the first mental hospital in Trenton, New Jersey, which Dix called "my first-born child." She continued her research and lobbying of legislatures in Pennsylvania, Kentucky, Maryland, Ohio, Illinois, Mississippi, Alabama, Tennessee, and North Carolina, managing to shame most states into opening mental hospitals. Because of her success, she was recruited in efforts to bring about prison reform and schools for the blind. For six years she lobbied the federal government to try to obtain income from public lands to fund care for the insane, but was unsuccessful. Disappointed, Dix went abroad where she worked to reform prisons and hospitals in Britain, France, Turkey, and Russia.

With the outbreak of the Civil War, Dix volunteered for service and was appointed superintendent of nurses for the Union Army. She organized the recruitment and training of thousands of nurses, and her development of the Army Nursing Corps greatly helped to legitimize women as health care providers. Although her imperiousness and autocratic behavior—she refused to accept members of religious sisterhoods or women under thirty—caused friction with army officials and doctors, and created controversy over her appointment, she remained chief of nurses until 1866. After the war Dix resumed her reform work of hospitals and prisons until she retired in 1881. She spent her last years living in the hospital in Trenton that she had helped into existence. Although she would probably be criticized today for her reliance on institutional rather than community care, there is no doubt that modern treatment of mental illness owes much to her pioneering work.

32

Hannah Arendt

1906–1976

Her penetrating analyses of totalitarianism and
democracy, the problems of mass society, the reasons
for revolution and political image making are widely
regarded as required reading for a thorough
understanding of modern political history.

—STEPHEN KLAIDMAN
Washington Post

Hannah Arendt is recognized as one of the twentieth century's
most brilliant and original political theorists. Her best-known
works, *The Origins of Totalitarianism, The Human Condition, Eichmann
in Jerusalem,* and *On Revolution,* written in a postwar climate of

reevaluation and uncertainty, are classics of political history and philosophy that have lost none of their relevance.

Born in Hanover, Germany, Hannah Arendt was the only child of Paul Arendt, an engineer, and Martha Cohn Arendt. Her father died in 1913; seven years later her mother remarried. Arendt was a precocious child who learned to read before entering kindergarten. After her expulsion from the gymnasium for a breach of discipline, she studied with a private tutor and audited courses at the University of Berlin to prepare for the final university entrance exam. At the University of Marburg, Arendt studied philosophy with Martin Heidegger and, after a semester at Freiburg, studied at Heidelberg with philosopher Karl Jaspers, who became a second father to her. Under Jaspers's supervision, Arendt completed her dissertation on St. Augustine's concept of love and, in 1929, received her doctorate in philosophy. Both Heidegger and Jaspers initiated Arendt's interest in existentialism, and their philosophies influenced her later work.

In 1933 Arendt began writing a biography of Rahel Vernhagen, an eighteenth-century Jewish salon hostess in Berlin. At the same time, she collected materials on German anti-Semitism for Zionist friends. The latter activity resulted in her arrest by the Gestapo. After a week's imprisonment, she left Germany for Paris, where she did social work for the Youth Aliyah, arranging for the emigration of orphaned and homeless European children to Palestine. In 1940 she married art historian Heinrich Blücher. Shortly after their marriage they were interned in separate camps in the south of France. Arendt and Blücher both managed to escape during the German occupation of Paris and, with Arendt's mother, obtained visas to come to America in 1941.

During the 1940s Arendt worked as a book editor, was a research director for the Conference on Jewish Relations and executive director of Jewish Cultural Reconstruction, and wrote articles for the *Partisan Review,* the *Review of Politics,* and *The Nation.* In 1950 she became a U.S. citizen. The following year she published *The Origins of Totalitarianism,* which firmly established her status as a major political thinker and historian. Based on a series of articles, this three-part work traces the origins of Nazi and Communist state theories back to the collapse of the eighteenth-century European nation-states with their stable class structures and to the rise of nineteenth-century anti-Semitism, imperialism, and nationalism. The book was the first significant postwar study of totalitarianism and was enormously influential.

Arendt's acclaimed second major work, *The Human Condition* (1958), explored humanity's historical-political shift from private and active public realms to a liberal social realm in which moral virtue is compromised. In 1961 *The New Yorker* sent Arendt to Jerusalem to cover the trial of Nazi war criminal Adolf Eichmann. The pieces she wrote for the magazine evolved into her 1963 book *Eichmann in Jerusalem: A Report on the Banality of Evil*. Arendt's argument that Eichmann was essentially a banal, thoughtless bureaucratic tool of Nazi state evil and not an inherently despicable man invested with the individual power to kill millions caused considerable controversy. Her assertion that the complicity of Jewish leaders was a contributing factor in the destruction of European Jewry further outraged many Jews.

Arendt's other works include *On Revolution* (1963), which focuses on the American political model of local township government; *Men in Dark Times* (1968), diverse portraits of modern men and women of courage; and *Crises of the Republic* (1972), a collection of political essays of the late 1960s and early 1970s. At her death Arendt left the nearly completed manuscript for two volumes of a proposed three-volume work, *The Life of the Mind*, an analysis of the thought process. The first two volumes, titled *Thinking* and *Willing*, were edited by Arendt's closest American friend, writer Mary McCarthy, and published in 1978. Arendt left notes for the third volume, titled *Judging*.

A teacher as well as a writer, Arendt served on the faculties of a number of American universities, including the University of Chicago, Cornell, Columbia, and Berkeley, and in 1959 was the first woman to hold the rank of full professor at Princeton. From 1967 until her death, she was a professor at the New School for Social Research in New York.

Arendt died of a heart attack in New York at the age of sixty-nine. The best-known theorist of her generation, Arendt articulated a new science of politics that ultimately reflected her abiding concern with personal integrity. Her works continue to instruct us on the wisdom of rational political and inner discourse.

33

Mother Teresa

1910–1997

The poor deserve not only service and dedication,
but also the joy that belongs to human love.

—MOTHER TERESA

Many consider Mother Teresa, founder of the Missionaries of
Charity and 1979 Nobel Peace Prize winner, to be a saint. And
with good reason. For over forty-five years she ministered to the
destitute, diseased, and dying of Calcutta and other parts of the

world with a selfless devotion that was remarkable even by the standards of a Roman Catholic establishment that expects nothing less from its nuns.

Mother Teresa was born Agnes Goxha Bojaxhiu in Skopje, Macedonia. She was the youngest of three children of Drana and Nikola Bojaxhiu, Albanians who had settled in Macedonia, then part of the Turkish Ottoman Empire. Nikola Bojaxhiu was a prosperous merchant, active in local politics and in the Albanian nationalist movement. Both Bojaxhius were deeply religious Catholics who instilled in their children the importance of helping the poor. In 1918 Nikola Bojaxhiu died, possibly as the result of poisoning by political opponents. To support the family, Drana Bojaxhiu became a dressmaker. She continued her charitable works, often taking young Agnes with her on visits to the sick, the elderly, and the lonely. These visits, as well as her mother's belief that "When you do good, do it unobtrusively, as if you were tossing a pebble into the sea," made a lasting impression on Agnes. She was a studious, contemplative, and solitary child, who frequently spent time alone in church praying. By the age of twelve, she was sure she wanted to became a nun. Her mother did not offer an opinion, preferring instead to wait and see if her daughter's desire for the religious life was a passing phase or a true calling.

The calling was real, and the teenage Agnes decided to join the Loreto order, a missionary group of nuns who taught Indian and Anglo-Indian girls in Calcutta. After spending two months at the Loreto Abbey in Dublin, Ireland, learning English, the language used by the nuns to teach the children, eighteen-year-old Agnes departed for India. During her novitiate at the Loreto convent in Darjeeling, she continued her English lessons and studied Scripture, the rules of her order, Hindi, and Bengali. She also received instruction in teaching and taught European and Indian girls for two hours a day at the convent school. In 1931 Agnes took her first vows as a nun, choosing the name Teresa, after Saint Therese, the patron saint of missionaries. She was then sent to teach at the convent school in Entally, a district of Calcutta. She took her final vows in 1937 and eventually become the school's principal.

Although Sister Teresa loved her work, she became increasingly disturbed about the wretchedness of the poor who lived in the teeming Motijhil slum outside the convent walls. She wanted to leave the convent to help ease the suffering in Motijhil, but was forbidden to do so by the order's rule of enclosure. Her concern for the plight of the poor intensified after she witnessed the human devastation that followed a massive four-day riot between Hindus and Muslims in 1946. The riot was one of many that erupted between the two religious groups during the country's move toward independence. Soon afterward, Sister Teresa experienced what she later termed "the call within a call," a conviction that she "was to leave the convent and help the poor while living among them. It was an order. To fail it would have been to break the faith." In 1947 she was granted an exclaustration by church officials in Rome. This meant that she would continue to be a nun but would also be free to leave the convent to start her own congregation dedicated to serving the poor.

In December 1948, after receiving three months of basic training from Mother Anna Dengel and her Medical Missionary Sisters in Patna, Sister Teresa returned to Calcutta. She spent a few days helping the Little Sisters of the Poor, who provided shelter for destitute elderly people, then ventured out alone into the streets of Motijhil. She decided to start an outdoor school and the first day managed to gather five children around her while she scratched out lessons in the dirt with a stick. Soon, in her classroom under a tree, she was teaching forty children language and number basics, as well as sanitation and hygiene. She spent the rest of the day tending the sick, comforting the dying, and doing whatever else she could to alleviate the suffering in a city where disease, death, gnawing hunger, and growing hopelessness were the daily portion of the desperately poor.

Sister Teresa became an Indian citizen in 1949. That same year she moved into the home of Michael Gomes, an Indian-Catholic teacher she had met through her work. Gomes helped her obtain medical supplies and provided much-needed moral support. When Sister Teresa became the mother superior of a new order, the Missionaries of Charity, in 1950, Gomes's home was the congregation's first official headquarters. In 1953 Mother Teresa and her nuns moved to a three-story house, purchased with money borrowed from the archdiocese.

Through funding provided primarily by donations, Mother Teresa founded the first Missionaries of Charity establishment, the Nirmal Hriday, the Home for the Dying, a residence where the poor could die with dignity. She next established a home for abandoned children and teenage girls called the Children's Home of the Immaculate Heart. In addition, the Missionaries of Charity organized a food-distribution program, provided a van that brought medical treatment into schools, set up clinics for lepers, and founded the Town of Peace, a community for lepers. By the early 1960s the mission was represented in thirty locations throughout India. After papal status was granted in 1965, the mission began to expand worldwide, first to Venezuela, and, by 1991, to ninety-five countries, including the United States. Adding strength and diversity to the order are the Missionary Brothers of Charity and the International Association of Co-Workers of Mother Teresa, a lay group of volunteers, which numbered twenty-six hundred members by 1985. In 1987 the Missionaries of Charity opened hospices for AIDS victims in New York and California.

Mother Teresa was frequently honored throughout her career, receiving such awards as the first Pope John XXIII Peace Prize; India's Nehru Award for her efforts in Bangladesh; the U.S. Presidential Medal of Freedom; the Templeton Prize for Progress in Religion; and the Nobel Peace Prize. Her death in 1997 was an occasion for worldwide mourning. Her body lay in state in Calcutta, and her funeral was televised internationally.

The late Indian prime minister, Indira Gandhi, once said of Mother Teresa that "to meet her is to feel utterly humble, to sense the power of tenderness and the strength of love." Yet, despite the boundless admiration felt for her around the world, Mother Teresa was sometimes accused of perpetuating the cycle of poverty rather than taking political action to end it. However, it could also be argued that political solutions, while often well-intentioned, have so far done little to truly alter the conditions that afflict the poor of the world. The simple mission of Mother Teresa and her followers has been to marshal the forces of compassion and love to comfort and sustain those who continue to suffer. As columnist Abigail McCarthy observed, "In a world of structures and technology in which no person seems to matter very much [Mother Teresa] has affirmed the preciousness of each human life."

34

Karen Horney

1885–1952

Man has potentialities for good and evil, and we see that he does develop into a good human being if he grows up under favorable conditions of warmth and respect for his individuality....Psychoanalysis has become for us a means for liberation and growth as a human being.

—KAREN HORNEY
From a 1945 address
to her colleagues

Despite psychoanalyst Karen Horney's traditional use of the masculine in the quote above, much of her influential work centered around female psychology. She was the first and best critic of Sigmund Freud's ideas about female neuroses and of many of his theories on neurosis in general. Horney's revisionist theories, including the belief that psychoanalysis should be a humanistic endeavor rather than a rigid science, were fiercely rejected by the majority of her inflexible, strictly Freudian colleagues. But the independent-minded Horney was not one to yield to the pressure of the psychoanalytic establishment and its founding father. She was, writes biographer Susan Quinn, "simply incapable of accepting someone else's version of her own experience, what she once called, 'the delicate vibrations of my soul.'"

Born in Hamburg, Germany, Karen Horney was the younger of the two children of Sonni and Berndt Danielsen. Her father, a Norwegian-born sea captain, was a strict Evangelical Lutheran who browbeat his wife and children, and was subject to fits of pious rage. Although he did not approve of education for women, his daughter was determined to study medicine. After attending the local high school, she went on to the University of Freiburg. Sonni Danielsen, who had left her husband, soon joined her daughter there. While at Freiburg, Karen met law student Oscar Horney. They were married in 1909, while Karen Horney was a medical student at the University of Berlin.

Horney's interest in the relatively new science of psychiatry began after she sought relief from bouts of nervous exhaustion and depression in sessions with therapist Karl Abraham. She gained her medical degree from the University of Berlin in 1915, with a thesis on traumatic psychoses. Between 1911 and 1915 she also gave birth to three daughters, whom she loved dearly if not exclusively. She raised them to be independent and once spoke of her approach to child rearing as a "good psychoanalytic upbringing."

During World War I, Karen Horney worked with shell-shocked soldiers and other psychiatric patients at the military neuropsychiatric hospital and the Berlin Sanitorium. After the war, she was active in the Berlin Psychoanalytic Institute and opened a private practice, where most of her patients were women. During the 1920s Horney concentrated on reforming the psychoanalytic view of women established by Freud, theorizing that women do not experience penis envy but instead envy the superior position of men in society. The castration complex in a young girl is generated, according to Horney, when she is ultimately frustrated in her desire to emulate her father, whose gender brings with it numerous social and sexual privileges. Horney's theory was well received, in part because it did not deviate too greatly from Freudian doctrine. It also secured her reputation as an intriguingly independent thinker and an expert in female psychology.

Horney separated from her husband in 1926, and in 1932 she moved to Chicago. There she cofounded and became associate director of the Chicago Institute for Psychoanalysis. In 1934 she moved to New York, where she taught at the New School for Social Research and joined the New York Psychoanalytic Society and Institute. During the 1930s and 1940s Horney developed a theory of personality and new concepts of neurosis that deviated from orthodox Freudian analysis by emphasizing environmental and cultural rather than biological factors in the genesis of neurosis. "There is no such thing as a normal psychology that holds for all people," Horney wrote in her first highly praised book, *The Neurotic Personality of Our Time* (1939). She also anticipated the later attention given by therapists to the narcissistic personality by describing in *Our Inner Conflicts* (1945) how neurotic individuals seek to deny their emotional pain.

Horney's break with the New York Psychoanalytic Society and Institute came in 1941, after publication of her second book, *New Ways in Psychoanalysis*. In each chapter, Horney examined Freudian concepts and laid out her own alternatives. She also concluded that neurotic individuals need not accept a life marked by personal turmoil, as Freud suggested, and that analysts should take a more active role in a patient's therapy to help free him or her from neurosis. Society members were so enraged by Horney's revisionist theories, they voted her out of her position as a training analyst. Equally enraged, Horney and four other members resigned from the society. They subsequently founded the Association for the Advancement of Psychoanalysis and its training arm, the American Institute for Psychoanalysis, which was renamed the Karen Horney Clinic after Horney's death.

Karen Horney's other works include *Self-Analysis* (1942), *Are You Considering Psychoanalysis?* (1946), *Neurosis and Human Growth* (1950), and *Feminine Psychology*, published posthumously in 1967. Throughout her career, Horney remained optimistic about a patient's capacity to heal psychic wounds in therapy and to continue the process once therapy ends. "Life itself," she once maintained, "still remains a very effective therapist."

35

Emily Dickinson

1830–1886

Her poetic strategy depended upon the "language of
surprise," wit, paradox, and irony, to reveal the naked
soul in dramatic conflict with established convention.

—JOHN B. PICARD
Emily Dickinson

The details of Emily Dickinson's life can be quickly summarized: born, lived, and died in Amherst, Massachusetts. During her lifetime, only a handful of her poems were published
anonymously. After her death, over seventeen hundred poems
were discovered hidden in her bureau. Their legacy was to earn
Emily Dickinson recognition as one of the world's greatest and

most innovative poets. If her life was sedate and quiet, her poems show depths of turmoil rarely visited by other writers. Her dramatic conflicts were played out internally and in her art. In her words, "The soul should always stand ajar, ready to welcome the ecstatic experience."

Emily Dickinson was one of the three children of Edward Dickinson, a lawyer, legislator, and the treasurer of Amherst College, whose father had been one of the school's founders. Her mother was an invalid, timid and completely subservient to her puritanical and authoritarian husband. The Amherst of Emily Dickinson's day was a rigidly conservative village of four hundred to five hundred families, in which the church wielded the highest authority. The rebel of the Dickinson family was Emily's brother, Austin, a lawyer who married a "worldly" New Yorker against his father's wishes and smuggled forbidden books to his sister, thus giving her access to a wider world. Emily was educated at Amherst Academy and attended Mount Holyoke Female Seminary for a short time. As a child and young adult, she enjoyed parties and the other social activities of Amherst, but after her schooling, she became increasingly reclusive, confining herself to a small circle of family and a few trusted friends, and attending to her household responsibilities. She rarely left home, except for brief visits to Washington, Philadelphia, and Boston. Dickinson rejected the Calvinist Protestantism of her family and kept her own counsel about her religious faith, as well as about much else.

It is speculated that Dickinson may have fallen in love with her father's law apprentice Benjamin Newton, who, in 1848, was living with her family. A brilliant freethinker, Newton introduced Emily to a new world of ideas, but was too poor to marry. He died of tuberculosis in 1853, after having begun his law practice in a town some distance away from Amherst. Another suspected emotional attachment was with the Reverend Charles Wadsworth, whom Dickinson met in Philadelphia in 1854, while she was on her way to visit her father, then in Washington serving a term in Congress. Although married, Wadsworth regularly visited Dickinson in Amherst until 1862, when he accepted a position in California. Following his departure from her life, Dickinson produced a flood of poetry depicting personal crisis and emotional turbulence. In her middle years, she acquired the reputation of an eccentric recluse who dressed perpetually in white and was rarely seen even by visitors to the Dickinson home. New evidence suggests, however, that her human contact and friendships were more varied and sustained than has been previously supposed.

Dickinson was encouraged in her writing by her girlhood friend, author Helen Hunt Jackson, and by author and abolitionist Thomas Wentworth Higginson, who examined her poems and tried to convert her to a more conventional style. She also received advice from Samuel Bowles, the editor of the *Springfield Republican*, who published seven of her poems. Her posthumous fame began when two volumes of her poetry and some of her correspondence were edited and published by Higginson and Mabel Loomis Todd, an author and friend of Emily Dickinson's, in 1890, 1891, and 1894. Later collections, beginning in 1914, established her as a major poet and an important influence on twentieth-century American poets. Dickinson's poetry, in turn, shows the influence of Calvinism and its preoccupation with the relationship between God, self, and nature. Her poetic style is compressed and emotional, harnessed by the narrow limits of the rhymed quatrains of Protestant hymn books, but pushed to a new expressiveness by rhythmic variations and unconventional rhymes. The emotional and intellectual weight she gives to her images transforms her verses from deceptively simple quatrains to wider, more cosmic speculations on God, death, and love, rendered with a lively, witty, and ironic intensity. She anticipated by several decades modern poetry's use of assonance and the power of elliptical thought and ambiguity. Throughout her work an intense, rebellious, and completely original poet is revealed. One of her own poems serves as a fitting testimony for this great poetic voice:

> This is my letter to the world,
>   That never wrote to me,—
> The simple news that Nature told,
>   With tender magisty.
>
> Her message is committed
>   To hands I cannot see,
> For love of her, sweet countrymen,
>   Judge tenderly of me!

36

Golda Meir

1898–1978

Golda Meir lived under pressure that we in this country would find impossible to understand. She is the strongest woman to head a government in our time and for a very long time past.

—WALTER CRONKITE
Quoted in Karen McAuley,
*World Leaders Past and
Present: Golda Meir*

Golda Meir, who began as a kibbutz worker in Palestine and rose from the ranks to become Israel's first, and to date, only, woman prime minister, was one of the most influential leaders in the Middle East. From Israel's birth in 1948 until her death thirty years later, Meir served her country's interests with an unflagging devotion that reflected her unswerving faith in the Zionist promise.

Golda Meir was born Golda Mabovitch in the Jewish quarter of Kiev, Ukraine. Her father, a carpenter, emigrated to the United States in 1903. In 1906 his wife and three daughters joined him. The family settled in Milwaukee, where Golda worked in her mother's small grocery store and attended school. When her parents refused to let her go to high school, fourteen-year-old Golda left home to live with her older sister, Sheyna, in Denver. She started high school and worked afternoons in a dry-cleaning shop. The sisters did not get along, and, after a year, Golda moved out. She dropped out of high school and supported herself with jobs in a laundry and a department store, then returned to Milwaukee after her parents promised not to interfere with her education. She finished high school in less than two years and went on to the Milwaukee Normal School for Teachers. At the same time, she became active in the Zionist labor movement.

In 1917 Golda married Morris Meyerson, whom she persuaded to emigrate to Palestine in 1921 as a condition of their marriage. After two years at the Merhavia kibbutz, the Meyersons moved to Jerusalem, where they both found jobs with the Histadrut, or Labor Federation. The marriage faltered, and Golda moved back to Merhavia for a time. When she returned to Jerusalem, she taught English in a private school and took in washing to supplement the family income, since her husband's health was poor, and the couple had two children. In 1928, after four years of devoting herself exclusively to her family, Golda decided to become more active in the political affairs of Palestine. As she wrote to her sister Sheyna, "My social activities are not an accidental thing: they are an absolute necessity for me." The Meyersons separated in 1941.

Golda began to work within the labor movement, becoming secretary of the Women's Labor Council and eventually a member of the executive committee of the Histadrut. In 1940 she became head of the Labor Federation's political department, representing the Histadrut at international conferences. As a delegate of the World Zionist Council, Golda undertook several fundraising missions to the United States and Britain. An eloquent and effective speaker, she was highly successful at generating support for the Israeli cause, and after 1946, for the new nation's very survival.

After the British Mandate was enforced in Palestine in 1946, Golda replaced the director of the political department of the Jewish Agency, who had been arrested by the British. She successfully negotiated the transfer to Palestine of thousands of families from British internment camps in Cyprus. In May 1948 she was one of the signatories of the Israeli Declaration of Independence and became the country's first ambassador to the Soviet Union. She was elected to the Knesset (Israel's parliament) in 1949 as a representative of the Labor Party and served as minister of labor under Israel's first prime minister, David Ben-Gurion. During her ministry, Israel's work force increased substantially. In 1950 she was named minister of foreign affairs. That same year, Morris Meyerson died, and Ben-Gurion asked members of his government to take Hebrew names. Golda wanted a name similar to Meyerson and chose Meir, which means "illuminate." From 1953 to 1966, Meir chaired the Israeli delegation to the United Nations. As U.N. delegate, she was placed in the delicate position of having to justify Israel's preemptive military action against Egypt during the Suez Crisis of 1956. Throughout her career, however, Meir was adamant and unapologetic concerning Israel's right to defend itself, once explaining to a *Life* magazine reporter, "We have always said that in our war with the Arabs we had a secret weapon—no alternative."

From 1965 to 1968, Meir was secretary-general of the Labor Party. She then retired, but on the death of Levi Eshkol in 1969 she was asked to take over as interim prime minister pending elections. She retained the post after elections were held in October. As prime minister of a coalition government, she dominated the Knesset and demonstrated toughness combined with humor and warm-heartedness during negotiations with hostile Arab nations and with the United States, Israel's greatest supporter. In 1971 Meir defeated a no-confidence vote engineered by her opponents in the Knesset, who felt that she had made excessive concessions to Egypt in peace negotiations. She still retained tremendous personal popularity.

After a surprise attack by Egyptian-Syrian troops, which took place on Yom Kippur in 1973, Meir rallied Israeli forces.

They finally managed to push back the aggressors and penetrate deeply into Syrian and Egyptian territory, but sustained heavy losses, and Meir's government was criticized for its unpreparedness. Meir resigned in 1974 after twice failing to form a new coalition government. She remained active in the Labor Party but became embittered when Egyptian president Anwar Sadat embarked on peace talks with the Conservative government of her political rival, Menachem Begin. She died in 1978 after a fifteen-year battle with cancer.

Despite the criticisms that dogged her at the end of her career, Meir's strength, vision, and lifelong dedication to building a Jewish nation have earned her a place as one of history's most remarkable women. As a *New York Times* editorial stated, "The miracle of Golda Meir was how one person could perfectly embody the spirit of so many."

37

Virginia Woolf

1882–1941

I do not know if she is going to exert an influence on
the future development of the novel—I rather suspect
that her style and her vision were so unique that
influence would only result in tame imitation—but I
cannot imagine a time, however bleak, or a writer,
whatever his school, when and for whom her devotion to
her art, her industry, her severity with herself—above
all, her passionate love, not only or chiefly for the big
moments of life but also for its daily humdrum "sausage-
and-haddock" details—will not remain an example that
is at once an inspiration and a judge.

—W. H. AUDEN
Forewords and Afterwards

If one were to compile a list of the most important twentieth-century English writers, Virginia Woolf's name, along with only a handful of other women, would certainly be included. Woolf, along with James Joyce, redefined the art of the novel, taking it from surface realism to the deeper reaches of consciousness, and profoundly influenced the majority of novelists who followed her. As an essayist and critic, she wrote convincingly about the fate of women artists and the restrictions from which they suffered.

Virginia Woolf was born in London, the third child in a family of two boys and two girls. She was the daughter of renowned Victorian critic, biographer, and scholar Leslie Stephen. Her mother, Julia, was a famous beauty and hostess to a distinguished literary circle that gathered at the Stephens' home. Leslie Stephen's impressive library was the locus of Virginia's education. The Stephen children, Virginia, Vanessa, Thoby, and Adrian, were encouraged in intellectual pursuits by both parents, but it was her father's training that had the greatest impact on Virginia. During the children's daily lessons, he instructed Virginia how to read sensitively and to appreciate fine writing. From her father, she learned that words and ideas were not only supremely important but endlessly fascinating. As Woolf later recalled about her father, "As he lay back in his chair and spoke the words with closed eyes, we felt that he was speaking not merely the words of Tennyson or Wordsworth but what he himself felt and knew. Thus many of the great English poems now seem to me inescapable from my father; I hear in them not only his voice, but in some sort his teaching and belief."

The family spent two months each summer in St. Ives in Cornwall, which Virginia loved "not only because it provided refreshment to the soul and stimulus to the imagination but because in that setting informal family life flourished." Julia Stephen died when Virginia was thirteen, and her father's deep mourning contributed to the first of several breakdowns that would recur throughout her life. Without the softening effect of his wife, Leslie Stephen ran the household as an inflexible and unforgiving Victorian patriarch. Woolf later remembered that "it was like being shut up in a cage with a wild beast." Her father died in 1904, which resulted in a second breakdown, as well as a suicide attempt. When Virginia recovered, she moved with her

brothers and sister to a home of their own in bohemian Bloomsbury. There they were at the center of an eccentric and talented
circle of artists, critics, and writers who would become famous as
the Bloomsbury Group. Included were such figures as critic and
biographer Lytton Strachey, writer Vita Sackville-West, novelist
E. M. Forster, and economist John Maynard Keynes.

In 1912 Virginia married Leonard Woolf, a critic and writer
on economics. The following year, she completed her first novel,
The Voyage Out, which she had been working on for six years. It
was published in 1915. In 1917 the Woolfs purchased a handpress
and founded the Hogarth Press, which would publish not only
some of Woolf's own books but other important modernist works,
including the poetry of T. S. Eliot. Woolf's second novel, *Night
and Day*, appeared in 1919, and like her first novel, was traditional
in method. In her subsequent novels, Woolf began to experiment
with less conventional form, using a more poetic, subjective style
to render a character's stream of consciousness, and turning the
novel inward to explore private thoughts and feelings. *Jacob's
Room* (1922), *Mrs. Dalloway* (1925), and her masterpiece *To the
Lighthouse* (1927), each written in her new style, center not on plot,
but on the inner, psychological world of her characters. Woolf's
love affair with Vita Sackville-West inspired her 1929 novel,
Orlando, a mock biography that pursues a single character from
Elizabethan times to the present, the protagonist changing sexes
to fit each age.

During the 1920s and 1930s, Woolf wrote several volumes of
criticism. In *A Room of One's Own* (1929), first presented by her as a
lecture at Oxford University, and in *Three Guineas* (1938), she took
up the cause of feminism and addressed the difficulties faced by
women writers. As she observed, "A woman's writing is always
feminine; it cannot help being feminine; at its best it is most
feminine." Long suppressed and ignored, this feminine perspective needed, in Woolf's famous formula, "five hundred pounds a
year and a room of one's own" to develop.

In 1941, depressed over the outbreak of war and sensing that
another breakdown was imminent, Virginia Woolf committed
suicide by drowning herself. In her distinguished career as a
writer, she had met the challenge urged by her father to make the
highest use of her intellect and emotions. Her influence on both
the history of the novel and on women writers who have re-

sponded to her call to give voice to the feminine, continues to be significant. "Her genius," wrote novelist and playwright Christopher Isherwood, "was intensely feminine and personal—private almost. To read one of her books was (if you liked it) to receive a letter from her, addressed specially to you...."

38

Queen Victoria

1819–1901

The finest and most poetic thing that can be said about
the Queen is...that her virtues and powers are *not* those
of a great woman like Elizabeth or Catherine II...but
are the virtues and powers of an ordinary woman:
things that any person, however humble, can appreciate
and imitate...an example inextricably precious to the
whole world.

—ALFRED MUNBY
Letter to Austin Dobson,
July 4, 1897

The England that Victoria came to rule in 1837 was still the largely agrarian, self-contained England of Elizabeth I, on the brink of a profound social and technological transformation. Upon her death nearly sixty-four years later, after the longest reign of any British monarch, the England she left was a modern, industrial nation whose colonial empire encompassed the globe. Victoria steadfastly oversaw this transformation and expansion, and in the process, set her stamp on the age that bears her name. She elevated the crown from partisan party intrigue and restored the prestige it had lost during the reigns of mad King George III, profligate George IV, and eccentric William IV. Moreover, she was a firm and secure presence in a turbulent century, a ruler who came to personify the prevailing values of duty, family, conscience, morality, and stability.

Alexandrina Victoria was the only child of Edward, Duke of Kent, and Princess Mary Louise Victoria of Saxe-Coburg Saalfeld. Her father, the younger brother of George IV and William IV, died when she was eight months old. Victoria grew up cloistered and protected, a pawn in the high-stakes political intrigue between her ambitious mother, aligned with her lover, Sir John Conroy, and a court in need of a respectable heir. Her mother isolated her from any influence other than her own. Throughout her childhood, Victoria was not allowed a room of her own and slept in her mother's room, and her education was carefully monitored by a German tutor. She was denied access to newspapers and any reading more intellectually stimulating than devotional and edifying books and poetry. Victoria was drilled daily in languages, religion, drawing, and singing. Her place in the succession, always in doubt by the possibility that William IV might father an heir, was carefully kept from her until she was eleven years old. When she was finally shown a book of the peerage, she is said to have remarked, "I see I am nearer to the throne than I thought....I will be good." Victoria was an affectionate, though at times a quick-tempered, girl, barely five feet tall and inclined to plumpness.

William IV died when Victoria was eighteen and legally able to succeed to the throne, disappointing her mother, who had hoped for a regency over the young queen. Victoria assumed her duties with an independence and confidence unusual in a young woman who had been so sheltered and controlled. She immediately distanced herself from her mother's influence, sleeping in a room by herself for the first time on the night of her accession, and impressed her ministers by her grasp of her responsibilities. She endured the five-hour coronation ceremony at Westminster with dignity, and followed it by giving her dog a bath. Thomas Carlyle observed that "she is at an age at which a girl can hardly be trusted to choose a bonnet for herself, yet a task is laid upon her from which an archangel might shrink." Victoria threw herself totally into her role as queen, relishing the power and the privileges of her rank. Her primary adviser and father-figure during the early years of her reign was the Whig prime minister, Lord Melbourne, to the embarrassment and distrust of the Tory opposition.

In 1840 the queen married her first cousin, Prince Albert of Saxe-Coburg Gotha, who was to become not only a devoted husband and father but also Victoria's closest adviser. At first denied a role in political and state affairs, Albert soon became the dominant influence on Victoria, helping to complete her education in his passions of science and technology, music, art, and statecraft. Their first child, Victoria, later empress of Germany, was born in 1840, followed a year later by Albert, the Prince of Wales, later Edward VII. Seven more children followed, though Victoria was not overly fond of babies, disliked pregnancy, and abhorred childbirth (she used chloroform during the birth of her seventh child, ending the moral controversy over the use of analgesics in obstetrics). Through marriage, Victoria's children would connect the British royal house with those of Germany, Russia, Greece, Denmark, and Romania, giving Britain a kind of parental status in Europe that would last into the next century.

In 1851, through Albert's patronage, the Crystal Palace Exhibition was held to immense popular acclaim. A showcase for the technological wonders of the century and the fruits of the Empire, the Crystal Palace became the symbol of the age, and represented the high-water mark of Victoria's reign. During the Crimean War of 1853 to 1856, the royal family was suspected of being pro-Russian, a charge Victoria countered by displaying a staunchly nationalistic fervor. She instituted the Victoria Cross for military bravery and supported war-relief efforts, including

Florence Nightingale's medical reforms. The tragedy of her life occurred in 1861 when Albert died of typhoid fever. The inconsolable queen disappeared from public affairs for three years and took on the mourning attire she was to wear for the rest of her life. The Widow at Windsor, as Rudyard Kipling called her, was persuaded to return to public life largely by Conservative prime minister Benjamin Disraeli, whose urbanity, wit, and aggressively expansionist foreign policy made him the queen's great favorite. Victoria disliked the other prominent prime minister of her reign, Liberal William Gladstone, whom she once described as "so very arrogant, tyrannical, and obstinate, with no knowledge of the world or human nature."

In 1876 Britain reinforced its control over India by giving Victoria the title of Empress of India. The queen was passionately interested in the welfare of her colonial subjects, though she never visited India or any other distant colony.

The fiftieth anniversary of Victoria's reign (the Golden Jubilee) in 1887 and the sixtieth in 1897 (the Diamond Jubilee) were grand occasions of great popular outpourings of affection for the queen who had reigned so long and so conscientiously. Her death in 1901 ushered in the new Edwardian era, when she and her age came to be seen as ponderous, old-fashioned, excessively moralistic, and repressed. It was only after the violence and chaos caused by two world wars in thirty years, followed by the collapse of the Empire, that the British began to once again appreciate the stability and prosperity Victoria had helped secure during her long reign. She had ruled over the most powerful nation on earth with an intriguing combination of majesty and bourgeois sensibility that would become the hallmark of succeeding British royals. As biographer Stanley Weintraub writes, "What Victoria had left behind as legacy was the sturdy ceremonial monarchy now ratified by public affection, by a yearning for continuity and tradition, and by the middle-class values that were her own and that remain beneath the fairy-tale veneer of royalty. She became England."

39

Martha Graham

1894–1991

In a dancer's body, we as audience must see ourselves, not the imitated behavior of everyday action, not the phenomenon of nature, not exotic creatures from another planet, but something of the miracle that is a human being.

> —MARTHA GRAHAM
> Quoted by Iris M. Fanger,
> "An American Modern,"
> *Christian Science Monitor,*
> June 9, 1986

Dancer, choreographer, and teacher Martha Graham has been described by her biographer, Agnes De Mille, as "a woman who made a greater change in her art...than almost any other single artist who comes readily to mind." Graham began by studying the Greek- and Oriental-inspired impressionistic and interpretive free-form movements of such modern dance pioneers as Isadora Duncan and Ruth St. Denis, and went on to create totally new forms of expression. She brought theater to modern dance and female sexuality from the female point of view to high art. Duncan and St. Denis changed the art of the dance, but Graham went even further: She changed the way we look at the world. Because of her singular influence on modern dance, an art form that would not have flourished without her, I have given her a relatively high ranking.

Martha Graham was born in Allegheny, Pennsylvania, the oldest of three daughters of George Graham, a psychiatrist, and Jane Beers Graham. The family moved to Pittsburgh and then to Santa Barbara, California, when Graham was fourteen. As a child, she was introduced to the world of the theater by her Irish nurse, Lizzie, who would make up musical plays for the Graham children to perform.

Graham was inspired to become a dancer after attending a recital given by Ruth St. Denis in 1911. As she later wrote: "Miss Ruth opened a door for me and I saw into a life." In 1916 Graham departed for Los Angeles to enroll in the Denishawn School of Dancing, run by St. Denis and her husband, dancer and choreographer Ted Shawn. Shy and awkward at first, Graham gradually gained confidence as a dancer, largely because of the encouragement of Denishawn's musical director, Louis Horst. "His sympathy and understanding, but primarily his faith, gave me a landscape to move in," she once said of him. Horst would continue with Graham, serving as her mentor and accompanist, for thirty years.

In 1920 Graham made her debut with the Denishawn Company, dancing the lead in *Xochitl*, an Aztec-inspired ballet that was created for her. She danced with the company until 1923, when, on the advice of Horst, she joined the Greenwich Village Follies. As a solo performer with the Follies, she worked with standard themes of modern dance and appeared in pieces that were basically moving *tableaux vivants*. After two years with the Follies, Graham accepted a teaching position at the Eastman School of Music in Rochester, New York. There she worked at training her body to move in ways and contexts different from any ever before attempted. She abandoned the lyrical, interpretive style of traditional modern dance for a sharper more dissonant form that would use the dancer's body to express inner feeling through movement and reflect a contemporary mood. "Life today is nervous, sharp and zigzag," she said. "It often stops in midair. That is what I aim for in my dances."

In 1926 Graham presented her new idiom in her first independent dance concert at the 48th Street Theatre in New York City. Her pieces, choreographed to the music of such Impressionist composers as Ravel and Debussy, were greeted with contempt by the traditionalists. However, Graham continued to draw audiences, which she claimed was her criterion for success. She went on to expand the themes of desire and conflict, creating stark studies in female ostracism, including *Revolt* (1927) and *Heretics* (1929). In 1930, at the invitation of conductor Leopold Stokowski, she danced the role of Élue, the Chosen One, in Leonide Massine's version of Stravinsky's *Rite of Spring*. She also created one of her most famous works, *Lamentations*, a solo piece in which she wore a long tube of material to indicate, as she put it, "the tragedy that obsesses the body, the ability to stretch inside your own skin, to witness and test the perimeters and boundaries of grief, which is honorable and universal."

During the 1930s Graham founded the Martha Graham School of Contemporary Dance and the Martha Graham Company of dancers, both of which would become world famous. In 1934 she began teaching summer workshops at Bennington College in Vermont. While at Bennington she created one of her most important works, *Letter to the World*, an interpretation of Emily Dickinson's poetry and a revelation of the poet's inner life. Graham's interest in American themes and archetypes, which she had explored in her dances, *Frontier* and *American Document*, culminated in her best-known ballet, *Appalachian Spring* (1944). She then moved on to produce works based on Freudian and Jungian themes, centering on historical and folkloric female archetypes such as Jocasta (*Night Journey*), Medea (*Cave of the Heart*), *Clytemnestra*, *Phaedra*, Joan of Arc (*Seraphic Dialogue*), and the biblical heroine Judith (*The Legend of Judith*). Her 1943 work *Deaths and Entrances* features characters drawn from the Brontë sisters and from Graham's own family. In 1949 Graham married Erich Hawkins, her dancing partner and longtime lover. The marriage was not a success and ended after two years.

Graham was frequently honored and spotlighted throughout her long career. A 1957 television documentary on Graham, *A Dancer's World*, received numerous awards, as did the film of her ballet *Night Journey*. She received numerous grants, and in 1981 was the recipient of the Scripps American Dance Festival Award, the largest grant ever awarded to anyone in the field of dance. She continued to dance until she was in her seventies and to create ballets and teach classes until her death at the age of ninety-six. Her last work was the uncharacteristically jazz-oriented *Maple Leaf Gala*, which premiered a few months before her death. In 1990 she wrote her autobiography, *Blood Memory*, published in 1991. In 1994, Graham's centenary, a documentary on her life and work was aired on PBS.

Graham choreographed over 160 ballets during her lifetime. She was a major influence on two generations of dancers: More than three-fourths of her performers went on to become choreographers and directors of dance companies, among them Paul Taylor, Merce Cunningham, and Graham's ex-husband Erich Hawkins. For Martha Graham, dance was "the hidden language of the soul of the body." Her technique continues to attract scores of disciples, who find in it, in the words of one young woman student, "the freedom to be bold."

40

Zora Neale Hurston

1901–1960

Zora Neale Hurston was...a woman who rejoiced in print about the beauty of being black. When her blues came, when bigots and rednecks and crackers and liberals and racial missionaries got her down, she retreated into a privacy that protected her sense of self; publicly, she avoided confrontation by announcing that she didn't look at a person's color, only one's worth. She personally believed in an integrated society, but she spent her career trying to preserve and celebrate black cultural practices. Her life testifies only for her particular black experience, but her career witnesses for contemporary black authors.

—ROBERT E. HEMENWAY
Zora Neale Hurston

One of America's most influential black writers, Zora Neale Hurston was a central figure in the Harlem Renaissance. She recorded and incorporated black folk tales and traditions into her work, invigorating literature with the power and expressiveness of the black vernacular. A brash and opinionated woman, she produced a series of novels and folklore collections that significantly gave voice to the black experience.

Zora Neale Hurston was born in Eatonville, Florida, the first incorporated black community in the United States. Her father, John Hurston, was the mayor of Eatonville and a Baptist preacher. The town's vibrant folk tradition and its frequent "lying" sessions of tall tales had a great impact on Zora, who absorbed many of the stories told by her elders and soon began to make up tales of her own. When her mother died and her father remarried, Hurston was passed about from boarding school to friends and relatives. At sixteen she worked as a wardrobe girl for a traveling light-opera troupe. She quit the show in Baltimore and went to work as a maid for a white woman who arranged for her to attend high school at the Morgan Academy.

From 1918 to 1924, Hurston studied part time at Howard University in Washington, D.C., while working as a manicurist. Her first writing appeared in the African-American magazine *Opportunity*, whose founder, Charles Johnson, encouraged her to come to New York to develop her writing and to finish her college degree. While studying anthropology at Barnard College, she wrote poems, plays, articles, and stories, and in 1925 she received several awards given by *Opportunity* to promising black writers. After her graduation from Barnard, Hurston went on to Columbia University to study with eminent cultural anthropologist Franz Boas, and this profoundly influenced her work. She then did field research in Eatonville, collecting data that she would include in her folklore collections and novels. After subsequent research in Haiti and Jamaica, she produced two important folklore collections, *Mules and Men* (1935) and *Tell My Horse* (1938). Her novels include *Jonah's Gourd Vine* (1934), *Their Eyes Were Watching God* (1937), *Moses, Man of the Mountain* (1939), and *Seraph on the Sewanee* (1948). Her autobiography, *Dust Tracks on the Road*, was published in 1942.

Hurston was a complex woman. Her literary biographer,

Robert Hemenway, described her as "flamboyant yet vulnerable, self-centered yet kind, a Republican conservative and an early black nationalist." African-American critics complained that the folk elements in her work were demeaning and one-dimensional. Seeking acceptance by mainstream literary standards, black writers feared that Hurston's evocation of rural black experience marginalized and diminished wider acceptance of African Americans. Few credited Hurston's work as a major source of vernacular strength and lyrical power. Critic Judith Wilson has observed that Hurston "had figured out something that no other black author of her time seems to have known or appreciated so well—that our homespun vernacular and street-corner cosmology is as valuable as the grammar and philosophy of white, Western culture."

Convinced of the vitality and promise of the black community—no doubt influenced by her experience in Eatonville—Hurston opposed legislation that forced integration, and her stand alienated her from other African Americans who pushed for assimilation into mainstream white culture. Her advocacy of the strength and vibrancy of black culture predated the black power and cultural movements that began in the 1960s. During Hurston's later years, her works were neglected and she lived in extreme poverty. She worked for a time as a maid, a librarian, and as a columnist for the *Fort Pierce Chronicle*. She was buried in an unmarked grave in a cemetery in Fort Pierce until writer Alice Walker, who has been instrumental in restoring Hurston's reputation, had a headstone erected.

Zora Neale Hurston is today acknowledged as one of the most important black writers of the twentieth century. Few college courses on African-American writing fail to include at least one of her books. Her masterpiece, *Their Eyes Were Watching God*, has been favorably compared to Richard Wright's *Native Son*, and is widely regarded, writes Robert Hemenway, "as one of the most poetic works of fiction by a black writer in the first half of the twentieth century, and one of the most revealing treatments in modern literature of a woman's quest for a satisfying life." Zora Neale Hurston remains a unique and influential literary ancestor to a later generation of African-American writers more sympathetic to this woman who defied a narrow categorization.

41

Harriet Beecher Stowe

1811–1896

To her who in our evil time
Dragged into light the nation's crime
With strength beyond the strength of men
And, mightier than their sword, her pen...
> —JOHN GREENLEAF WHITTIER
> Quoted in Johanna Johnston,
> *Runaway to Heaven, the Story*
> *of Harriet Beecher Stowe*

It was only half in jest that Abraham Lincoln called Harriet Beecher Stowe "the little lady who made this big war." Stowe's novel of slavery, *Uncle Tom's Cabin*, had, for a vast American and world audience, crystallized the abolitionist sentiments of the North and elucidated the moral purpose of the Civil War. Few, if any, works of fiction have wielded such influence.

Harriet was born in Litchfield, Connecticut, the seventh of nine children born to Lyman Beecher, a leading clergyman of the time. Harriet's mother died when she was five, and her father remarried shortly thereafter and produced four more children. Her childhood was generally happy amidst a large family circle that was dominated by a Calvinist father for whom God was a wrathful though attentive spirit. Like all the Beecher children, Harriet early developed an interest in theology and in schemes for improving humanity. She was educated at the Litchfield Academy and at the Hartford Female Seminary, where she assisted her sister Catherine, the school's founder, as a student-teacher.

In 1832 the Beecher family relocated to Cincinnati, where Lyman Beecher served as the first president of the Lane Theological Seminary. It was in this border city, across the river from the slave state of Kentucky, that Harriet was first exposed to the institution of slavery. Her brothers were violently opposed to slavery, and Harriet had aided a runaway slave, but she was not yet moved to write on the subject.

In 1836 she married Calvin Stowe, a biblical scholar and professor at the seminary. The couple had six children. Harriet began writing for the *Western Monthly Magazine*, the *New York Evangelist*, and other religious publications, and in 1843 published her first book of fiction, *The Mayflower: Sketches and Scenes and Characters Among the Descendants of the Puritans*.

In 1850 the Stowes and their children relocated to Brunswick, Maine, where Calvin Stowe had been offered a position on the faculty of Bowdoin College. The same year saw the passage of the Fugitive Slave Act, which mandated that slaves who escaped to freedom in the North be returned to their masters. Stowe's outrage over the act led her to write *Uncle Tom's Cabin or, Life Among the Lowly*, first published serially in an abolitionist newspaper, the *National Era*. Stowe began with the climactic scene of Tom's beating and death for refusing to reveal the hiding place of two escaped slaves and then worked her way back in a series of vivid scenes of slave life she felt she had not created but only described. "My vocation," she declared, "is simply that of a *painter*, and my object will be to hold up in the most lifelike and graphic manner possible, slavery, its reverses, changes, and the Negro character, which I have had ample opportunities for studying." She meant to persuade her readers of the evil of slavery, but she was careful in her depiction, intending to show "the best side of the thing, and something approaching the worst." Two of her slave owners, for example, are portrayed as kindly and honorable, while the third, the brutal, degenerate Simon Legree, is a renegade New Englander.

Stowe had modest expectations for her novel; what happened instead was a publishing phenomenon. Published in book form in 1852, a first edition of five thousand sold out in two days; twenty thousand copies were sold in less than three weeks. It has been estimated that three million copies of the book were eventually sold in the United States alone. *Uncle Tom's Cabin* appeared in forty different editions, and was translated into many foreign languages. Longfellow wrote in his journal: "How she is shaking the world with *Uncle Tom's Cabin*.... Never was there such a literary *coup-de-main* as this." English historian Thomas Macaulay called the novel, "the most valuable addition America has made to English literature." Tolstoy considered it the highest achievement of moral art, on the same level as *Les Misérables* and *A Tale of Two Cities*. Dramatizations of the novel flooded the stage, and it is said that between 1853 and 1930, it never ceased to be performed. Stowe had written the first genuine American bestseller, eliminating former Puritan prejudice against fiction as worthless entertainment.

Stowe also had her critics. She was predictably reviled in the South, where George F. Holmes, writing in the *Southern Literary Messenger*, stated that she "has shockingly traduced the slaveholding society of the United States...as the mouthpiece of a large and dangerous faction which, if we do not put down with the pen, we may be compelled one day...to repel with the bayonet." In the twentieth century, the novel's depiction of African Americans was criticized, and Uncle Tom become a synonym for black servility and accommodation under oppression. Stowe met criticism of the novel's innaccuracies with a defense published as *A Key to Uncle Tom's Cabin* (1853), which documented the abuses she had dramatized. Her most frequent defense, however, was her continual assertion that the Lord wrote the book, and she merely transcribed His words.

As a result of her novel's great success, Stowe found herself at the center of the antislavery crusade, although she never allied herself with the abolitionists, whom she considered extremists. She developed an interest in other reform movements, such as temperance and women's suffrage. Stowe continued to explore the issue of slavery by writing *Dred: A Tale of the Great Dismal Swamp*, which was published in 1856. Her later novels are set mainly in the New England of her childhood. She also wrote volumes of poetry, books for children, articles, and travel memoirs. A popular writer, Stowe aptly expressed the attitudes of nineteenth-century middle-class Americans. In the 1870s she thrilled audiences with public readings from her works. During the 1880s and 1890s her health and lucidity declined, and she spent her last years in the Hartford home she had built with the profits from *Uncle Tom's Cabin*.

Harriet Beecher Stowe's best-known novel is regarded today more as a significant cultural document than as a literary masterwork. But Stowe's "despairing appeal to a civilized humanity," as she put it, served its era well by galvanizing public opinion, as no other piece of writing had, in the great debate over slavery.

42

Rosa Luxemburg

1870–1919

She gave herself completely to the cause of socialism, not only in her tragic death, but throughout her life, daily and hourly, through the struggles of many years. She was the sharp sword, the living flame of the revolution.

—CLARA ZETKIN, close colleague of Rosa Luxemburg

One of history's greatest revolutionary leaders, Rosa Luxemburg's politics, forged in the cauldron of a Poland dominated by Russia and coveted by Germany, would lead her toward the proletarian promise of socialism and eventually to the founding of the Polish Socialist Party, the radical socialist Spartacus League, and the German Communist Party.

Rosa Luxemburg was born in the small Polish town of Zamość, the youngest of five children of a Jewish merchant. A hip disease as a child kept her in bed for a year. It was incorrectly treated, and Luxemburg had a pronounced limp for the rest of her life. Although she was small and fragile-looking, she was a bright, active, self-confident child who was particularly fond of reading, especially poetry. When Rosa was three years old, her family moved to Warsaw, where her father became a member of leading intellectual circles. In 1881 she experienced a pogrom against the Warsaw Jews, a frightening event that left her with a permanent terror of crowds. Growing up doubly oppressed by the Russian rulers and by the Polish Catholic majority, Luxemburg's refuge was the patriotic idealism of Polish poet and playwright Adam Mickiewicz. She was further influenced by the first Polish socialists and their illegal "proletariat" group, which she joined in 1887. In 1889, because of her revolutionary activities, she was forced to flee Warsaw for Zurich, home to many Polish émigrés and revolutionaries. There she met Leo Jogiches, a Lithuanian revolutionary, with whom she lived off and on for the next twenty years, and studied philosophy, economics, and law at the university. She earned her doctorate with a thesis on the industrial development of Poland. With Jogiches, she founded the Polish Socialist Party in 1892 and a splinter group, the Social Democratic Party of Poland in 1894.

In 1898 Rosa Luxemburg married German anarchist Gustav Lubecks in order to obtain German citizenship. In Berlin, she began to organize workers in the German Social Democratic Party, and with characteristic confidence wrote "I am convinced that in six months I'll be one of the best speakers in the Party." She was, in fact, an excellent speaker, able to mesmerize audiences with her zeal and expert political analysis. In 1904 she served a three-month prison sentence for insulting Emperor Wilhelm II in a public speech. The following year she returned to Poland on a false passport to organize workers' revolts in a Polish uprising against Russian troops. She was arrested by czarist police and imprisoned but was eventually rescued by the German Social Democratic Party (SPD), which bribed Russian officials to release her on bail. This experience with actual revolution made Luxemburg impatient with the theorizing and abstract debate of the German socialists, and in an influential pamphlet, *The Mass*

Strike, she called for full-scale action from the workers. In 1907 she was appointed instructor of economics at a school for SPD officials. She continued to write, publishing an important economic textbook in 1912 and her most famous work, *The Accumulation of Capital*, in 1914.

The outbreak of the First World War was a serious setback for Luxemburg, who feared that nationalism would undermine worker solidarity. She spent most of the war in prison, where she organized the Spartacus League with fellow socialist inmates Karl Liebknecht and Clara Zetkin. Led by Luxemburg and Liebknecht, the Spartacists demanded the establishment of a dictatorship of the proletariat, opposed the postwar democratic government, and engaged in sporadic acts of terrorism. Despite her commitment to Spartacist ideals, Luxemburg advocated gradual, spontaneous political change and was critical of Lenin's triumph in assuming power after the Bolshevik revolution. In an editorial criticizing Lenin and Trotsky's suspension of democratic rights, she wrote that "[Lenin] is completely mistaken in the means he employs: decree, the dictatorial power of a factory overseer..."

At a meeting held during the last days of 1918, Luxemburg was instrumental in transforming the Spartacists into the German Communist Party. In January 1919 Luxemburg and Liebknecht were arrested for taking part in a Communist uprising. They were taken from the police by soldiers, interrogated, beaten, and then shot. Luxemburg's body was thrown into a canal. Her murderers were eventually charged but acquitted.

The German Communist Party Rosa Luxemburg founded with such devotion to the socialist ideal grew in political strength only to perish in the flames of Nazi ambition. The communism of the Soviets would expire in its turn. Luxemburg, the astute political theorist, was certainly ahead of her time when she wrote, "Socialism by its very nature, cannot be dictated, introduced by command....Without general elections, without unrestricted freedom of press and assembly, without a free range of opinions, life dies out in every public institution and only bureaucracy remains active."

43

Mary McLeod Bethune

1875–1955

What does the Negro want? His answer is very simple. He wants only what other Americans want. He wants opportunity to make real what the Declaration of Independence and the Constitution and the Bill of Rights say, what the Four Freedoms establish. While he knows these ideals are open to no man completely, he wants only his equal chance to obtain them.

—MARY MCLEOD BETHUNE
"Certain Inalienable Rights,"
from *What the Negro Wants,*
1944

Mary McLeod Bethune is primarily known as a prominent educator who greatly enhanced educational opportunities for African-American girls. However, her outstanding efforts on behalf of the black community at the national and government level further enhance her status as one of America's most influential leaders and the most important African-American woman of her time.

Born in Mayesville, South Carolina, Bethune was one of the seventeen children of former slaves Sam and Patsy McLeod. As a child, Mary picked cotton on a plantation and walked ten miles to school, an experience that partly motivated her to later found a school for African-American children. A scholarship enabled her to attend the Scotia Seminary (later Barber-Scotia College), a Presbyterian school for black girls that emphasized religious and industrial education. Again with the help of scholarships, she studied at the Bible Institute for Home and Foreign Missions (later the Moody Bible Institute) in Chicago. Mary was the only black student at the institute. She graduated in 1895 with the intention of working as a missionary in Africa, but was told by the Presbyterian Mission Board that there were no available assignments for blacks in Africa.

Mary took a teaching job at the Haines Normal and Industrial Institute in Augusta, Georgia, whose founder and principal was Lucy Laney. Laney's success inspired Mary to strongly consider opening a school of her own. After teaching at the Kindell Institute in Sumter, North Carolina, where she met and married sometime teacher and salesman, Albertus Bethune, she moved with her husband and baby son to Palatka, Florida. There she accepted a teaching position with the Palatka Mission School for blacks, a Presbyterian Mission School, and separated from her husband.

In 1904 Bethune founded the Daytona Normal and Industrial Institute in Daytona Beach with money raised from cake and ice-cream sales to local construction workers. Her first students were five girls and her son; by 1923 there were three hundred girl students and twenty-five faculty and staff members. That year, with the sponsorship of the Board of Education for Negroes of the Methodist Episcopal Church, the Daytona Institute merged with the Cookman Institute in Jacksonville to become a coeducational college. In 1929 it was renamed Bethune-Cookman College, and in 1943 the fully accredited college awarded its first four-year degrees. Bethune stepped down as president of the college in 1942 to concentrate on fundraising for the school. She resumed the presidency in 1946 after a highly successful fundraising campaign and retired from the college as president emeritus in 1947.

Bethune was also active in several associations for African-American women. From 1917 to 1924, she served as president of the Florida Federation of Colored Women and in 1920 founded and was president of the Southeastern Federation of Colored Women. In 1924 she became president of the National Association of Colored Women, considered by many to be the highest position to which a black woman could aspire.

From the 1930s until her death in 1955, Bethune assumed many leadership roles. In 1935 she founded the National Council of Negro Women (NCNW), which united the major black women's associations nationally, and served as the council's president until 1949. She became the first African-American woman to be a presidential adviser when Franklin Roosevelt named her director of Negro Affairs of the National Youth Administration in 1936. In addition, she served as special adviser to FDR on minority affairs. She created the Federal Council on Negro Affairs, a group of African Americans working to strengthen black support of FDR's New Deal, to decrease discrimination, and to increase the number of government jobs for black Americans. Bethune also assisted the secretary of war on the selection of officer candidates for the Women's Army Auxiliary Corps, established in 1942. She represented the NCNW at the founding conference of the United Nations in 1945. Bethune also served as vice-president of the NAACP from 1940 to 1945, and later became vice-president of the National Urban League.

Despite Bethune's many achievements and success in voicing black concerns to the highest levels of government, she was not complacent regarding the future of African Americans. She fought energetically for equality, but her era, while paving the way for an awareness of minority issues, did not represent a watershed in black history. Bethune died the same year that Rosa Parks took her heroic stand against segregation. Perhaps Bethune presaged that historic moment and the civil rights movement that followed it when she stated in *What the Negro Wants*, "If we accept and acquiesce in the face of discrimination, we accept the responsibility ourselves and allow those responsible to salve their conscience by believing they have our acceptance and concurrence. We should, therefore, protest openly everything...that smacks of slander."

Charlotte Brontë

1816–1855

What passion, what fire in her!
—GEORGE ELIOT
   On Charlotte Brontë

Emily Brontë

1818–1848

Stronger than a man,
simpler than a child,
her nature stood alone.

—CHARLOTTE BRONTË
   On Emily Brontë

Almost as compelling as Charlotte and Emily Brontë's singular achievements as literary artists is the adversity that both women endured and transcended to produce their work. Each writer affected the course of English fiction in significant ways. As writers steadfastly devoted to their visions the Brontës continue to inspire; as women who struggled against a stifling and hostile environment, their achievement is magnified. Each woman managed to create unique and powerful reflections of a world rarely expressed or experienced as intensely by other novelists.

Charlotte and Emily Brontë were the third and fourth daughters in a family of five girls and one boy. Their father, Patrick Brontë, was the vicar of the parish of Haworth in the West Riding of Yorkshire, a wild and picturesque countryside of desolate moors. Their mother died in 1821, and the children were raised by an aunt and their puritanical and tyrannical father. Elizabeth Gaskell, Charlotte's biographer, has written of Patrick Brontë that his "strong, passionate Irish nature was, in general, compressed down with resolute stoicism....He did not speak when he was annoyed or displeased, but worked off his volcanic wrath by firing pistols out the back door in rapid succession." After the two eldest Brontë daughters, Maria and Elizabeth, died of tuberculosis, contracted at school, Charlotte and Emily, also at school, were brought home. There, the children were left largely to themselves. The major imaginative event of their young lives took place when Patrick Brontë brought home a box of wooden soldiers for his son, Branwell. Each child claimed one for his own. The soldiers became the dramatis personae in an ever-lengthening series of fantasy stories in which the children invented imaginary kingdoms and populated them with historical and literary figures. Charlotte's and Emily's first poems and stories, written in tiny script on small pieces of paper, were about these invented kingdoms and provide a key to the development of their remarkable genius. The Brontës' obsession with the worlds they created stayed with them well beyond childhood, causing them to become, as one critic has observed, not precocious children but retarded adults.

Economic circumstances forced them, however, to enter the real world. Both Charlotte and Emily worked as teachers, and their youngest sister, Anne, became a governess. Branwell was expected to become a portrait painter; instead, he became the family embarrassment, succumbing to drink and opium. To keep the family together, the girls concocted a plan to open their own school. In order to perfect their French, Charlotte and Emily obtained teaching positions in Brussels. Emily became so home-sick for Yorkshire that she soon returned. Charlotte, isolated and alone, eventually returned to Haworth after developing an ide-alized attachment to the school's owner, whose wife disapproved. The sisters' next venture was to collaborate on a volume of poetry, which was published at their own expense under the pseudonyms of Currer, Ellis, and Acton Bell. Only two copies were sold. Each sister then attempted a novel designed to please a publisher. Anne wrote *Agnes Grey*, based on her experiences as a governess. Emily transferred her imaginary childhood kingdom to a Yorkshire setting in *Wuthering Heights*, and Charlotte used her experiences in Brussels in a novel called *The Professor*. Anne's and Emily's novels were accepted, but Charlotte's was rejected by several publishers. Encouraged by one editor, however, she went on to recast some of the themes from her childhood stories into a new pattern, colored by her experience. The result was *Jane Eyre*, accepted and published in 1847.

Jane Eyre depicts the development, in Charlotte Brontë's words, of a "heroine as plain and simple as myself." After enduring a troubled childhood, Jane becomes a governess who is loved by her enigmatic employer, Mr. Rochester, a man in possession of a secret that blights their chance for happiness. The story became a phenomenal success and sensation: The novel's first edition was sold out in six weeks. It was also attacked as seditious and un-Christian, one reviewer charging that the "book might be written by a woman but not by a lady." The main offense of Charlotte Brontë's heroine was her frank avowal of her love for Rochester and her willingness to listen sympathetically to his rake's history. However, the controversy generated by the book can be seen in the context of the time in which it appeared: 1848 was a year of revolution in Europe, during which the govern-ments of five nations were overthrown. It was a time when the whole fabric of society seemed to be collapsing. Jane Eyre's independence and insistence on following the dictates of her own heart, as opposed to authority and custom, were seen as an echo of the assault on traditional authority occurring throughout

Europe. Even more revolutionary was the way in which Brontë laid bare the deepest recesses of self and emotion in the novel, subjects previously reserved for poetry. In the view of critic Kathleen Tillotson, Charlotte Brontë is "the first subjective novelist, the literary ancestor of Proust and Joyce—a historian of private consciousness."

The popular success of *Jane Eyre* obscured the reception of *Wuthering Heights*. Readers and critics incorrectly assumed that Emily Brontë's novel was the earlier apprentice work of Charlotte Brontë and ignored it. This was a colossal oversight. A tragic story of the doomed love between the headstrong Catherine Earnshaw and the gypsy foundling, Heathcliff, *Wuthering Heights* is an extraordinary tale of two people caught in the grip of impossible passions, never before depicted as frankly and intensely in fiction. The novel's originality of vision and sophistication of structure makes it one of the greatest novels ever written.

The commercial failure of *Wuthering Heights* was a profound disappointment to Emily. In the same year as Charlotte's great success and Emily's failure, Branwell died, and at his funeral, Emily caught a cold that developed into consumption. She died at the end of the year. Anne Brontë also died of tuberculosis, in the spring of 1849, leaving Charlotte alone. She wrote two other novels, *Shirley* and *Villette*, and in 1855 married her father's curate. She lived for another year before dying of tuberculosis while pregnant. Patrick Brontë survived them all, living to the ripe old age of eighty-four.

Both Charlotte and Emily Brontë remain two of the most-read and admired writers of the nineteenth century. Both have been claimed as feminist heroes and as artistic influences. "They aimed at achieving through prose fiction," writes literary critic Q. D. Leavis, "something as serious, vital, and significant as the work of their favorite poets, which should voice the tragic experience of life, be true to the experience of the whole woman, and convey a sense of life's springs and undercurrents."

Catherine the Great

1729–1796

Catherine acquired her title of the Great largely in terms
of her accomplishments in foreign affairs. She was
operating in a value system of her century, which judged
the achievements of monarchs largely in terms of their
frontiers and the magnitude of their military victories.

—L. JAY OLIVA
Catherine the Great

Popular history has made much of the libidinous lifestyle of
Catherine II, empress of Russia. While she had many lovers, her
reputation for concupiscence has tended to overshadow her

brilliance and influence as a ruler. An enlightened and progressive leader, Catherine completed what Peter the Great had begun: the transformation of Russia from a relatively backward country into a powerful nation and a player in European politics.

Born Sophie Augusta Frederica, Catherine was a princess of Anhalt-Zerbst, one of the many small, independent Prussian states later absorbed into the German Empire. She was a high-spirited, intelligent girl, whose French governess raised her on French classics and encouraged her to question authority and rely on her common sense. In 1739 she met her second cousin, Peter Ulrich, the grandson of Peter the Great, who would later become the heir to the throne of Russia. Despite an aversion to his childish behavior, Sophie "gradually began to think of myself as being destined to become his wife." To accomplish this marriage necessitated the compliance of the formidable Empress Elizabeth, daughter of Peter the Great, who required an heir for Peter but did not want a royal alliance with anyone powerful enough to cause diplomatic difficulties later on. Sophie, a princess of a minor German state, seemed to be an ideal choice, and in 1744 she was invited to visit Russia with her mother to prepare for the marriage.

The Russian court that the fifteen-year-old Sophie discovered was barely civilized by Western European standards. The courtiers were unmannerly, often lice-ridden, and, as the young princess later observed, "It would have been safe to wager that half the company did not know how to read, and I am not entirely sure that a third of them knew how to write." The Empress Elizabeth was alternatively autocratic and fanatically devout. Sophie attempted to ingratiate herself with Elizabeth. She studied Russian, took instruction in the Russian Orthodox faith, changed her name to Catherine Alekseyevna at her baptism, and even shared with her future husband his passion for toy soldiers. She won Elizabeth's favor and in 1745 married her cousin, then the Grand Duke Peter. Neglected by the doltish, immature tsarevitch, Catherine filled her time by reading widely, especially the works of such writers as Voltaire and Montesquieu, and informing herself about Russian conditions. She also took a succession of lovers, one of whom, Sergei Saltykov, was likely the father of her son Paul, whom Elizabeth immediately seized to raise as Peter's heir.

Catherine's successful attempt to become completely Russian made her popular with powerful political and military factions opposed to the capricious behavior of her eccentric husband. In 1762, after the death of the empress, Catherine and a group of conspirators led by her lover, Count Grigory Orlov, acted to depose the new tsar. Catherine went from barracks to barracks to rally support, and her troops soon gained control of the capital, St. Petersburg. Peter, too confused to act decisively to maintain his power, gave up the throne and was placed under house arrest. Seven days later it was announced that he had died of a hemorrhage. In fact, he had been strangled by Catherine's guards.

Catherine began her reign in a spirit of reform guided by the thinkers of the Enlightenment. She instituted numerous cultural and educational reforms, founding new universities and the nation's first school for girls. She modernized Russian commerce and banking, was an enthusiastic patron of literature and the arts, and encouraged some reasoned debate on social and political issues.

Although initially appalled by the misery of Russia's peasants, she did little to alleviate or end serfdom. After the peasant uprising of 1773–1774, a rebellion that seriously threatened her throne, Catherine strengthened the provincial nobility's administrative powers and increased the central government's control over rural areas, thus creating a feudalistic society in which the instutition of serfdom became even more firmly entrenched. As historian James H. Billington observed, "Few other rulers of her time had such sweeping plans for reform and attracted so much adulation from the *philosophes*, yet few others were so poor in practical accomplishments. In her failure, however, she created the conditions for future change—posing vexing questions for the aristocracy while creating intolerable conditions for the peasantry." In a fundamental way, the seeds for the Decembrist uprising of 1825 and the Russian Revolution of 1917 were planted by Catherine's neglect of the peasants and by her pragmatic support of an autocratic aristocracy, together with the emergence of a new Russian intellectual class.

Catherine's outstanding achievements were in the realm of foreign affairs. She increased Russian control over the Baltic provinces and the Ukraine; established a virtual protectorate over Poland, and then secured the largest portion of that country in a three-way partition of Poland among Prussia, Austria, and Russia; annexed the Crimea, which allowed Russian control of both the Caspian and Black Seas; and encouraged the colonization of Alaska. During Catherine's reign, Russia added millions of square miles to its empire and its population rose from twenty to thirty million. By her skillful diplomacy, which included acting as mediator between Prussia and Austria in the War of the Bavarian Succession (1778–1779), and by extending Russia's western boundary into Central Europe, Catherine greatly enhanced Russia's power and prestige, as well as its influence in European affairs.

Ten years before she died, Catherine wrote her own epitaph, which read in part, "At age fifteen, she made the threefold resolution to please her husband, Elizabeth, and the nation. She neglected nothing to accomplish this.... Having ascended the throne of Russia, she wished to do good and sought to procure for her subjects happiness, liberty, and prosperity." Catherine's legacy was not quite as benign as she might have wished, but there is no doubt that the "enlightened despotism" of her reign produced a world power of lasting influence.

47

Ida M. Tarbell

1857–1944

Tarbell joins the select company of propagandists like Thomas Paine and Harriet Beecher Stowe whose works were like bugle calls to battle.

—MARY E. TOMKINS
Ida M. Tarbell

The first woman to become a muckraking writer, Ida Tarbell is recognized for her pioneering role in investigative journalism and especially for her classic 1904 study of corruption in the oil industry, *The History of Standard Oil.* That two-volume work spurred federal investigations into the company, which ultimately led to the breakup of the Standard Oil monopoly in 1911 under the Sherman Anti-Trust Act.

Ida Minerva Tarbell was uniquely suited to write on the subject of oil. Her father, Franklin Tarbell, was a shrewd businessman who made a fortune after the 1859 discovery of oil in Titusville, Pennsylvania, by anticipating the need for oil containers and becoming the first manufacturer of wooden tanks for the industry. When iron replaced wood, Franklin Tarbell used his capital to become an oil producer. Both Franklin and his wife, Esther, who had been a teacher before her marriage, encouraged their daughter's intellectual curiosity, and inculcated in her the traditional virtues associated with the nineteenth-century American Dream: hard work, thrift, honesty, and moral purpose. At the age of fourteen, Ida decided never to marry and she early cultivated what would be a lifelong need for independence and freedom—especially freedom from entanglement in groups such as the suffragists.

In 1876 Ida Tarbell entered Allegheny College to study biology. Her mentor, Professor Jeremiah Tingley, the head of the department of natural sciences, taught her research methods and advocated experimental learning outside of books, which no doubt explains the solid research skills and analytical precision Tarbell brought to journalism. She graduated from college in 1880 as one of only five women students. She then took a job teaching English, languages, and science at the Poland Union Seminary in Ohio. Discouraged by this work, she left after two years and returned to Titusville, where she became an associate editor and writer for the *Chautauquan*, a magazine connected with the Chautauqua literary and scientific movement and its home studies program. In 1891 she quit her job, traveled to Paris, and enrolled at the Sorbonne. To help support herself, she wrote occasional articles for American magazines. Her work attracted the attention of S. S. McClure, who was starting his own magazine, *McClure's*, and he published her articles and interviews with such French luminaries as Louis Pasteur, Emile Zola, Alphonse Daudet, and Alexandre Dumas, *fils*. Tarbell also wrote a series of articles on Napoleon, which were published in book form in 1895 as *A Short Life of Napoleon* and brought her national acclaim. She followed this success with a series on Abraham Lincoln, a subject that had fascinated her since childhood and to which she would return, writing eight books on Lincoln's life.

From 1894 to 1906 Tarbell worked as an assistant editor for

McClure's, which had gained a reputation as the leading muckraking magazine of the day. The term *muckraker* had come from Theodore Roosevelt, who compared such writers as Tarbell, Lincoln Steffens, and Upton Sinclair to the "man with a muck rake" in John Bunyan's *Pilgrim's Progress*. Tarbell's landmark study attacking John D. Rockefeller's oil trust, first published as a series of articles in *McClure's*, was the result of an exhaustive, two-year research effort and included information supplied to her by an employee of Standard Oil and by Rockefeller's disgruntled brother, Frank. In the book, Tarbell recognizes Rockefeller's genius while at the same time regarding the corporation as guilty of "commercial sin" because of its immoral attempts to stifle individual business endeavor. Rockefeller derisively called Tarbell "Tarbelly" and forbade any reference to "that misguided woman." Beyond that, he had no reply to the book.

In 1906 Ida Tarbell and Lincoln Steffens bought *American Magazine,* and Tarbell turned her attention to tariffs, which she attacked as another way trusts gained monopolistic control. President Woodrow Wilson said about her war on tariffs that "She has written more good sense, good plain common sense...than any man I know." Wilson appointed Tarbell a delegate to his Industrial Conference in 1919. President Harding later named her to his Unemployment Conference.

Tarbell's other works include *The Business of Being a Woman* (1912), *The Nationalizing of Business: 1878–1898*, and her autobiography, *All in the Day's Work* (1939).

During her career, Ida Tarbell showed no reluctance to take on powerful corporations whose greed was in direct contrast to her own highly developed moral sense. She was, writes Mary Tomkins, "the journalist who bested the robber barons in a fair fight and scotched the reptilian principle of special privilege that they had attempted to substitute for the historic American principle of equal opportunity."

48

Jane Goodall

1934–

Yes, man definitely overshadows the chimpanzee. The chimpanzee is, nevertheless, a creature of immense significance to the understanding of man.... He has the ability to solve quite complex problems, he can use and make tools for a variety of purposes, his social structure and methods of communication with his fellows are elaborate, and he shows the beginning of self-awareness. Who knows what the chimpanzee will be like forty million years hence? It should be of concern to us all that we permit him to live, that we at least give him the chance to evolve.

—JANE GOODALL
In the Shadow of Man

A zoologist-ethologist who revolutionized field research on animals in nature, Jane Goodall has devoted her long career to extending human understanding of animal behavior. She is particularly noted for her groundbreaking six-year study of chimpanzees, conducted by the shores of Lake Tanganyika. There, after gaining the acceptance of a group of chimpanzees, she was able to discover and record the animals' social hierarchy and complex system of communication. Goodall's painstaking studies of chimpanzees, the animals most closely related to humans, have also provided invaluable glimpses of the social, biological, and cultural connections between the two species across the evolutionary barrier.

Born in London, Jane Goodall is the daughter of Mortimer Goodall, a businessman and racing-car driver, and Vanne Joseph Goodall, an author. From her earliest childhood, Jane was fascinated by animals and would disappear into a hen coop to wait for the chickens to hatch from their eggs. She cherished a toy chimpanzee someone had given her and read with delight the Dr. Doolittle series of animal stories. During World War II, Jane and her mother relocated to Bournemouth on the English coast, where they remained after her parents divorced. After graduating from school, Goodall took secretarial courses and worked at a series of jobs. Having always dreamed of going to Africa, she was given the opportunity in 1957, when a friend invited her to visit her parents' farm in Kenya. Determined to stay in Africa, Goodall sought out anthropologist Dr. Louis Leakey, then curator of the National Museum of Natural History in Nairobi. Leakey hired her as an assistant secretary and allowed her to accompany him on his paleontological expedition to Olduvai Gorge on the Serengeti Plain. Although Goodall found the work fascinating, her main interest continued to be the study of animals. Leakey suggested that Goodall research a group of chimpanzees living on a reserve in Tanzania. An earlier study of chimpanzee behavior in the wild had been made by Professor Henry W. Nissen, whose research had been carried out for only two and a half months, too short a time for a truly comprehensive understanding of these primates. The project proved irresistible to Goodall, but she felt that her lack of formal training would be an obstacle in undertaking such a serious scientific study. Leakey convinced her that it was to her advantage to enter the project unburdened by predetermined theories and that she needed only what she already possessed: a desire for knowledge and a sympathetic understanding of animals.

In 1960, accompanied by her mother, Jane Goodall embarked on what would become a six-year first encounter with chimpanzees in the Gombe Stream Chimpanzee Reserve. Living in a tent beside Lake Tanganyika, and battling the threats of malaria, cobras, insects, and thieving baboons, Goodall spent months roaming the dense, rugged terrain and gained only fleeting glimpses of the chimpanzees, who were frightened away by her approach. With patience and determination she persisted until she was finally accepted by a group of chimpanzees, each of whom she named. From her close observations, Goodall made a number of new and fascinating discoveries about wild chimps. She learned that they make and use simple tools, hunt small animals for food, engage in troop battles to establish territorial dominance, and cooperate as a group when hunting or defending terrain. Goodall's careful documentation of "her" chimps ended speculation and corrected earlier accounts of wild chimpanzee behavior.

Her field study was interrupted by trips back to England, where she began work on her doctorate in ethology at Cambridge University. In 1964 she married the Dutch photographer and naturalist Hugo von Lawick, and together they continued to chronicle the history of Goodall's chimpanzee group. Their son, Hugo, born in 1967, was raised in the camp that became the Gombe Stream Research Centre. In 1970 Goodall and von Lawick published a joint study of wild dogs, jackals, and hyenas, titled *Innocent Killers*, and a year later, Goodall published a summary of her research on chimpanzees, *In the Shadow of Man*, which included photographs taken by her husband. The book was enormously popular, and its success gave Goodall a worldwide reputation, which she has used to campaign for better treatment of animals in captivity and in the wild. Goodall and Von Lawick eventually divorced, and in 1973 she married Derek Bryceson, a politician and director of the Tanzania National Parks. In 1977 she founded the Jane Goodall Institute to increase awareness about the harm done to animals by poachers and hunters and the destruction of wilderness areas. Her other works on chimpanzees include *The Chimpanzees of Gombe: Patterns of Behavior* (1986) and *The Chimpanzee: The Living Link Between "Man" and "Beast"* (1992).

Before Jane Goodall's work in the field, scientists believed that only humans possessed the complex skills and social organization that she observed for the first time among chimpanzees. Goodall's work changed the way scientists conduct research on animal behavior and fundamentally altered the prevailing view of human characteristics as unique and exclusive in nature. For Goodall, the right of chimpanzees and other creatures in the wild to coexist with humans is a reflection of her lifelong love of animals. As she once told an interviewer, "I want to make [people] aware that animals have their own needs, emotions, and feelings—they matter."

49

Emma Goldman

1869–1940

For the cause of free speech in the United States Emma Goldman fought battles unmatched by the labors of any organization.

—ROGER BALDWIN,
    Quoted in Richard Drinnon,
    Rebel in Paradise, 1961

It was once said of Emma Goldman that she was born to ride a whirlwind. This is an apt description of a woman who, as an anarchist, radical feminist, and advocate of birth control, free love, and free speech, agitated more fiercely and deliberately stirred up more controversy than any other social or political activist of her day. Red Emma, as she was popularly known, was reviled and scorned for her radicalism. A consummate rebel, she

170

fought for the freedom of the individual at a time when the organization was fast becoming paramount.

Goldman was born in the Jewish ghetto of Kovno, Russia (now Kaunas, Lithuania), the only child of Abraham, a shopkeeper, and Taube Goldman. Her father was disappointed at the birth of a daughter, and her mother considered her an additional burden. Emma endured an unhappy childhood caught between her father's bitter and fiery temper and her mother's cold indifference. Dogged by business failure, the family moved to Königsberg, Prussia, where Emma attended school. One of her teachers took an interest in her, cultivated her taste for music and literature, and helped her prepare for the gymnasium entrance examination. Although Emma passed the exam, her religious instructor refused to provide the necessary certificate of good character. In 1881 the Goldmans moved to St. Petersburg, where, her formal education at an end, Emma took a job in a cousin's glove factory. She also began to associate with radical university students and to read the new radical texts that advocated political dissent.

In 1885 Emma escaped an arranged marriage by emigrating to America with her half-sister, Helena. They settled in Rochester, New York, and began work in a clothing factory for $2.50 a week. Goldman's treatment by sweatshop owners happy to exploit the hard work of immigrants, destroyed her faith in the American Dream, fostered her distrust of capitalism, and formed her politics. She was also deeply affected by the execution of four anarchists in connection with the 1887 Haymarket Square riot in Chicago.

Goldman liked to say that her real life began in 1889 when she moved to New York City and met Johann Most, editor of the radical newspaper *Freiheit*, and Alexander Berkman, an émigré Russian revolutionary. She joined their anarchist movement, which for her—a survivor of the harsh authority of her parents, the ethical demands of Judaism, and the brutality of Russian anti-Semitism who had quickly become disenchanted with American democracy—had an immediate appeal with its promise of a classless, nonauthoritarian society. During the early years of her political activism Goldman endorsed the notion that the ends justify any means—including acts of violence. In 1892, after a strike at the Carnegie Steel Company at Homestead, Pennsylvania, was put down with the loss of several workers' lives, Goldman assisted Berkman in his plot to kill Henry Clay Frick, the Carnegie factory manager. Frick survived the attack, but Berkman served a fourteen-year prison sentence. Goldman, in turn, served a one-year prison term in 1893 for inciting unemployed workers in New York's Union Square to riot. In prison, Goldman took up nursing, and after her release studied midwifery and nursing in Vienna.

By the beginning of the new century, Goldman had begun to renounce her earlier calls for violence, especially after learning that President McKinley's assassin, Leon Czolgosz, claimed to have been inspired by her. Her outspoken, almost manic support of diverse causes was, however, undiminished. An accomplished and electrifying speaker, she traveled throughout the United States, lecturing on anarchism, the revolt of women, and the socially and stylistically progressive works of dramatists Henrik Ibsen and August Strindberg. She constantly battled police and vigilante attempts to censor her. As the editor, with Berkman, of the radical monthly *Mother Earth* (1906–1917) and the publisher of many pamphlets, Goldman raised the concerns of radicals and liberals over threats to freedom of speech. Under Ibsen's influence, Goldman trumpeted the cause of the independent New Woman and attacked the narrowness and hypocrisy of conventional marriage (although she married twice). She advocated "free love," by which she did not mean promiscuity but rather love unencumbered by legal sanctions, and she criticized feminists who wished to banish men from women's emotional lives. At the same time, she rejected the call for suffrage as insignificant and a sham. A firm believer in voluntary motherhood and family limitation, she campaigned on behalf of birth control for over two decades, influenced by the work of Margaret Sanger. She, like Sanger, was arrested for publicly lecturing on the subject.

In 1917 Goldman and Berkman were arrested for opposing the draft and sentenced to two years in prison. Two years later, with the aid of J. Edgar Hoover, government officials, who had long attempted to have Goldman deported, took advantage of wartime legislation to send her to Russia along with 248 other victims of the postwar Red Scare. In Russia Goldman became an outspoken critic of the Russian Revolution and the Bolshevik suppression of civil liberties, much to the shock of her radical colleagues who were unwilling to speak out against the autocratic policies of a socialist nation. During the 1920s and 1930s, Goldman lectured and wrote such books as *My Disillusionment in Russia* (1923) and her autobiography, *Living My Life* (1931). During the Spanish Civil War, she labored tirelessly for the doomed Loyalist cause against fascist Francisco Franco. In 1940, while on a fundraising mission to Canada, she died of a stroke. U.S. officials allowed her body to be brought back for burial in a Chicago cemetery. As Robert Drinnon writes in *Rebel in Paradise*, Emma Goldman "had lived to the end a life of unique integrity."

50

Coco Chanel

1883–1971

In eclipse at those times when fashion favored eccentricity and exaggeration and in demand during periods of self-doubt and quest for certainties, Chanel's fashion is once more called eternally modern. Coco Chanel, who died on a Sunday—the only day, her friends said, that could kill her—was a force and legend in her time. She ruled for long periods over almost six decades. Posthumously, her reign is stretching to cover the century. Chanel No. 1.

—AXEL MADSEN
Chanel: A Woman of Her Own

Ranked fairly high at midpoint is Coco Chanel, the influential fashion designer whose look, for many, is embodied in her signature suit—a straight knit skirt and collarless cardigan-shaped jacket accessorized with pearls or gold chains, black- or white-tipped sling-back shoes, and a quilted purse. But Chanel's fashion legacy goes beyond the classic elegance of her suits, or indeed, the enduring popularity of her fragrances, Chanel nos. 5 and 19. She freed women from corsets and long skirts and put them into short skirts, simple jerseys, suits, dresses, chemises, turtlenecks, cardigans, trousers, low-heeled shoes, and the "little black dress," still considered eminently suitable for any occasion. Chanel designed haute couture for the rich and created ready-to-wear casual, comfortable clothes for everyone else. Her sportswear, widely imitated by scores of other fashion designers, came to define the essence of the modern, liberated woman, a reflection of Chanel herself.

Gabrielle Bonheur Chanel managed to liberate herself from more than just her corsets. Born in the poorhouse at Saumur, a town on the Loire River, Chanel was the second illegitimate daughter of itinerant peddlers Albert Chanel and Jeanne Devolle. Her mother, who would give birth to another daughter and two sons, died when Gabrielle was twelve. After Albert Chanel disappeared, the boys became unpaid farm laborers and the girls were sent to an orphanage run by nuns. Although her parents had married soon after she was born, all her life Chanel worried that her illegitimacy would be discovered. "She could never live with the truth," writes Madsen, "and spent her adult years perpetually revising her life story."

After six years at the orphanage, Gabrielle and her older sister, Julie, were accepted as charity cases at a convent finishing school in Moulins. At twenty, Gabrielle joined her young aunt Adrienne as an assistant in a Moulins clothing and fabric shop, where she waited on customers and gained a reputation as an excellent seamstress. To make extra money, she moonlighted in a tailor shop and did private alterations. She also dated young army officers, who took her to a local nightclub where she sometimes performed as a chanteuse. The story goes that she gained her nickname from a popular song about a Parisienne who lost her dog, Coco.

In 1905 Chanel moved in with Etienne Balsan, a wealthy young ex-army officer turned horse breeder. At Balsan's estate and in the fashionable racing venues near Paris, Chanel mingled with the kept women, aristocrats, nouveaux riches, artistes, and staid horse breeders who frequented the track during France's *belle époque*. She took advantage of her status as a beautiful social upstart and echoed the emergence of feminism by developing her own style of dress, which masculinized feminine fashion in direct contrast to the current mode. "If ladies at the grandstand at Longchamp came in feather hats and skirts that swept the grass," writes Madsen, "she was at the racetrack in strict tailor-made and boater." Instead of a riding skirt, Chanel would wear britches. Her hats were the first of her creations to attract notice, and she began designing millinery for friends. By 1913, with the financial help of her new lover, Arthur "Boy" Capel, a British diplomat and wealthy scion of a coal-mining family, she opened millinery boutiques in Paris and Deauville. She soon added sportswear to her collections, and in 1915 opened her first fashion house in the French resort of Biarritz.

The 1920s and 1930s represented the height of Chanel's success. The casual liberating elegance of her clothes made her enormously popular with the youthful boyish-looking New Woman of the 1920s. During the 1930s, despite heavy competition from such flamboyant newcomers as Elsa Schiaparelli, Chanel's simple, classic suits, dresses, and evening wear, as well as her sportswear, continued, to reign supreme. In addition, she designed clothes for theater and ballet productions and films, including Jean Renoir's *Rules of the Game* and several Hollywood movies. By the late 1930s Chanel was the wealthiest couturier in France, famed not only for her fashions but also for her celebrated friends, among them Igor Stravinsky, Winston Churchill, Pablo Picasso, Jean Cocteau, and Colette.

At the outbreak of World War II, for reasons that remain unclear, Chanel closed the House of Chanel and laid off her entire staff. Only the boutique selling her Chanel No. 5 remained open. Chanel's wartime conduct was less than exemplary, although it was certainly consistent with that of many French luminaries during the Occupation. She spent the war years as the mistress of a German diplomat, Hans Gunther von Dincklage, nicknamed Spatz, and in one bizarre episode used her German connections to convince a high-ranking SS officer to send her to Madrid with a peace proposal for Winston Churchill. Chanel made the journey to Madrid, but was not allowed to see Churchill. After the war, she was arrested as a collaborator and detained by the British for three hours, then released. Her quick release was probably due to her knowledge of Nazi collaborators highly placed in British society, including the Duke and Duchess of Windsor.

Eclipsed by Christian Dior's "New Look" and such up-and-coming young designers as Givenchy and Pierre Cardin, and considered, writes Madsen, "a prewar fashion designer without a fashion house in a postwar era of diminished perspectives," Chanel stayed on the fashion sidelines during the postwar years. In 1953 she reopened the House of Chanel and brought out a new collection, a refined version of the simple, classic line she had designed in the 1930s. Her comeback led to a resurgence of popularity that lasted until her death, and continues today. Coco Chanel was, writes Madsen, "the Pied Piper who led women away from complicated uncomfortable clothes to a simple, uncluttered, and casual look that is still synonymous with her name."

51

Dorothy Thompson

1894–1961

Americans were used by now to the potent views of former sportswriters...nasty gossips...blustering reactionaries...and the lofty male highbrows...But...the nation was also ready for Dorothy Thompson, whose particular blend of solid reporting and naked emotion had never before been seen in a syndicated column....Her call to conscience, her emergence on the American scene as an almost mythic heroine, "half-mother and half firebrand," gave Dorothy a place in the history of journalism that was entirely her own.

—PETER KURTH
American Cassandra:
The Life of Dorothy Thompson

At the height of her popularity as a journalist, Dorothy Thompson was, arguably, the most influential woman writer in the English-speaking world. Her syndicated column "On the Record" had a readership of seven to eight million people. In 1941, *Time* magazine declared that she and Eleanor Roosevelt had "the most power and prestige of any women in America." Thompson, known as "the First Lady of American Journalism," used her influence to mold public opinion during some of the most tumultuous times of the twentieth century. Celebrated and notorious in her day, she remains a model of the passionately opinionated, committed reporter. As her fellow journalists joked, the news happened where Dorothy was.

Dorothy Thompson was the oldest of three children. Her father, Peter Thompson, was a Methodist minister who had come to America from England for a visit, met his wife, Margaret Grierson, the daughter of Scottish immigrants, and thereafter worked as an itinerant preacher around the suburbs of Buffalo. By the time Dorothy was twelve she had lived in five different homes. She was a restless, adventurous child given at an early age to running away from home, "following my own will and passion," as she later wrote. When she was seven, her mother died, and her father, as Dorothy had predicted, married his church's organist. Relations between Thompson and her stepmother were strained, and in 1908 Dorothy was sent to live with an aunt in Chicago. There she attended Lewis Institute, a private school that combined a high school and junior college. In 1912 she transferred to Syracuse University on a scholarship available to children of Methodist minsters. At Syracuse, Thompson developed a strong interest in the women's suffrage movement and won a reputation as a gifted, articulate, and outspoken student.

After her graduation in 1914, Thompson tried to become a teacher, but failed the state test in grammar, a remarkable setback for a future journalist. She worked as a publicist and lecturer for a Buffalo women's suffrage group, and in 1918 took a job in Cincinnati as publicity director for the Social Unit, a New York–based reform organization committed to raising political consciousness in the slums. Thompson became increasingly interested in international issues and decided to seek a career in journalism, but she could not find a job. Undaunted, she sailed for Europe in 1920, and within months, without previous experience or press credentials, was filing major stories for the International News Service (INS), including a major scoop, the final interview with Sinn Fein leader Terence McSwiney.

During the early 1920s Thompson worked as a publicist for the American Red Cross and as the Vienna correspondent for the *Philadelphia Public Ledger*. In 1924, after scoring a journalistic coup by writing a first-hand account of the attempt to restore the Hapsburg monarchy, she was hired by the *Ledger* and the *New York Evening Post* as their chief of Central European Services. Thus began what one of her biographers, Marion Sanders, has called "the Thompson legend in which the intrepid girl reporter, braving unimaginable perils to get the news, becomes as much a part of the story as the events she is covering." While headquartered in Berlin, Thompson met author Sinclair Lewis, whom she married in 1928. Their son was born in New York in 1930. Later that year Thompson returned to Europe, where she wrote articles documenting the ominous prewar situation. A 1931 interview with Adolf Hitler, which was expanded into a 1932 book titled *I Saw Hitler!*, greatly enhanced her reputation. However, she had seriously underestimated the Nazi leader, whom she portrayed as insecure, insignificant, and incapable of seizing power. The book caused her much-publicized expulsion from Nazi Germany in 1934.

In 1936 Thompson accepted an assignment from the *New York Herald Tribune* to write three columns a week interpreting political events for women readers. "On the Record" was a phenomenal success, syndicated in more than 150 newspapers nationwide. A monthly column for the *Ladies Home Journal* and a successful NBC radio program added to her audience, as did lecture tours. Shrewdly intuitive, Thompson showed a remarkable ability to translate complex political events and topics into easily grasped analysis, interpreting a wide range of subjects for her readers. As one critic observed, "She took virtually every phase of human life under her supervision, untroubled by any inner doubts and adopting from the first an air of authority that her clients found irresistible." Some critics found her strident and emotionally self-indulgent and charged her with being "against everybody." However, the "Thompson Philosophy" is better understood by her defense against the charge that she hated

Franklin Roosevelt: "When he is right, I am for him; when he is wrong, I'm against him." Thompson was frequently her own best revisionist, tending to take the long view on issues, and completely unencumbered by doubts over what was right or wrong.

In 1937, at the height of her fame, Thompson separated from Lewis, who abhorred the political interests that sustained his wife, was drinking heavily, and whose writing career was on the wane. Thompson worked on her column in bed, where she remained until noon, reading newspapers, drinking black coffee, and chain-smoking, popular emblems of the imperious newspaperwoman. During the war years before 1941, she campaigned vehemently for U.S. involvement in the Allied cause to the censure of those advocating neutrality, and she endorsed Roosevelt for reelection, a stance which resulted in the termination of her contract with the Republican *Tribune*. She transferred her column to the liberal *New York Post*. After America entered the war, Thompson broadcast a series, *Listen Hans*, over CBS shortwave radio to the German people, attacking the aberration of Nazism, but defending the humanity of the German people. After the war Thompson turned her attention to the Middle East. Her views on the creation of a Jewish state in Palestine had shifted from strong support of Israel to criticism of Zionist militancy, and she gradually moved toward a pro-Arab position. She wrote her last newspaper column in 1958 but continued her column for the *Ladies Home Journal*, writing on education and family issues.

Thompson died of a heart attack in Lisbon, Portugal, in 1961. In 1939 she wrote what can stand as her testament: "One cannot exist in full consciousness—without having to have a showdown with one's self, without having to define what it is that one lives by, without being clear in one's mind what matters and what does not matter."

52

Grace Murray Hopper
1906–1992

They told me quite frequently that a computer could not write a program; it was totally impossible; that all that computers could do was arithmetic...that it had none of the imagination and dexterity of a human being. I kept trying to explain that we were wrapping up the human being's dexterity in the program that he wrote...and that of course we could make a computer do these things so long as they were completely defined.

—GRACE HOPPER
From her keynote address at History of Programming Languages Conference, 1978.

Known to her colleagues and subordinates as Amazing Grace, mathematician, naval officer, and computer pioneer Grace Hopper greatly influenced the future of computer technology by developing the concept of automatic programming that led to the COBOL (Common Business Oriented Language) programming language. Hopper's work simplified computer technology and ultimately made it accessible to a significantly larger and more diverse group of users. That achievement makes Hopper more than worthy of inclusion here.

Born in New York City, Grace Hopper graduated from Vassar College in 1928 and received her Ph.D. in mathematics from Yale University in 1934. She taught mathematics at Vassar from 1931 until 1943, when she enlisted in the WAVES (Women Accepted for Voluntary Emergency Service) branch of the navy. After attending the U.S. Naval Reserve Midshipman School, she graduated with the rank of lieutenant junior grade and was assigned to the Bureau of Ordnance Computation Project at Harvard, where she developed programs for the Mark I, the first automatically sequenced digital computer and a forerunner of today's electronic computer.

In 1946 Hopper joined the Harvard faculty as a research fellow in engineering sciences and applied physics at the Computation Laboratory. There she worked on the second and third series of Mark computers for the navy. She left Harvard in 1949 to take a position at the Eckert-Mauchly Computer Corporation, which was involved in building the first commercial large-scale electronic computer, UNIVAC. While at Eckert-Mauchly, Hopper and her staff created the first computer language compiler—a program that translates programming codes into a machine language a computer can understand. In 1955 Hopper began work on a language that would be suitable for doing business data processing on computers and would also be easy to use. The result was COBOL, which is still widely used today.

While pursuing her industrial career, Hopper maintained close contact with the naval reserve. She retired in 1966, but was recalled by the navy to supervise the organization's computer languages and programs. In 1969 she became the first person to receive computer science's Man of the Year award from the Data Processing Management Association. In 1973 she became the first woman to be promoted to captain while on the navy's retired reserve list. She was one of two women to be named a fellow of the Institute of Electrical and Electronic Engineers, winning the institute's McDowell Award in 1979, and in 1983 was appointed rear admiral by President Ronald Reagan. Upon her retirement from the navy in 1986, Hopper, at eighty, was the oldest officer on active duty in the armed services. She subsequently served as a senior consultant to the Digital Corporation, a position she held until her death. In 1991, she became the first woman to receive, as an individual, the United States Medal of Technology, awarded to her "for her pioneering accomplishments in the development of computer programming languages."

A combative and unorthodox presence in the computer science community, Grace Hopper fought hard to convince "the Establishment," as she called the computer science hierarchy, that computers were capable of becoming more than just highly efficient calculators. It is largely due to her efforts that computer technology made the great leap forward from the lab to the laptop.

53

Barbara McClintock

1902–1992

One of the remarkable things about Barbara McClintock's surpassingly beautiful investigations is that they come solely from her own labors. Without technical help of any kind, she has by virtue of her boundless energy, her complete devotion to science, her originality and ingenuity, and her quick and high intelligence made a series of significant discoveries unparalleled in the history of crytogenetics.

—MARCUS RHODES
In Evelyn Fox,
The Life of the Organism

Nobelist Barbara McClintock is recognized as one of the most influential geneticists of the twentieth century. Her revolutionary work on gene and chromosome behavior has come to be acknowledged as a fundamental concept of gene functioning. An individualist, McClintock, unlike others in her field, worked alone and with corn, instead of using the preferred research object, *Drosophila*, the fruit fly. She never gave lectures to build her career or consulted with her colleagues, and she chose not to publish her findings for years, believing that no one would accept them. Her belief proved to be correct.

In 1951 McClintock delivered a paper at the Cold Spring Harbor Symposium for Quantitative Biology entitled, "Chromosome Behavior and Genic Expression." That paper detailed the results of McClintock's ten-year observations of the changes in color patterns in kernels of Indian corn and her correlation of these changes with changes in chromosome structure. Some genes, she explained, appeared to shift their locations in the chromosomes from one generation to the next. In response to external stimuli received from the developing organism, these "transposable elements," as McClintock termed them, seemed to jump to specific places on chromosomes to insert themselves into genetic material and alter it.

McClintock's colleagues, steeped in the Darwinian tradition of changes occurring randomly in genes, and working at a time when the structure of DNA had not yet been described, were not impressed with McClintock's theory of purposeful "jumping genes." With characteristic patience, McClintock returned to her solitary research at the Cold Spring Harbor laboratory, working her usual twelve-hour-a-day, six-day week.

McClintock's capacity to work alone began in childhood. She was the third of four children born to Brooklyn doctor Thomas McClintock and Sara Hardy McClintock. As a child, Barbara enjoyed such solitary activities as reading and, according to biographer Evelyn Fox Keller, "she loved to sit alone, intensely absorbed, just 'thinking about things.'" She preferred engines to dolls and sports to the traditional girls' pursuits of the era. Her parents, strong proponents of self-determination, supported their daughter's independent spirit until adolescence, when, writes Keller, "the passion for sports gave way to the passion for knowledge." At Erasmus Hall High School she developed a love of science, which especially worried her mother. She feared her daughter would become, according to McClintock, "a strange person, a person that didn't belong to society."

Overriding parental objections, McClintock enrolled at Cornell University's College of Agriculture in 1919. When she was a junior, she was invited to take the university's graduate course in genetics. She received her Ph.D. in botany in 1927 and stayed on at Cornell to teach. In the 1930s McClintock was awarded two fellowships and worked at the University of Missouri. During this period she established her reputation by becoming one of the few scientists to develop an understanding of chromosomes as the basis of heredity. She also discovered the nucleolar organizer of the chromosome, a structure that seemed to order genetic material during cell division. Again, McClintock was ahead of her time; her finding was not explained by molecular biologists until thirty years later. In 1941, after continually being denied promotions, she left the University of Missouri to work at the Cold Spring Harbor Laboratory. She was elected to the National Academy of Sciences in 1944 and was the first woman to become president of the Genetics Society of America. She remained at Cold Spring Harbor until her death in 1992.

McClintock received numerous awards in the 1960s and 1970s, including the National Medal of Science. Such recognition was likely the result of researchers catching up to McClintock at long last; molecular biologists had finally isolated transposable elements in bacteria. In 1983 McClintock became the first woman to win an unshared Nobel Prize in Physiology and Medicine. Once described by DNA codiscoverer James Watson as the third most important geneticist in history, along with Gregor Mendel and Thomas Hunt Morgan, McClintock was characteristically self-effacing concerning her Nobel stature. "It might seem unfair," she said, "to reward a person for having so much fun over the years."

54

Elisabeth Kübler-Ross

1926– 2004

The fear of death is the most inescapable fear of human beings and the most unavoidable one....Dying is still a distasteful but inevitable happening which is rarely spoken about. One might think that the scientific man of the twentieth century would have learned to deal with this uniform fear as successfully as he has been able to add years to his life span....[Yet] advancement of science has not contributed to but rather detracted from man's ability to accept death with dignity.

—ELISABETH KÜBLER-ROSS,
From a paper for the Chicago
Theological Seminary, 1966

A pioneer in the field of thanatology, psychiatrist Elisabeth Kübler-Ross has effected a much-needed revolution in the way we think about death and dying. Her important first book, *On Death and Dying*, explored the process by which people cope with death, a subject long suppressed or ignored. By daring to confront one of humankind's greatest fears, Kübler-Ross has helped countless dying patients achieve a liberation of the spirit. Her work has also had lasting influence in the medical community, which has become more responsive to the emotional needs of the dying and their families.

Elisabeth was one of a set of triplets born to Emmy Kuebler Villiger and Ernst Villiger, a prominent businessman in Zurich, Switzerland. The trio of girls, identically dressed, were expected to develop uniformly and to behave decorously, but as Elisabeth grew older, she began to differ in character from her sisters. She was full of energy, outgoing, and rebellious, an average student whose intellect was insufficiently challenged by her plodding and uninspired teachers. At fifteen she left home rather than submit to her imperious father's demand that she work for him as a secretary and bookkeeper. She took a job as a housekeeper to a widow in Romilly on Lake Geneva, but soon returned home to Zurich. There, she worked at a small laboratory and in the dermatology department of the canton hospital. After doing postwar relief work in Europe, which included a harrowing visit to the Maidenek concentration camp, Elisabeth returned home only to be banished from the family by her father who disapproved of her activities.

Having already decided to become a physician, Elisabeth applied to the University of Zurich Medical School and was accepted. After her graduation in 1957, she married Emmanuel Ross, an American medical student, and moved with him to the United States, where she interned at the Community Hospital in Glen Cove, New York. She decided to specialize in pediatrics, feeling that children were the "most deprived minority," too often spoiled and insulated from reality. She was accepted as a resident at New York's Columbia Presbyterian Medical Center, but her pregnancy ruled this out. On such short notice her only option was a residency at a public mental institution, and she went to work at Manhattan State Hospital. Her work there with patients deemed "hopeless" led her to become a psychiatrist. After further residency work and a fellowship at the Psychopathic Hospital in Denver, she taught psychiatry at the medical schools of the University of Colorado and the University of Chicago.

It was while teaching psychiatry that Kübler-Ross began to address the issue of death in case observation of her dying patients. As she has written, "To be with a dying patient makes us conscious of the uniqueness of the individual to this vast sea of humanity, aware of our finiteness, our limited life span."

In 1965, she instituted an interdisciplinary seminar on death at the Billings Hospital in Chicago in which she proposed "a series of conversations with the terminally ill which would make it possible for them to talk about their feelings and thoughts in this crisis situation. [By] these conversations...others would learn too how better to work with the dying." *On Death and Dying*, published in 1969, grew out of this seminar. In the book, Kübler-Ross describes how treatment of the dying has changed over time. Instead of taking place at home in the comforting presence of family and friends, most deaths now occur in impersonal institutional settings and are seen as failures of the technological expertise of physicians. She also identifies the five stages dying patients go through: denial, anger, bargaining, depression, and acceptance. This book and Kübler-Ross's subsequent works have profoundly affected our view of death and paved the way for more humane treatment of the terminally ill by medical personnel. Hospice care has been established as an alternative to dying in a regular hospital, and there has been more emphasis on counseling for the families of dying patients.

A recent work, *AIDS: The Ultimate Challenge* (1987), focuses on the medical, moral, and social implications of the disease and the need for compassion in dealing with the thousands of men, women, children, and babies who are victims of this pandemic.

In *On Death and Dying*, Kübler-Ross writes: "Those who have the strength and the love to sit with a dying patient in *the silence that goes beyond words* will know that this moment is neither frightening nor painful, but a peaceful cessation of the functioning of the body." Through her work, Elisabeth Kübler-Ross made it possible for the dying and those who love them to overcome their fear of death and to experience the peace that can and should accompany the ultimate human act.

55

Joan of Arc

1412–1431

Her strength came from the fact that in her were
combined for the first time the old religious faith and
the new force of patriotism. God spoke to her through
the voices of St. Catherine, St. Michael, and St.
Margaret, but what he commanded was not chastity nor
humility nor the life of the spirit but political action to
rescue her country from foreign tyrants.

— BARBARA TUCHMAN
A Distant Mirror

Jeanne d'Arc, the French saint and national heroine, also known as Joan of Lorraine, the Maid of Orleans, and simply *la Pucelle* (the Maid), was born into a France devastated by the Black Death and the defeats of the Hundred Years War. The English, supported by their Burgundian allies, occupied Paris, and by 1429 would secure all of France north of the Loire. French resistance against the invaders was minimal due to a lack of coordinated leadership and a national loss of courage. There was no king to unite his people and inspire them with patriotic fervor (Charles VI had died in 1422, two years after he was forced to name Henry V of England his heir), only a timid, feckless dauphin controlled by unscrupulous, apathetic ministers. Surprisingly, the paladin who would pull the French out of their collective malaise was not a chivalrous noble experienced in military strategy but an illiterate young peasant woman who claimed to have a direct line to God.

Joan of Arc grew up in the town of Domremy on the border of the provinces of Champagne and Lorraine. She was the third of five children of farmer Jacques d'Arc, a devout man and a locally prominent one, who sometimes collected taxes and tributes for neighboring landowners. Joan's childhood was spent driving her father's herds to the fields and learning housewifery and religion from her mother, Isabelle, an intensely pious woman. Domremy, which lay across the Moselle River from the Duchy of Lorraine, allied with Burgundy, was fiercely loyal to the French cause. Village children would often throw stones at their traitorous Lorranien neighbors and play at being soldiers in a nearby abandoned castle. According to biographer Vita Sackville-West, Joan was "a perfectly ordinary little peasant girl, accustomed to take the rough with the smooth." Charles Dickens characterized her somewhat differently in *A Child's History of England* as a "moping, fanciful girl," given to spending long hours on her knees praying in the gloomy village church. Other chroniclers of Joan of Arc have also stressed her childhood attachment to prayer. What finally emerges is the picture of a lively but lonely village girl with more intelligence and imagination than most, and probably one who was deeply affected by her mother's piety and religious teaching.

Joan was about twelve when she began to hear "voices" sent

by God—those of St. Michael, St. Catherine, and St. Margaret. The voices told her that her divine mission was to free France from the English and ensure that the dauphin was crowned king. She was to cut her hair, dress like a man, and carry arms. The voices continued their exhortations throughout her adolescence. Explanations for the voices have ranged from the belief that they were the result of a truly mystical religious experience to the suggestion that the hormonal imbalances of puberty led to auditory hallucinations. Sackville-West wrote that Joan was "determined, impatient, and frequently rough-tongued," and quoted her as saying, "I was admonished to adopt feminine clothes; I refused, and still refuse. As for other avocations of women, there are plenty of other women to perform them." Without denying the validity of a true religious calling, it seems clear that Joan also sought a destiny for herself far removed from the traditional lot of young peasant women. The use of religious imperative to justify behavior has always been a historical convenience.

In 1429 Joan convinced Robert de Baudricourt, captain of the dauphin's forces at Vaucouleurs, of her calling, and he agreed to take her to the dauphin, Charles, at Chinon Castle. Joan made the journey in male clothing with six companions. At Chinon she conquered Charles's skepticism as to her sacred mission, but was ordered to undergo examinations by theologians at Poitiers. After proving her divination, Joan persuaded Dunois, the illegitimate son of Louis d'Orleans, known as the Bastard of Orleans, and others of the dauphin's circle to attack Orleans, then under siege by the English. She was furnished with troops and given the rank of captain. Throughout the attack, her inspirational leadership provided spirit and morale more than military expertise, although she is described in Alice Buchan's *Joan of Arc and the Recovery of France* as "most expert in war, as much as in carrying the lance as in mustering a force and ordering the ranks, and in laying the guns."

After the May 1429 victory at Orleans, which many viewed as miraculous, Joan and her army took other English posts along the Loire and routed the enemy at Patay. She urged the dauphin to be crowned Charles VII at Rheims; and after considerable persuasion on her part, he agreed. Joan stood near him during the coronation. This represented the pinnacle of her fortunes. In September 1429 she unsuccessfully besieged Paris. The following spring, she tried to defend Compiègne but was captured by the Burgundians. She attempted to escape but was recaptured and ransomed to the English, who were eager to destroy her influence by putting her to death. In order to exempt themselves of responsibility for killing her, however, the English turned her over to the ecclesiastical court at Rouen.

Joan bravely fought her inquisitors and was shown to be humorous and forthright during her interrogation and trial on charges of witchcraft, heresy, and wearing male clothes, an offense against the church. She was tried before Pierre Cauchon, the bishop of Beauvais, whose violent partisanship for the English made a fair trial impossible. Joan was convicted and burned at the stake in the Rouen marketplace on May 30, 1431. The executioner is reported to have said afterward, "I greatly fear that I am damned for I have burnt a holy woman." Charles VII made no attempt to ransom or save her, possibly, writes Barbara Tuchman in *A Distant Mirror*, because of the "nobility's embarrassment at having been led to victory by a village girl." However, Charles made a tardy recognition of her service in 1456 by staging a rehabilitation trial that annulled the proceedings of the original one.

Joan of Arc was beatified in 1909 and canonized in 1920. Her life has lent itself to numerous legends, and she has been represented in many paintings and statues. French-Italian poet Christine de Pisan, who died in 1430, wrote a poem in praise of her, and she has long been a favorite subject for fiction writers, biographers, and historians, as well as for composers and filmmakers.

While Joan of Arc's life and death did not instantly lead to a national resistance, it nevertheless renewed the hope and energy of the French and helped demoralize the English and the Burgundians, who by 1435 were back in the French camp. But the phenomenon of Joan of Arc defies categorization. "Perhaps it can only be explained," writes Tuchman, "as the answer called forth by an exigent historic need. The moment required her and she rose."

56

Indira Gandhi

1917–1984

To many, Indira Gandhi remains a magnetic, enigmatic, and fascinating personality, while to others, she is a sinister specter hovering in the political wings.

—MARY C. CARRAS
Indira Gandhi:
In the Crucible of Leadership

Indira Gandhi, India's first woman prime minister, was both admired for her strength and resolve, and reviled for her abuse of power. She considerably expanded India's role as an international force and a major voice among the countries of the Third World.

A tireless advocate of democracy for India, her administration was eventually marred by self-preservation and the abrogation of democratic rights. She was faced with the difficult task of governing the second most populous nation on earth, a country fragmented by intense religious and political partisanship, and although her achievements fell short of the goals she set, she remains a world leader eminently worthy of recognition.

Indira was born into the first family of independent India. Her father, Jawaharlal Nehru, and her grandfather, Motilel, were, along with Mohandas Gandhi (no relation), the major players in India's struggle to free itself from British rule. One of Indira's first childhood memories "was of burning foreign cloth and imported articles in the courtyard of the home: the whole family did it." The bonfire was held in response to Mohandas Gandhi's call for a nonviolent campaign of noncooperation with the British and a boycott of European-made goods. Indira consigned her favorite, foreign-made doll to the flames, perhaps a fitting sacrifice for a child whose hero was Joan of Arc. At the age of twelve, she gathered a thousand children together to form the "Monkey Brigade," her version of the revolutionary Indian National Congress, India's largest and most influential political party. Both of Indira's parents spent long periods in jail, which made her childhood a lonely and insecure one. She attended school in Poona and later studied with Indian poet and philosopher Rabindranath Tagore. After her mother contracted tuberculosis, Indira interrupted her studies to accompany her parents to Switzerland for her mother's treatment.

In 1938 Indira entered Somerville College of Oxford University to study modern history. She was in London during the worst part of the blitz, driving an ambulance and tending casualties. Ironically, at the same time, her father was languishing in a British jail in India. While in England, Indira became engaged to Feroze Gandhi, a family friend and a student at the London School of Economics. When the couple returned home to marry in 1942, they found themselves in the middle of the fiercest and bloodiest fighting of the independence movement. The Indian National Congress had endorsed a "Quit India" policy that called for the immediate withdrawal of the British and a massive campaign of nonviolent civil disobedience if the British did not comply. With the Japanese to contend with, the British showed no willingness to negotiate. They attacked protesters and jailed most of the National Congress leaders, including Indira, who spent nine months in prison.

After India won its independence in 1947, Indira's father, Jawaharlal Nehru, became the nation's first prime minister and minister of foreign affairs. Indira served as one of his trusted advisers and accompanied him on diplomatic missions around the world. In 1955 she accepted an important post on the Congress Working Committee. Four years later she was elected president of the Indian National Congress, a position previously held by both her father and grandfather. When Nehru died of a stroke in 1964, Indira was considered too young and inexperienced to succeed him. Her gender was also a liability. She accepted instead a position in the cabinet of Prime Minister Lal Shastri. When Shastri died suddenly in 1966, Indira was put forward as prime minister by Congress party leaders, who believed she could be easily manipulated by them.

Indira, however, proved to be a forceful and decisive prime minister, skillfully balancing off the United States and the Soviet Union, each of whom wanted India under its sphere of influence. She defeated Pakistan in the 1971 war that produced the independent state of Bangladesh and mounted a domestic "Remove Poverty" campaign, with limited success. Corruption and the strong-arm tactics of Indira's son and designated successor, Sanjay, fostered strong opposition to her government. In 1975 she was indicted for minor election fraud during the 1971 campaign, and there were calls for her resignation. She responded by declaring a state of emergency, during which her opponents were jailed and the press was censored. Indira relaxed the state of emergency in 1977, after the Supreme Court overturned her conviction. However, in the general election that followed, she was voted out of office. The new coalition government had no program except its opposition to her, and in 1980 she was reelected prime minister for the third time.

Sanjay's 1980 death in a plane crash forced his older brother, Rajiv, an airline pilot, into politics to become his mother's successor. In 1984 Indira's order to surpress Sikh extremists who held the Golden Temple in Amritsar created an outbreak of violence from the Sikh minority, and resulted in her assassination by her Sikh body guards.

Described by Indian historian M. Chalapathi Rau as "an idealist without illusion," Indira Gandi strove to lead her country away from poverty and religious extremism and failed. Her turbulent and contradictory career, marked by the pragmatic, not to say autocratic, exercise of political power, illustrates the challenge of democratic leadership in a relatively young nation that continues to struggle for economic parity and cultural balance.

57

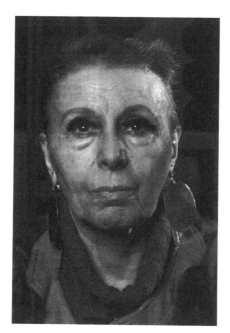

Louise Nevelson

1899–1988

In getting to this pitch of achievement, she, like Georgia O'Keeffe, has also redrawn the assumptions that surround the role of women in art. In that respect she belongs to the culture as a whole, not just to the art world and its concerns.

—ROBERT HUGHES
Quoted in C. S. Rubinstein,
American Women Artists, 1982

A pioneer in the art of sculpture, Louise Nevelson is best known for her monumental box assemblages of complex, rhythmic abstract shapes. Her sculptures, constructed from odd pieces of wood, found objects, cast metal, and other materials, and completely covered with black, white, or gold paint, have a uniform tone that gives them a mysterious quality and accentuates the structural importance of the shadows within them.

Nevelson spent three decades struggling for recognition of her work. She willingly sacrificed marriage, family, and financial security for the freedom to fully devote herself to the search for her personal artistic vision. Today she is recognized as one of the major sculptors of the twentieth century, and toward the end of her life she received more public commissions than any other American sculptor.

Nevelson was born Louise Berliawsky in Kiev, Russia, the second child in a family of three girls and one boy. In 1902, her father, Isaac Berliawsky, a lumber merchant, emigrated to the United States and settled in Rockland, Maine, where he established a successful lumber and construction business. Three years later, his family joined him in Rockland. The Berliawskys were one of only thirty Jewish families in what Nevelson later described as "a WASP Yankee town," and as immigrants and Jews were excluded from much of the community's social life.

Nevelson's feelings of isolation and her shyness in school were mitigated by her happy home life. "I adored my parents," she later told her biographer and friend, Arnold Glimcher. "My mother was freethinking and had strong socialist ideas. My father believed in equal rights for women." The Berliawskys stressed the value of education and encouraged their children's interest in the arts. In addition to her schoolwork, Louise took dancing, piano, voice, and painting lessons. She was a mediocre student but she excelled in art and knew by the age of nine that she wanted to be a sculptor. Her chance to fulfill her dream of studying art in New York City came in 1917, when she met wealthy Jewish cargo ship owner Charles Nevelson, whose home was in New York. The couple married in 1920, and two years later their son, Mike, was born. Although she plunged into a study of all the arts, including dance, voice, and drama, Nevelson felt increasingly stifled by her marriage. "My husband's family thought they were terribly refined," she later wrote. "Within their circle you could know Beethoven, but God forbid if you *were* Beethoven. You were not allowed to be a creator, you were just supposed to be an audience."

In 1931, after spending two years at the Art Students League, Nevelson left her husband, entrusted her son to her family in Maine, and went to Munich, Germany, to study with legendary art teacher Hans Hoffman. Soon after Nevelson arrived, however, Hoffman left for the United States to escape fascism. Nonetheless, Hoffman's Cubist teachings left a great impression on Nevelson and permanently affected her work. After studying for a time in Paris, where she became entranced by the work of Picasso and by the power of the African sculpture in the Museé de L'Homme, Nevelson returned to New York to begin working as a sculptor.

The 1930s were difficult years both financially and professionally for Nevelson. She resumed study with Hans Hoffman, who was now teaching at the Art Students League, and worked as an assistant to WPA muralist Diego Rivera, who introduced her to the art of pre-Columbian Mexico. She sculpted compulsively, creating blocky figures of plaster that show the influence of pre-Columbian art and Cubism. Nevelson began to exhibit her work at group shows, and in 1936 showed five wooden sculptures at an art gallery in Greenwich Village. That same year her son came to live with her while he finished high school. Despite their long separation, Nevelson and Mike were able to establish a close relationship that lasted for the rest of her life.

By 1941 Nevelson had gained a small amount of recognition for her work but had achieved no significant success and was in acute financial distress. With a courage born of desperation, she stormed into the prestigious Nierendorf Gallery, and insisted that Karl Nierendorf look at her work. He agreed, visited her studio, and, impressed, scheduled her first solo exhibition. Nierendorf became Nevelson's close friend and a major source of professional support. When he died in 1948, she sank back into obscurity. Nevelson did not exhibit again until 1955, when her sculptures, constructed of orange crates and painted black, were featured in the first of several one-woman shows at the Grand Central Moderns Gallery.

In 1957 Nevelson began to assemble "found objects"—moldings, jagged scraps of crates, furniture legs—within stacked boxes to create rich, encrusted walls. With her "Moon Garden + One" exhibition in 1958, which featured her matte black sculpture wall *Sky Cathedral*, Nevelson fully came into her own style.

Critics called *Sky Cathedral* "marvelous"; Nevelson characteristically called it "a feast—for myself." Art collectors began to show interest in her work, and she was offered a contract with the prestigious Martha Jackson Gallery. For the first time, Louise Nevelson was financially secure.

In 1959 she was invited to exhibit in the Museum of Modern Art's "Sixteen Americans" show, for which she created a massive all-white environment, *Dawn's Wedding Feast.* Nevelson defined the sculpture as "a marriage with the world." In 1962, she produced the all-gold wall assemblage, *Dawn,* which she had filled with furniture sections, baseball bats, and rifle stocks. The same year, she represented the United States in the sculpture section of the Venice Biennale. In 1967 she presented a major retrospective exhibition of her work at the Whitney Museum of American Art in New York.

Among Nevelson's many other notable works are *Ice Palace I* (1967), a Plexiglas sculpture; *Bicentennial Dawn* (1976), a large three-part white-wood sculpture; *Mrs. N's Palace* (1977), her largest assemblage; and *Shadows and Flags* (1978), a group of huge steel sculptures created for the newly named Louise Nevelson Plaza in downtown Manhattan. She received the National Medal for the Arts in 1985.

Nevelson's appearance was almost as dramatic as her sculptures. She fringed her eyes with three layers of thick, black artificial eyelashes made of fur and costumed herself in wildly unconventional ensembles. A typical Nevelson outfit might consist of a Chinese embroidered robe over a denim workshirt and a Mexican skirt, topped by a head-scarf or jockey cap. Nevelson's personal style was yet another expression of her fierce individualism. As she once said, "It's a hell of a thing to be born, and if you're born you're at least entitled to your own self."

58

Emmeline Pankhurst

1858–1928

We woman suffragists have a great mission—the
greatest mission the world has ever known. It is to free
half the human race, and through that freedom to save
the rest.

—EMMELINE PANKHURST
Speech in *Votes for Women*,
October 25, 1912

In 1903 the women's suffrage movement in England turned
militant with the formation of the Women's Social and Political
Union (WSPU). Organized and led by Emmeline Pankhurst and
her daughter, Christabel, the WSPU dissidents mounted a tactical
campaign of violence and disruption of public life designed to

harass legislators into adopting women's suffrage as a party measure. The WSPU's "guerrilla warfare," as Mrs. Pankhurst called it, resulted in only limited success for the movement. Nevertheless, the Pankhurst strategy represents an important historical moment in which women, after having finally lost patience with an intransigent male establishment, felt compelled to resort to violence to gain the political equality they had been denied.

Emmeline Pankhurst was a most unlikely candidate to lead a movement or a revolution. Born Emmeline Goulden in Manchester, England, she grew up in a household dominated by her Victorian father, a self-made man who had risen from office-boy to master cotton spinner and bleacher to factory owner. When she was fourteen, Emmeline was sent to Paris for her education. Upon her return to Manchester, she was courted by Richard Pankhurst, a barrister and supporter of radical causes, particularly women's suffrage. Emmeline devoted the next six years to managing their household and raising four children— Christabel, Sylvia, Frank, and Adela. There was little to suggest a different direction for Pankhurst from that of any other conventional, genteel Victorian matriarch. She had merely exchanged her role as dutiful daughter for that of dutiful wife and mother.

However, the influence of her husband's advocacy of liberal causes increasingly had an impact on Pankhurst's thinking. For a time she joined the progressive socialist Fabian Society and the Independent Labour Party. She also held local office as a Poor Law Guardian, as a school board member, and as a registrar of births and deaths. Through these experiences she began to observe the inferior position of women and their legal and social oppression by men. She concluded that it would be necessary to increase women's political power in order for them to achieve emancipation and to reform society at large.

In 1889 Pankhurst gave birth to her fifth and last child, and, while recovering she decided with a group of women friends to form a Women's Franchise League to work toward gaining the vote for women. Her husband strongly supported her activities, and when he died in 1898, she was left without his guidance and influence. Her activism waned until it was rekindled by the strong political interests of her eldest daughter, Christabel.

Disappointment in the lack of interest shown by the Liberal and Independent Labour parties in women's suffrage led the Pankhursts to form the Women's Social and Political Union. From the start, the WSPU's membership was exclusively female and its sole issue was women's suffrage. As suffragist Emmeline Pethwick-Lawrence wrote of Mrs. Pankhurst at the time, "She was, as she instinctively knew, cast for a great role. She had a temperament akin to genius. She could have been a queen on the stage or in the salon. Circumstances had balked her in the fulfillment of her destiny. But the smoldering spark leapt into flame when her daughter Christabel initiated militancy."

The WSPU distrusted all party promises and called for immediate parliamentary action to extend the franchise to women. To force an unwilling and condescending government to act, they also instituted a strategy of confrontation that included disrupting election meetings and organizing massed processions to the Houses of Parliament. In 1908 Pankhurst announced an escalation of tactics to convince the government to accede to their demands. The WSPU smashed windows in central London, burned letters in post boxes, set fire to unoccupied buildings, and defaced other buildings, stopping just short of committing actual violence to individuals. The WSPU's violence against property was aimed at making, in Pankhurst's words, "England and every department of English life insecure and unsafe." As Pankhurst stated, "The argument of the broken pane of glass is the most valuable argument in modern politics."

The government responded with arrests and imprisonments, and Emmeline Pankhurst was jailed for the first time in 1908. The women prisoners began hunger strikes, which were followed by brutal forced feedings and releases, and then, under the "Cat and Mouse" Act, the rearrest of fasting prisoners once they had recovered. The cycle of violence and brutal countermeasures continued until 1914 when a "Conciliation Bill" was accepted that excluded working-class women from the vote and fell short of the universal suffrage Pankhurst and the WSPU had desired. However, the government's pledge of support was accepted, to be redeemed at the end of World War I. In 1918 women over the age of thirty were enfranchised, and by 1928, the year of Emmeline Pankhurst's death, all English women were given the vote on the same terms as men.

Emmeline Pankhurst stands as an exceptional example of a woman committed to the cause of women's rights, although the efficacy of her methods continues to be debated. British Prime Minister David Lloyd George decried Pankhurst's strategy, saying, "What an extraordinary mixture of idealism and lunacy! Hasn't she the sense to see that the very worst method of campaigning for the franchise is to try and intimidate or blackmail a man into giving her what he would gladly give her otherwise." Yet it was not at all clear that the British government was prepared to gladly give women the vote, and Pankhurst's advocacy of force to create change would become an important legacy in future agitation in India and in the United States. Pankhurst was able to mobilize support for the cause of women's suffrage and risked a great deal to ensure its eventual success. She joins an important group of women that includes Susan B. Anthony and Elizabeth Cady Stanton who pressed the cause of increasing political power for women, inspiring succeeding generations of women activists.

59

Dorothea Lange

1895–1965

Through her photographs the symptoms of the Depression are clearly set forth and through them we can better understand the tragic events of those times. She made intimate contact with the victims....Her pictures were effective for they were believed. Nothing about them was contrived or artificial; her warmth was so contagious that her subjects were virtually unaffected by the presence of the camera...

—VAN DEREN COKE, photographer
In Milton Meltzer, *Dorothea Lange*

In the early 1930s, no longer able to ignore the misery of the unemployed men she daily witnessed on the streets of San Francisco, Dorothea Lange abandoned her lucrative career as a society photographer to chronicle the victims of the Depression. Her first attempt resulted in one of her best-known photographs, *White Angel Breadline*, which shows a man in the foreground, staring down at the cup he holds in his hands, his back to the crowd of men in line for food. Lange went on to produce exceptionally powerful images of destitute rural Americans, which helped to create a national awareness of their plight and became classics of documentary photography.

Born in Hoboken, New Jersey, Dorothea was the eldest daughter of Joan and Howard Nutzhorn. At the age of seven she came down with polio, which left her with a lifelong limp and an early sense of shame at being disabled that gradually gave way to acceptance in adulthood. When she was twelve, her father, a lawyer, abandoned the family, (possibly, suggests Lange's biographer, Milton Meltzer, because he had embezzled a client's funds and had been forced to leave town.) The family moved in with Joan Nutzhorn's mother, and Dorothea was transferred to a public school on the Lower East Side of Manhattan, near the library where her mother worked. In 1907 the Nutzhorns divorced, and Joan resumed her maiden name, Lange, which her daughter and son also adopted.

Unhappy at school and treated badly at home by her tyrannical grandmother, Dorothea frequently spent her days wandering through the city, carefully observing what she saw. She graduated from high school in 1913 determined to become a photographer, although she knew little about the work and had never used a camera. From 1914 to 1917, while attending the New York Training School for Teachers, Lange apprenticed herself to portrait photographers, including Arnold Genthe, known for his photographs of San Francisco's Chinatown and the devastation caused by the 1906 earthquake, and Charles H. Davis, a theatrical photographer. She also studied with renowned artist-photographer Clarence H. White at Columbia University.

When her course with White ended, Lange bought a large camera and two lenses and began to work on her own, using a converted chicken coop as a darkroom. In 1918 she left New York with the intention of earning her way around the world making photographs and got as far as San Francisco. There she worked as a photo finisher and joined a camera club. She started a portrait business in 1919 with money given to her by a friend. Her studio became a gathering place for many artists, including painter Maynard Dixon, whom Lange, twenty-one years his junior, married in 1920. Throughout the decade, her thriving portrait business provided the main support for the couple and their two children.

In 1934 Lange met social economist Paul Taylor at an exhibit of her documentary photographs. The two began working together to record in words and pictures the living conditions of migrant workers for the California State Emergency Relief Administration. Their reports resulted in the establishment of the first state-built camps for migrants. Lange and Taylor were married in 1935, two months after Lange's divorce from Maynard Dixon.

From 1935 to 1942 Lange traveled throughout the United States documenting the effects of the Depression on rural Americans for the Farm Security Administration. Her photographs, reproduced in numerous magazines and newspapers, as well as in illustrated books and exhibits, had an enormous impact on the public. Her famous study, *The Migrant Mother*, a photograph of a prematurely aged woman holding a baby while two children lean on her shoulders, was published worldwide to raise funds for medical supplies. Lange's work appeared in a book titled *An American Exodus: A Record of Human Erosion*, coauthored by Paul Taylor and published in 1939.

Soon after the United States entered World War II, Lange was hired by the War Relocation Authority to document the mass internment of Japanese Americans in concentration camps. Her sympathy for the internees caused suspicions among her supervisors, and many of her photographs were impounded until after the war. In 1945 she photographed delegates to United Nations conferences for the State Department. While covering the San Francisco conference, she had to be hospitalized for ulcers. She did not photograph again until 1951, when she began to focus on aspects of everyday life, using her family as her favorite subjects. She also produced photo essays for *Life*, including "Three Mormon Towns" and "Irish Country People," and worked with

Edward Steichen on his prodigious "Family of Man" exhibit. In the late fifties and early sixties, she traveled overseas with Taylor, whose work took him to Asia, Venezuela, Ecuador, and Egypt. Although she was frequently in poor health, she photographed when she could, documenting what she felt were universal similarities in human expression.

Lange died in San Francisco of cancer of the esophagus in 1965. The following year, a retrospective exhibition of her work, which she had designed in 1964, opened at the Museum of Modern Art, and her study of American women, *The American Country Woman*, was published.

Dorothea Lange's photographs profoundly affected American photojournalism by their simplicity and directness. In the words of Edward Steichen, "Hers are among the most remarkable human documents ever rendered in pictures."

60

Agnes De Mille

1909–1993

Ours is an upbeat, a hurried, hasty beat. It keeps pressing us to go farther, to include everything so that we can savor everything, so that we can know everything, so that we will miss nothing. Partly it's greed, but mainly it's curiosity. We just want to experience it. And we do.

—AGNES DE MILLE

When dancer, choreographer, teacher, and author Agnes De Mille spoke those words in January 1990, at a gala honoring the fiftieth anniversary of the American Ballet Theatre, she might have been describing her own unique contribution to American dance. De Mille's ballets gave new scope and breadth to dance by combining classical and modern movement with the spirited rhythms of American folk dance. She brought ballet to musical comedy for the first time, ending the era of high kicks and chorus-line turns. At the core of De Mille's work was her cardinal belief that dance meant communication, and to that end she presented audiences with an innovative mix of movement and story for them to fully experience and savor.

Agnes De Mille was born in New York City to playwright-director William De Mille (brother of film producer-director Cecil B. DeMille) and Anna George De Mille. When Agnes was nine, the family moved to Hollywood. At the age of ten she saw Anna Pavlova perform and immediately decided to become a great dancer. Her decision was greeted less than enthusiastically by her parents, who stressed academic achievement and did not want either of their daughters to pursue careers on stage. Nevertheless, they allowed Agnes to take one private and one group dance lesson a week as good physical training. De Mille's teacher, Theodore Kosloff, was pessimistic about the ten-year-old's prospects. He told her she had weak knees, was overweight, and was too old to start ballet. De Mille persisted, and in time Kosloff conceded that she showed an extraordinary talent for pantomime. In her mid-teens, De Mille pleased her father by announcing her intention to give up dance lessons to attend college. At the University of California, she danced in productions and majored in English literature, graduating cum laude.

When the De Milles divorced, twenty-year-old Agnes moved to New York with her mother and sister. She was determined to forge a career as a dancer and choreographer. But Broadway during the Jazz Age was dominated by the Schubert brothers, who marketed salable, proven theatrical entertainment and beautiful showgirls. Agnes, despite the powerful De Mille connection in Hollywood, did not meet the Broadway criteria of the era and was turned down by every agent she approached. Discouraged, but not defeated, De Mille did a tour with dancer Adolph Bolm and shared a series of programs with dancer Jacques Cartier. Her first successful effort at choreography was a well-received dance called *49*, one of the first dances to make use of American folk material on the concert stage. In 1932, after De Mille was fired as choreographer from the Broadway show *Flying Colors*, she decided to try her luck in Europe. A brief, moderately successful season in Paris, Brussels, and London followed, during which British dance critic Arnold Haskell singled out De Mille as "the first real idiomatic American dancer."

The thirties were watershed years for De Mille. She studied, worked, and performed with Marie Rambert at the Mercury Theatre in London, where her colleagues included young dancers and choreographers who would become world famous, such as Alicia Markova, Antony Tudor, and Frederick Ashton. Her first successful paying job was as choreographer for a Cole Porter musical, *The Nymph Errant*, which starred Gertrude Lawrence, the reigning queen of musical comedy. De Mille was then invited to Hollywood by her Uncle Cecil to choreograph and perform a nude dance on the back of a live bull for his 1934 epic *Cleopatra*. Agnes walked off the set when told by "Uncle C" that her dance had "no excitement, no thrill, no suspense, no sex." While in Hollywood, she also took classes with dancer Carmalita Maracci, whom she greatly admired, and taught a class of her own, in which she experimented with gesture and pantomime.

In 1939 De Mille was asked to join a new ballet company in New York, Ballet Theatre. For the first time, De Mille was working with a true corps de ballet and a truly eclectic company, whose members would eventually include Antony Tudor, Adolph Bolm, Michel Fokine, Alicia Alonso, Lucia Chase, Jerome Robbins, and Robert Helpmann. "Diaghilev may have established higher standards artistically," writes De Mille of the early days of what would become the American Ballet Theatre, "but our scope and verve were unmatched." Among the works De Mille choreographed for Ballet Theatre was *Black Ritual*, the first ballet performed entirely with black dancers in a classic American ballet company. But it was with *Rodeo*, a ballet she created for Serge Denham of the Ballet Russe de Monte Carlo, that De Mille firmly established her place as one of the most innovative choreographers in dance history. A celebration of the American West with music by Aaron Copland, and featuring an amalgam of folk dancing, modern dance, and classical ballet, *Rodeo* made ballet history. Its premiere at the Metropolitan Opera House garnered twenty-two curtain calls, and critics compared De Mille to Mark Twain.

Five months later, De Mille again made history with her ballets for the Rodgers and Hammerstein musical *Oklahoma!* The show featured smoothly integrated dance and plot for the first time in a musical comedy and marked a new era of sophistication in the genre. De Mille went on to choreograph such classic musicals as *Carousel, Brigadoon, One Touch of Venus, Bloomer Girl, Gentlemen Prefer Blondes,* and *Paint Your Wagon* and to create ballets, most notably *Fall River Legend.* Throughout this period, De Mille managed to successfully juggle her career with her role as a wife and mother.

During the 1960s Agnes De Mille worked to obtain basic minimum salaries for dancers and helped to repeal the New York State law prohibiting Sunday dance performances. As cofounder and president of the Society of Stage Directors and Choreographers, De Mille was the first woman president of a labor union in the United States. She served as the only American judge at the International Ballet Competition in Moscow and on the first National Advisory Council on the Arts. In 1973 she founded the Heritage Dance Theatre, which was devoted to dances of American traditional and historical interest. Besides *Dance to the Piper,* her volumes of memoirs and books on the art of dance include *And Promenade Home, Speak to Me, Dance With Me, The Book of the Dance, To a Young Dancer,* and a biography of Martha Graham, *Martha: The Life and Work of Martha Graham.* In 1981 De Mille published *Reprieve,* a moving account of her recovery from the near-fatal cerebral hemorrhage she suffered in 1975.

Agnes De Mille's artistic essence was probably best described by another dance innovator, Martha Graham, who told her, "There is a vitality, a life-force, and energy, a quickening that is translated through you into action and because there is only one of you, this expression is unique." De Mille used that unique expression to transform the dance and its place in the musical theater.

61

Sappho

c. 613 B.C.–c. 570 B.C.

All is so rhythmically and sublimely ordered in the
poems of Sappho that supreme art lends solemnity and
grandeur to the expression of unmitigated passion.

—DAVID M. ROBINSON
Sappho and Her Influence

Facts are scant and contradictory concerning the life of Sappho, the greatest of the early Greek lyric poets, whom Plato called "the tenth Muse." She was born in either Eresos or Mytilene on the Greek island of Lesbos into an aristrocratic, socially prominent family, and was orphaned at the age of six. Her father, Skamandronymous, is believed to have been a prosperous wine merchant. The eldest of her three brothers, Charaxos, was a wine merchant as well, and another brother, Larichos, held the prestigious job of wine pourer for the Mytileneans at their town hall.

Sappho had a daughter, Cleïs, named after her mother, according to the tradition of the time; the child's father may have been a wealthy merchant named Cercylas. Some sources claim that Cercylas was her husband and died when Sappho was about thirty-five. Sappho lived mainly in Mytilene but was exiled to Sicily for a time, probably because of her family's political activities. She is reputed to have been short and dark-haired in an era when the feminine ideal was tall and fair-haired. Although her romantic preference was for women, she is said to have had male as well as female lovers, including the poet Alcaeus. Legend has it that she threw herself off a cliff for the unrequited love of a man named Phaon, but this is generally considered by scholars to be untrue.

Lesbos, in Sappho's day, was a brilliant cultural center with a strong poetic tradition. Its society was markedly less misogynous than that of many of the Greek city-states; Lesbos's women mixed freely with men, were highly educated, and formed clubs for the cultivation of poetry and music. Sappho wrote her poetry for her circle of friends and disciples, mostly, but not exclusively, young women. She wrote in the Aeolic dialect in a great many meters, one of which has been called, after her, the Sapphic stanza. The principal subject of her poetry is love with all its passion, joy, sorrow, jealousy, frustration, and longing. Sappho's verse is a classic example of the love lyric and expresses the poet's feelings for women, her daughter, and nature, written with a direct simplicity and a perfect control of meter. Sappho also composed, and probably performed, epithalamiums, songs or poems written to celebrate a marriage that usually tell of the happenings of the wedding day.

In the third and second centuries B.C., Aristophanes of Byzantium and Aristarchus of Samothrace collected and edited Sappho's poetry in nine books, according to meter. Her work continued to influence readers, scholars, and the Roman poets Catullus, Ovid, and Horace. By the fifth century A.D., when scholars began to transcribe works from papyrus scrolls to books, Sappho's poetry was left out and largely forgotten. It was not until the 1890s that a concerted effort was begun to collect and arrange her works. The first modern collection of Sappho's poetry was published by the Oxford University Press in 1925.

Of Sappho's nine books of poetry, only fragments survive. The most complete poem consists of seven stanzas and is an invocation to the goddess Aphrodite to help the poet in her relationship with a woman:

> Thorned in splendor, beauteous child of mighty
> Zeus, wile-weaving, immortal Aphrodite,
> smile again; your frowning so affrays me
>   woe overweighs me.

> Come to me now, if ever in the olden days
> you did hear me from afar, and from the
> golden halls of your father fly with all speeding
>   unto my pleading.

> Down through mid-ether from Love's highest regions
> swan-drawn in car convoyed by lovely legions
> of bright-hued doves beclouding with their pinions
>   Earth's broad dominions.

> Quickly you came; and, Blessed One, with
> smiling countenance immortal, my heavy heart
> beguiling, asked the cause of my pitiful condition—
>   why my petition:

> What most I craved in brain-bewildered yearning;
> whom would I win, so winsome in her spurning;
> "Who is she, Sappho, so evilly requiting
> fond love with slighting?

> "She who flees you soon shall turn pursuing,
> cold to your love now, weary with wooing,
> gifts once scorned with greater gifts reclaiming
>   unto her shaming."

> Come thus again; from cruel cares deliver;
> of all that my heart wills graciously be giver—
> greatest of gifts, your loving self and tender
> to be my defender.

Sappho's influence through the ages has been threefold. As a Greek lyric poet of epic proportions, she can rightly be considered the first known woman author and the founder of women's literature. Her work influenced not only the Romans but later poets, such as Thomas Campion, Philip Sidney, Swinburne, and Ezra Pound. Finally, because of her sexual preference, she has achieved immortal status as the patron saint and muse of lesbian lovers. Sappho was unfailingly accurate when she wrote of herself and her followers, "I think that someone will remember us in another time."

62

Nadia Boulanger

1887–1979

There are those names which escape from the cyclone of
indifference and the ogre of daily events. The name of
Nadia Boulanger is one of these, for it has attained a
position of nobility that makes it invisible to the
mediocre. It is rare that a young musician intrigues us,
or that his work at least partially opens a door, without
his disclosing that he is a pupil of Nadia Boulanger.

> —JEAN COCTEAU
> In a 1957 tribute to Boulanger

Nadia Boulanger, French composer, conductor, and teacher, was one of the most influential figures in music in the twentieth century. Although she achieved acclaim as a composer and was the first prominent woman conductor of major orchestras, it was her role as a music teacher that earned her the most lasting distinction. As composer Virgil Thomson declared, Boulanger was "a one-woman graduate school so powerful and so permeating that legend credits every U.S. town with two things—a five-and-dime and a Boulanger pupil." Thomson summarized Boulanger's pervasive impact on American music by saying that she was, particularly for American musicians, "our Alma Mater."

Boulanger was born in Paris, where her father, Ernest Boulanger, like his father before him, taught singing at the Paris Conservatory. Her mother, Raissa, a Russian-born princess, had been one of her father's pupils. Nadia began studying at the conservatory at the age of ten, and by the time she completed her training at seventeen had won numerous first-prize awards for composing. She achieved some success in composing instrumental and vocal pieces, winning second place in France's Prix de Rome competition with a cantata, *La Sirène*. Around 1912 she abandoned composition and turned her attention increasingly to teaching. One of her first pupils was her younger sister, Lili, who became the first woman to win the Prix de Rome, in 1913. It is likely that Boulanger gave up her own composing in recognition of her sister's greater talent. As Boulanger later recalled, "I had to give it up because I wrote music that was not even bad, just useless. My calling is to teach." Lili's early death in 1918 proved to be a turning point in Nadia's career, solidifying her vocation as a teacher.

During her long career, Nadia Boulanger taught at the Ecole Normale, at the American Conservatory in Fontainebleau, where she was appointed director in 1950, and at the Paris Conservatory. She traveled to the United States in the 1930s and 1940s to teach at Wellesley College, Radcliffe, and Juilliard. Her list of pupils reads like a who's who of modern music: Aaron Copland, Virgil Thomson, Roy Harris, Elliott Carter, David Diamond, and many others. Aaron Copland, the celebrated composer of such classic American works as *Appalachian Spring* and *The Red Pony*, said of her that she "knew everything there was to know about music; she knew the oldest and the latest music; pre-Bach and post-Stravinsky, and knew it cold. All the technical know-how was at her fingertips." Boulanger's teaching regimen and discipline were legendary; starting her teaching day at 8:00 A.M., sometimes earlier, she would continue teaching until 10:00 P.M. Although she never pursued conducting as a major activity, she did conduct regularly and became the first woman to conduct the Royal Philharmonic, the New York Philharmonic, the Philadelphia Orchestra, and the Boston Symphony Orchestra. In 1938 she was asked how it felt to be the first woman conductor of the Boston Symphony. She replied with typical candor, "I've been a woman for a little more than fifty years, and I've gotten over my original astonishment."

Boulanger's great genius as a teacher was to uncover the original talent of each of her students measured against her own exacting standards. As Virgil Thomson explained, "Preconceiving the kinds of work her pupils were to write was never the Boulanger method." She both cultivated new compositions and led the revival of interest in early music through her many performances and recordings of Baroque and Renaissance vocal music. For fifty years she offered weekly Wednesday afternoons in her Paris apartment for musical discussion, analysis, and performances by her pupils and invited guests. At the age of eighty she was asked about retiring. Her response: "I never think of age. I've no time. I work. Retirement? I don't know what that is. One works or one cannot work—that would be death." Nadia Boulanger continued to work, though blind and confined to a wheelchair, until her death in 1979 at the age of ninety-two.

63

Gwendolyn Brooks

1917– 2000

Her greatest impact has been as key player in the
literature of African-American people.
> —HAKI MADHUBUTI
> *Say That the River Turns:*
> *The Impact of Gwendolyn Brooks*, 1987

One of the most significant poets of the twentieth century,
Gwendolyn Brooks was the first African American to win a
Pulitzer Prize for poetry, and in 1976 she became the first black
woman inducted into the National Institute of Arts and Letters.
Able to move comfortably between formal structure and eloquent
language and street talk and the rhythm of black urban life,
Brooks has produced a treasury of important poems, all in-
formed by her humanistic vision.

Gwendolyn Brooks was born in Topeka, Kansas, and grew up on the South Side of Chicago. Her mother, Keziah, had been a teacher. Her father, David, was a janitor who had hoped to become a doctor and had studied premedicine at Fisk University for a year and a half. Both parents inculcated the value of literature and learning in Gwendolyn and her younger brother, Raymond, and kept the children on a strict regimen: rough play in the morning, quiet play, reading, and drawing in the afternoon. Brooks began to write at the age of seven, composing her first poem, a two-line verse. She writes, "I have notebooks dating from the time I was eleven, when I started to keep my poems in composition books. My mother decided that I was to be the female Paul Laurence Dunbar." At thirteen, her poem "Eventide," was published in *American Childhood* magazine. As payment she received six copies of the magazine and an encouraging letter from the editor. Brooks's school years were largely unhappy ones. Teased for her timidity and social awkwardness, she was also ridiculed for her dark skin by blacks, who considered light skin the standard of beauty, and shunned by whites for being black. Brooks used her school experience as the basis for her 1953 novel *Maud Martha*, one of the first novels to explore the theme of a black girl's coming of age. After her graduation from high school, Brooks attended Woodrow Wilson Junior College, where she published *News Review*, a newspaper focusing on racial and cultural issues. In 1939 she married writer Henry Lowington Blakely, whom she had met through her involvement with the NAACP. The first of the couple's two children was born in 1940.

During the early 1940s, Brooks perfected her craft in poetry classes run by Inez Cunningham Stark and given in the South Side Community Art Center. Her first book of poetry, *A Street in Bronzeville*, was published in 1945, the same year that she was selected as one of the ten women to receive a *Mademoiselle* magazine Merit Award for Distinguished Achievement. The 1950 Pulitzer Prize for poetry was awarded to her for her volume *Annie Allen*, published in 1949. Her subject matter dealt with the values of the black community, but her style was the sophisticated literary language of such modernist poets as Ezra Pound and T. S. Eliot. During the 1950s and 1960s, Brooks published volumes of children's poetry and adult collections, including *The Bean Eaters* (1960), *Selected Poems* (1963), and *Riot* (1969). In *The Bean*

Eaters Brooks allowed herself the full range of poetic involvement in the lives of African Americans, writing of the murder of Emmett Till and cutting through the bravura of young black boys in the remarkable "We Real Cool."

In 1967 Brooks attended the Second Black Writers' Conference at Fisk University and was influenced by the energy and perspective of the black writers she met there. As she recalls, "Until 1967 my own blackness did not confront me with a shrill spelling of itself. I knew that I was what most people were calling a 'Negro'; I called myself that, although always the word fell awkwardly on a poet's ear." She began to deliberately explore the implication of her black identity. Before 1967, she remembers, "I wasn't writing consciously with the idea that blacks *must address* blacks, *must write* about blacks.... I'm trying to create new forms, trying to do something that would be presented in a tavern atmosphere." Rather than simplify her style, Brooks began to, as she put it, to "clarify my language." She declared that she wanted "these poems to be free. I want them to be direct without sacrificing the kinds of music, the picture making I've always been interested in." Her first book in her new style was *In the Mecca* (1968), subtle portraits of black urban life. Prior to her shift in style and subject, Gwendolyn Brooks was a confirmed integrationist; now she celebrated the power of black identity. As she summarizes her career, "The forties and fifties were years of high poet-incense, the language-flowers were thickly sweet. Those flowers whined and begged white folks to pick them, to find them lovable. Then—the sixties: independent fire!"

Brooks has continued to publish important volumes: *Aloneness* (1971), *Beckonings* (1975), *Primer for Blacks* (1980), *Blacks* (1987), *Winnie* (1988), and *Children Come Home* (1991). In all her works an original and unique poetic voice is heard capturing the experience of daily life. As Brooks describes her method, she "scrapes life with a fine-tooth comb." The result is the gold lying beneath the surface.

64

Maria Montessori

1870–1952

The transformation of the school must be
contemporaneous with the preparation of the teacher.
For if we make of the teacher an observer...then we
must make it possible for her to observe and experiment
in the school. The fundamental principle of scientific
pedagogy must be, indeed, the *liberty of the pupil*—such
liberty as shall permit a development of individual,
spontaneous manifestations of the child's nature.

—MARIA MONTESSORI
The Montessori Method

225

At the core of Maria Montessori's educational philosophy is her belief in self-motivation and auto-education for preschool-age children and kindergartners. Her method places the child in a noncompetitive, cooperative environment, in which he or she will learn naturally with the help of proper materials. The materials, which include developmentally appropriate "learning games" tailored to the individual child's interests and abilities, are set up by the teacher-observer who only intervenes when a child needs help. Montessori's aim was to reverse the traditional approach of an active teacher imposing arbitrary tasks upon a passive class, thus facilitating spontaneous, individual self-development and independence.

Maria Montessori's dedication to reform can be traced back to her childhood and young adulthood in a newly unified Italy torn between parochialism and a national commitment to social progress. She was the only child of Renilde Stoppani Montessori, a well-educated, socially liberal woman from a well-off family, and Alessandro Montessori, an army officer turned civil servant. Like his wife, Alessandro Montessori supported liberal causes; unlike Renilde, he strongly disapproved of education for women beyond elementary school.

Maria spent her early childhood in the agricultural town of Chiaravalle, whose quiet provincialism contrasted sharply with the noisy, crowded, sprawling tenements of its more modern neighbor, the Adriatic seaport of Ancona. Maria's mother, a strict disciplinarian, stressed the values of hard work and the importance of helping the less fortunate, and the young girl was assigned a daily quota of knitting for the poor. She gave herself the task of washing sections of the tile floor in the Montessori home, "an experience she must have enjoyed," writes her biographer, Rita Kramer, "and which sounds strikingly like what later came to be known as 'exercises of practical life' in the Montessori school."

When Maria was five, her family moved to Rome. At six, she was enrolled in public school where she won awards for good behavior and, in second grade, for "women's work," which meant sewing and cooking. Montessori was an outspoken, authoritative, independent-minded child, who was usually the leader in games with other children. She loved to study, and although she was not a brilliant student, she did well in exams. Her mother encouraged her academically and was delighted when, at twelve, Maria decided to attend a technical school to study a general curriculum that included French, history, geography, mathematics, and science. Her father was predictably outraged at his daughter's "unfeminine" decision but did not interfere. Montessori did well at the school and went on to another technical institute, graduating in 1890. She continued her education at the University of Rome, where she became the first Italian woman to study medicine and, upon graduating with honors in 1896, the first to obtain a medical degree.

While practicing medicine, Montessori became increasingly interested in helping children with learning disabilities. She studied the work of the French educators Jean-Marc-Gaspard Itard, who had pioneered the use of sensory stimuli with the learning disabled, and Edouard Sequin, whose exercises using physical activity to stimulate perception resulted in the ability of his students to learn to read and write. She was also influenced by the philosopher Jean-Jacques Rousseau and his prioritization of the process of learning over what is learned. From 1897 to 1898 Montessori took classes in pedagogy and anthropology at the University of Rome. In addition, she published articles in professional journals with her colleague Dr. Giuseppe Montesano and lectured on such diverse topics as war and peace, women's issues, education, and the need for a medical-pedagogical institute to train teachers in the care and education of mentally disabled children. In 1899 she gave birth to a son, Mario, whose father was Giuseppe Montesano. Maria and Giuseppe never married, and Mario kept his mother's name throughout his life.

In 1900 Maria Montessori was appointed the director of the Orthophrenic School, a teacher-training institute of the kind she had advocated in her lectures. There she pioneered in the instruction of learning-disabled children, especially in the use of an environment rich in manipulative, sensory-stimulating materials. She left the institute in 1901 to continue her studies, and in 1904 was appointed a lecturer in natural sciences and medicine at the University of Rome, a position she held until 1908.

The success of Montessori's program at the Orthophrenic School inspired her to adapt her methods to the education of children without disabilities, and in 1907 she opened the first

Casa dei Bambini (Children's House), a day-care center for preschool children in the San Lorenzo slum district of Rome. The success of her venture and the increasing interest in her method led Montessori and her followers to establish similar schools in other parts of Europe, as well as in the United States, where the first Montessori school opened in Tarrytown, New York, in 1912. As her method became more popular, Montessori began to dedicate her time to training teachers and to writing and lecturing. By 1923 she had given up her academic and medical careers in order to devote herself fully to what had become the "Montessori movement."

By 1929, however, interest in Montessori education had declined in several countries and especially in the United States, where opponents argued that the method was destructive of discipline. In Fascist Italy, Montessori schools were officially banned. For the next twenty-two years, Maria Montessori continued to train teachers in her method and to travel on behalf of the movement. After her death, the Montessori method experienced a renaissance in many American schools, and in 1960 the American Montessori Society was formed. Today almost every early-childhood teacher uses ideas, learning techniques, and objects (the most familiar of which is child-sized furniture) that can be traced back to Maria Montessori. "She belongs," writes Kramer, "on any list of those whose existence shaped our century, and the fact that she was a woman, born in Italy thirty years before the end of the last century, makes that fact even more remarkable."

65

Marian Anderson

1897–1993

At age ten I heard, for the first time, the singing of
Marian Anderson on a recording. I listened, thinking,
"This can't be just a voice, so rich and beautiful." It was
a revelation. And I wept.

—JESSYE NORMAN, soprano

Marian Anderson is justly considered to be one of the outstanding vocal talents of the twentieth century. Her wide-ranging
contralto excelled equally at lieder, arias, oratorio selections, and

the Negro spirituals that were the centerpiece of many of her concerts and recordings. The combination of her powerful voice and the stateliness of her stage presence—closed eyes and minimal gestures—electrified audiences around the world. From the beginning of her career as the gifted "Baby Contralto" to her status as the first African-American singer to become a permanent member of the Metropolitan Opera Company, Anderson's artistic achievements and triumph over racial discrimination were a moving testament to talent, determination, patience, and an undaunted spirit.

Marian Anderson was born in Philadelphia, the oldest of three daughters of John and Annie Anderson. The family was poor, but close and loving, and, as Anderson later wrote in her autobiography, *My Lord, What a Morning*, she never missed what she could not have because she "had the things that really mattered." At six she joined the junior choir at the Union Baptist Church, where she impressed the director by learning all the vocal parts in the hymns. As a teenager she performed at churches and local organizations, often accompanying herself on the piano, and sang with the Philadelphia Choral Society, a black ensemble. Her singing attracted the attention of celebrated black tenor Roland Hayes, who suggested voice lessons for Anderson and obtained singing engagements for her out of town. At fifteen Anderson began to study with local African-American soprano Mary Patterson, who had offered to teach her for free. Sensing the need for a more formal music education, Anderson tried to enroll in a Philadelphia music school but was told, "We don't take colored." Having grown up in a mixed neighborhood and been surrounded by affection and encouragement, Anderson's first contact with blatant racism made her feel "as if a cold, horrifying hand had been laid on me."

Members of Philadelphia's black community began the "Fund for Marian's Future," which enabled Anderson to study for a year with Agnes Reifsnyder, the most famous contralto in the area. Shortly before her graduation from high school, Anderson auditioned for voice teacher Guiseppe Baghetti, who immediately accepted her as his pupil. A benefit concert featuring Roland Hayes was held at the Union Baptist Church to raise money for Anderson's lessons. Baghetti became Anderson's primary teacher and can be credited with refining her technical skills, further broadening her already remarkable range, and expanding her repertoire to include classical songs and arias. Anderson enjoyed acting and wanted to try opera, but was discouraged by the virtual exclusion of African Americans from that field. She continued to perform and embarked on her first concert tour at nineteen. While traveling through the South with her accompanist and manager, Billy King, Anderson experienced first hand the grim realities of segregation embodied by the Jim Crow laws of the era. But she also emerged from her tour with greater confidence in her vocal abilities and with the certainty that "with continued study and concentration, I would be able to do whatever I undertook." Despite this, after a coolly received recital at New York's Town Hall, Anderson, at twenty, felt her career was over. It took many months of soul-searching and the gentle council of her mother before she was ready to resume her lessons with Baghetti and begin touring again.

In 1925 Baghetti entered Anderson in a New York Philharmonic voice competition. She competed against three hundred other singers and won first prize. Her debut with the Philharmonic at Lewisohn Stadium on August 26, 1925, was a critical success. Shortly after performing at Carnegie Hall as soloist with the Hall Johnson choir, Anderson signed with Arthur Judson, who headed one of the nation's top concert agencies. But the prestige attached to being known as a "Judson artist" did little to expand Anderson's career. "I have no doubt," she writes, "that the Judson office was encountering resistance in selling a young Negro contralto to its normal concert circuits." In search of a wider audience, Anderson, like many black performers before her, decided to go to Europe to study and sing. From 1930 to 1935 she toured Europe and Scandinavia with great success. In 1935 the impresario Sol Hurok heard Anderson sing in Paris and offered to manage her. Despite her misgivings, he persuaded her to return to the United States to sing at another Town Hall concert. This recital, in December 1935, was the critical success Hurok had promised it would be. "Let it be said from the outset," wrote the *New York Times*'s music critic, "Marian Anderson has returned to her native land one of the great singers of our time."

During the late 1930s Anderson sang for the Roosevelts at the White House and toured the United States, performing before sell-out crowds in seventy cities. In 1939 the most famous racial incident of her career occurred: The Daughters of the American Revolution forbade her to perform at Constitution Hall, their national headquarters. Eleanor Roosevelt resigned from the D.A.R. in protest, and other prominent women followed suit. Harold Ickes, the secretary of the interior, offered Anderson the Lincoln Memorial for a concert on Easter Sunday. A crowd of seventy-five thousand assembled to hear her sing, and millions more listened to a radio broadcast of the event. In the years to come, photographs and films of Anderson singing in front of Lincoln's statue would poignantly symbolize the struggle of African Americans for equal rights. Four years later, the D.A.R. invited Anderson to take part in a concert for China Relief at Constitution Hall. "There was no sense of triumph," Anderson later wrote. "I felt that it was a beautiful concert hall, and I was happy to sing in it."

In 1955 Anderson debuted at the Metropolitan Opera as Ulrica in Verdi's *The Masked Ball.* Although she was fifty-seven and past her vocal prime, she was greeted with a tumultuous ovation. As the first African-American member of the Metropolitan Opera Company, she shattered the racial barrier that had kept black singers from pursuing careers in opera.

During the latter part of her career, Marian Anderson was appointed an alternate delegate to the Human Rights Committee of the United Nations and gave benefit concerts for the Congress of Racial Equality, the NAACP, and the America-Israel Cultural Foundation. She sang at the inaugurals of Presidents Eisenhower and Kennedy and performed again at the Lincoln Memorial during the 1963 civil rights March on Washington. In 1964 Anderson began her farewell tour at Constitution Hall, and in 1965 she gave her last recital at Carnegie Hall. Through the Marian Anderson Awards, which Anderson started in 1943, many young singers have realized their dreams of a professional career. "She was," said Shirley Verrett, an African-American soprano and Marian Anderson Award winner, "a dreammaker, giving us the right to dream the undreamable, reach for the unreachable, and achieve the impossible. Her courage has indeed changed the course of history, and she has cast a shadow that embraces us all."

66

Anne Frank

1929–1945

So we walked in the pouring rain...each with a school satchel and shopping bag filled to the brim with all kinds of things thrown together anyhow. We got sympathetic looks from people on their way to work. You could see by their faces how sorry they were they couldn't offer us a lift; the gaudy yellow star spoke for itself....

When we arrived at the Prinsengracht, Miep took us quickly upstairs and into the "Secret Annexe." She closed the door behind us and we were alone.

—ANNE FRANK
Diary entry, July 1942

233

When Anne Frank opened the small, red-and-white-checked book to begin her diary, she wrote that "no one will be interested in the unbosomings of a thirteen-year-old schoolgirl." From 1942, when the Frank family and four other Jews went into hiding, until 1944, when they were discovered and sent to concentration camps, Anne used her diary to express her innermost thoughts and feelings, to grapple with the contradictory aspects of her personality, and to chronicle life inside the *achterhuis*, as she called it. She could not know that her prodigious literary effort, what *New Yorker* writer Judith Thurman has termed "an epistolary autobiography" (Anne wrote her diary as a series of letters to an imaginary friend she named Kitty), would become the most influential human document of the most inhuman period in history.

Annelies Marie Frank was born in Frankfurt, Germany, the second daughter of Otto and Edith Frank. In 1934 the family emigrated to Amsterdam, hoping to escape the Nazis. In Amsterdam, Otto Frank started a business selling pectin and spices to Dutch housewives and leased a warehouse and offices on the Prinsengracht, in the old part of the city, several miles from the Franks' suburban home. When Amsterdam fell to the Germans in 1940, Otto Frank quietly made preparations to go into hiding.

In July 1942 Anne's sister, Margot, was ordered to report for deportation. Shortly thereafter, the Franks made the trek on foot from their home to their hiding place, an empty attic apartment occupying three floors above Otto Frank's warehouse. For the next two years they shared their hideout with the van Pelses and their son, Peter, and a dentist named Pfeffer. The group's links to the outside world were a radio, which could only be played softly at night, and Otto Frank's employees, who gallantly protected them and brought them supplies obtained with forged ration coupons.

It was in this paradoxical atmosphere of increasing stress and relative comfort that Anne lived and wrote about her adolescence. With complete honesty, she described her bodily changes and budding sexuality, her detached feelings toward her sweet but somewhat priggish older sister, her resentment of her mother, and her faith in her beloved father, to whom she had given the pet name of Pim. Like most adolescents, she struggled to reconcile her "lighter, superficial self" with what she called "the deeper side of me." She was, writes Thurman, "a strong, canny, fluent, truthful writer, who escaped the preciousness that generally mars the work of young people."

In August 1944 the group in the secret annex was betrayed, probably by the warehouse clerk, and on August 4 the security police raided the hideout and arrested the inhabitants. While searching for valuables, the police emptied Otto Frank's brief-case, with Anne's diary hidden inside, onto the floor. A week later, Miep Gies, one of the group's protectors, returned to the hideout, retrieved the diary, and kept it in the event that Anne should return. The Franks, the van Pelses, and Pfeffer were held in a Dutch transit camp for a month and then shipped to Auschwitz. A Dutch woman survivor who shared the same barracks as Edith Frank and the girls later described to an interviewer Anne's response to the horrors of that hell: "She...saw to the last what was going on all around us. We had long since stopped seeing....Something protected us, kept us from seeing. But Anne had no such protection, to the last....She cried. And you cannot imagine how soon most of us came to the end of our tears." Anne and Margot were transported to Bergen-Belsen in the fall of 1944. The following spring, they both died in a typhus epidemic that decimated the camp.

When Otto Frank, the group's only survivor, returned to Amsterdam, he was given Anne's diary, which he published in 1947 under a title Anne herself had chosen for a future book about the secret annex, *Het Achterhuis*. In 1953 the journal was published in the United States as *The Diary of a Young Girl*. A new edition was published in 1995. A perennial bestseller, Anne's diary has been translated into more than thirty languages and was adapted into a hugely popular play. Anne also wrote fables, stories, and essays, which were published in 1957. In 1989 a seven hundred page critical edition of the diary was published in the Netherlands, primarily as a response to Holocaust revisionists, those who deny that the Holocaust took place and have attacked Anne Frank's character and credibility.

In one of her last and most quoted diary entries, Anne wrote that "in spite of everything I still believe that people are really good at heart." Such faith shames the revisionists and reminds us that Anne Frank's life and work represent a triumph of the human spirit of life over the purveyors of death.

67

Babe Didrikson Zaharias

1914–1956

My goal was to be the greatest athlete that ever lived.
— BABE DIDRIKSON ZAHARIAS,
This Life I've Led

Called by sportswriter Grantland Rice "the greatest athlete of all...for all time," Babe Didrikson Zaharias was an athletic phenomenon—a champion in basketball, track-and-field, and golf who excelled also in baseball, tennis, and swimming. Brash and supremely confident, Babe Didrikson set out to become the greatest athlete who ever lived. Her tenacious pursuit of this goal changed women's sports forever.

236

Born Mildred Didrikson, Babe was the third child of Ole and Hannah Didriksen, emigrants from Norway who settled in Beaumont, Texas. Her father was a seaman and carpenter who found occasional work in the Texas oil fields. Her mother was an accomplished skier and skater. Babe showed enormous athletic gifts at an early age, surpassing any child—girl or boy—in town, at any sport. Nicknamed Babe after Babe Ruth, the era's reigning sports hero, Didrikson's first organized sport was basketball. At eighteen, after her outstanding performance on the all-city and all-state teams brought her to the attention of the manager of the Houston Employers Casualty Company's women's athletic teams, she was hired as a stenographer for the company and the forward for the company's women's basketball team, the Golden Cyclones. She next took up track-and-field, and in an unprecedented move, entered the Amateur Athletic Union women's national track-and-field championship in 1932, not as the member of a sponsored team, but as an individual contestant. She won six events, broke four women's world records, and also won the team championship by herself, scoring twice as many points as the second-place team. Not surprisingly, she was immediately heralded as the Wonder Girl.

Two weeks later, as a member of the U.S. Olympic Team in Los Angeles, Didrikson won gold medals and broke world records in the javelin throw and the eighty-meter hurdles. The next day she took the silver medal in the high jump.

As an amateur athlete during the 1930s, Didrikson had few outlets and means to support herself in sports, and she was forced to turn professional. She performed in exhibitions and on the vaudeville circuit, she toured with an all-star basketball team. Increasingly, she was seen less as an athlete worthy of respect and more as a freak of nature, a woman who used strength and competitive prowess to challenge the popular image of the petite and powerless female.

After the Olympics, Didrikson was invited to play golf by sportswriter Grantland Rice. Though she had played golf infrequently, Didrikson's natural ability caused Rice to declare that "she is the longest hitter women's golf has ever seen, for she has a free lashing style backed up with championship form and terrific power." In 1934 Didrikson, with typical self-confidence, set out to establish a golf career, practicing with relentless determination.

She won the Texas Women's Amateur Championship in 1935, but she was subsequently ruled ineligible to play in amateur tournaments because of her professional sports activities. She then played in exhibitions and entered the men's Los Angeles Open, where she failed to qualify. It was there, however, that she met George Zaharias, whom she married in 1938. Zaharias, a professional wrestler, provided Didrikson with the financial cushion she needed to reclaim her amateur status. After waiting the requisite three years without making any money from athletic endeavors, Didrikson was reinstated as an amateur in 1943. She went on to win the U.S. Golf Association amateur tournament in 1946 and fifteen tournaments in a row between 1946 and 1947.

In 1947 Didrikson became the first American woman to win the British amateur title, and, after turning professional the same year, won thirty-four professional tournaments, including three U.S. Open victories. Her participation in the Ladies Professional Golf Association (LPGA), which she helped to found in 1946, served to attract other women to the professional ranks of sports. She continued to compete in the 1950s, despite having cancer, winning five tournaments in 1954 and a sixth award as Woman Athlete of the Year. In 1956, she succumbed to the disease at the age of forty-two.

In 1982 a poll was taken among America's leading sports historians to name the ten most outstanding and influential athletes or administrators in American sports history. Didrikson ranked second, right below her namesake, Babe Ruth. She deserves that ranking, not only because of her remarkable athletic achievements, but also for her impact on the future of women's sports. By gaining credibility and respect for her fierce determination and competitive style, Didrikson redefined the role of women athletes, opening up what had formerly been a narrow world and legitimizing professional sports for women.

68

Margaret Thatcher

1926–2013

"Is he one of us?" became the emblematic question of the Thatcher years. Posed by Mrs. Thatcher herself, it defined the test which politicians and other public officials aspiring to her favour were required to pass. It epitomised in a single phrase how she saw her mission. This was to gather a cadre of like-minded people who would, with her, change the face of the Conservative Party and launch the recovery of Britain.

—HUGO YOUNG
*The Iron Lady: A Biography
of Margaret Thatcher*

Margaret Thatcher was the first woman prime minister of Great Britain, the second longest-serving prime minister in that nation's history, and the first woman ever to head a major Western democracy. The most famous English politician since Winston Churchill, her name is synonymous with a political philosophy— Thatcherism. Adored by conservatives, she was reviled by the Left as, during her years in office, she sought to dismantle the postwar welfare state and reinvent Britain for the next century. Her legacy continues to be felt in Britain, and the wisdom and value of her leadership continues to be debated.

Margaret Thatcher was born Margaret Hilda Roberts in the small town of Grantham in the Midlands of England. Her father, Alfred, was a grocer, and the family, consisting of Margaret, her sister, Muriel, and their mother, lived above the store. Alfred Roberts was self-educated and dedicated both to the values of education and public service. Margaret inherited her interest in politics from him. He served on the town council as alderman and as mayor.

As a student Margaret Thatcher was hard-working and competitive, and in 1944 she gained admission to Oxford University, where she studied chemistry to help insure her of a career upon graduation. She was an adequate, if unexceptional, chemist. Her main passion at Oxford was the Conservative Association, which she joined on her arrival and eventually chaired.

After graduating in 1947, Thatcher went to work as a research chemist and also became active in the local Conservative Party. In 1950 she ran for parliament in a predominantly Labour district and lost the election, although she impressed Conservative party officials with her energy and debating skills. During the campaign, she met Denis Thatcher, a prominent businessman, whom she married in 1951. In 1953 she gave birth to twins—a boy and a girl—and qualified as a barrister with a specialty in tax and patent law. She practiced law until 1959, when she won a seat in the House of Commons for the affluent London suburb of Finchley.

Thatcher's rise in the Conservative Party was steady. She was appointed a junior minister in the Ministry of Pensions and National Insurance in 1962 and two years later was promoted from the junior back bench to the front bench of senior party leaders. When Edward Heath was elected prime minister in 1970, bringing the Conservative Party back into power after six years, Thatcher was named minister of education and science. She was the only woman in Heath's cabinet. She worked for more local autonomy in educational policy, and though she was opposed to more government spending, actually increased the education budget. Heath's government was defeated in 1974, after showing itself largely unable to deal with the powerful labor unions or to cope with the recession brought on by the energy crisis of 1973. Thatcher believed that the Conservatives had lost faith in a free economy and needed to roll back government controls and spending. In 1975 she stood for Conservative Party leader and won, becoming the first woman leader of a major political party in seven hundred years of English parliamentary history.

In 1979 Margaret Thatcher successfully passed a no-confidence vote on the Labour Party government of James Callahan, which forced a general election. As she readied herself for the campaign, she said, "I've got fantastic stamina and great physical strength, and I have a woman's ability to stick to a job and get on with it when everyone else walks off and leaves." The election focused on the status quo of Labour versus the change offered by the Conservatives. Thatcher pledged to combat inflation, higher in Britain than in any other European country; deal with the nation's 1.3 million unemployed; and she insisted that economic growth would come only with tax cuts and curbing the power of the trade unions. She proclaimed that "the slither and slide to the socialist state is going to be stopped, halted, and turned back," and warned that "Unless we change our ways and our direction, our greatness as a nation will soon be a footnote in the history books." Thatcher and the Conservatives won a stunning victory.

During Thatcher's eleven years as head of state, she mounted the Thatcher Revolution, which included attacking inflation by controling the money supply, sharply cutting government spending and taxes for higher-income individuals, and privatizing government industries. Her anti-union policies forced coal miners to return to work after a year on strike. Unemployment levels continued to rise to postwar levels, although the decline in Britain's economic output was reversed.

In foreign affairs, Thatcher was dubbed the Iron Lady by the Russians for her outspoken opposition to Communism, yet she was an early supporter of Mikhail Gorbachev, stating, "We can do business together." In 1982 she successfully mounted a military campaign to retake the Falkland Islands from the Argentines, proclaiming upon receiving word of Argentina's surrender, "Today has put the Great back in Britain." In 1985 she forged an accord with Ireland, giving it a consulting role in governing Northern Ireland. A close ally of President Ronald Reagan, she allowed the United States to use British air bases to bomb Libya in 1986, a decision that prompted Liberal Party leader Dennis Healey to comment, "[She has] turned the British bulldog into a Reagan poodle."

Thatcher's record on social welfare was uniformly weak. Regarded by her critics as indifferent to the fate of Britain's poor, her response to widespread riots in London's economically depressed borough of Brixton and elsewhere in 1981 was to call for more police power rather than to try to correct the root causes of the disturbances. Her advocacy of a poll tax to fund local government, largely seen as a regressive tax on the poor, led to rioting and was responsible for the challenge to her leadership in 1990 that resulted in her resignation.

Throughout her years in office, Margaret Thatcher showed the iron determination of her convictions. She relished political debate with the opposition and rarely retreated from positions that were unpopular, once stating, "I cheer up immensely if an attack is particularly wounding because I think...if they attack one personally, it means they have not a single political argument left." Her major influence may lie less in the success or failure of the Thatcher revolution than in forever putting to rest the doubt that a woman can ably lead a major world power.

69

Mary Cassatt

1845–1926

At last I could work in complete independence without considering the opinion of a jury. I had already recognized who were my true masters. I admired Monet, Courbet, and Degas. I hated conventional art. I began to live.

> —MARY CASSATT
> Recalling how she felt when invited
> to exhibit with the Impressionists,
> In Achille Ségard, *Un Peintre
> des Enfants et des Mères: Mary Cassatt*

243

The only woman in the Impressionist group of artists who helped to redefine modern art, Mary Cassatt is universally regarded as the greatest woman artist of the nineteenth century. She has also been called "the most significant American artist, male or female, of her generation." As her friend, the influential art editor and critic, Forbes Watson, said, rejecting her title as "America's best woman painter": "Much more interesting and revealing would be a list of men who painted better than Mary. It would be a very short list."

Born in Pittsburgh, Mary Cassatt was the daughter of Robert Simpson Cassatt, a successful stockbroker and real estate speculator, and Katherine Cassatt. She was inspired to become a painter when, at the age of seven, she accompanied her family on an extended, four-year European trip to France and Germany and was exposed to the great European works of art for the first time. While there, Cassatt developed an enduring love for Paris and for French culture and became determined to return to Europe to study painting.

In 1861 the sixteen-year-old Cassatt enrolled at the Pennsylvania Academy of Fine Arts, a somewhat daring but respectable-enough endeavor for a woman at the time. However, when she declared her intention to become a professional painter, her father, who believed that it was acceptable for his daughter to dabble in art but not earn a living from it, is reported to have said: "I would almost rather see you dead." Nonetheless, he supported her decision to return to Europe to study, and in 1866 she moved to Paris and began her training by copying paintings in museums.

At the insistence of her parents, Cassatt returned to America during the Franco-Prussian War, but in 1872 she left for Italy, where she was greatly influenced by the sixteenth-century artist Correggio. She also visited Spain, Belgium, and Holland to absorb the techniques and styles of Diego Velázquez, Peter Paul Rubens, and Frans Hals. By 1873, Cassatt was exhibiting regularly at the Paris Salon and selling her work. She stopped exhibiting at the Salon after the jury disapproved of the avant-garde direction she was taking, and forced her to paint out the light colors of one of her submissions to conform to their conventional taste.

In 1877, painter and sculptor Edgar Degas visited Mary Cassatt's studio and invited her to exhibit with the Independents (called Impressionists by hostile critics). The typically acidic Degas told Cassatt, "Most women paint as though they are trimming hats...Not you." Cassatt accepted Degas's invitation and also began a forty-year relationship with him, which continued until his death in 1917. Through their association with one another, Degas, Cassatt, and the other Impressionists began the greatest redefinition of art since the Renaissance. Committed to the truthful depiction of ordinary life, the Impressionists sought to recreate the artist's or viewer's impressions of a scene and explored the effect of light on a subject. Cassatt's works are characterized by their unusual angles of vision and natural and unposed portraits.

In 1877, the same year that she met Degas, Cassatt's family came to Paris to live with her. Cassatt spent the next seventeen years caring for and nursing her father, mother, and sister through long and ultimately fatal illnesses. These obligations drastically affected her output, and she produced only half as many paintings as Degas. During these years Cassatt began her series of pictures of mothers and children. Her honesty and sympathy in the informal poses of her subjects bring a freshness to this well-worked theme. In addition to several versions of *Mother and Child*, Cassatt's best-known paintings include *Lady at the Tea Table, Modern Women*, a mural painted for the Women's Building at the 1893 Chicago Exposition, and a portrait of the artist's mother. Cassatt also produced widely admired pastels, etchings, drypoints, and aquatints. During the 1890s, her work began to show the influence of Post-Impressionism and Japanese art.

In 1893 Cassatt bought a chateau in Oise, where she lived and worked until her death, and had a successful one-person show in Paris. However, the lack of critical respect shown her work in America annoyed her greatly. Still, she served the cause of art in the United States by advising wealthy American friends, such as philanthropist and suffragist Louisine Havemeyer, on purchases of works of art, which later became major bequests to American museums. In 1904 Cassatt was made a Chevalier of the French Legion of Honor. Her greatness was finally recognized in the United States when the Pennsylvania Academy and the

Chicago Institute awarded her several prizes, all of which she rejected.

Tall, thin, and aristocratic, Cassatt was described by British author Vernon Lee as "very nice, simple, an odd mixture of self-recognizing artist...and the almost childish garrulous American provincial." Opinionated and outspoken, Cassatt was an ardent feminist who donated the proceeds from an exhibition of her work in New York to the suffrage movement. She lost her eyesight in later years and was forced to stop painting. Although increasingly alone and bitter, she used her prestige to help better conditions for women workers at a button factory near her home, once declaring, "If I weren't a weak old woman, I'd be a Socialist." She died at her chateau at the age of eighty-two after having achieved during her long life the double distinction of pioneering a new art and a new role for women artists.

70

SARA BERNHARDT.

Sarah Bernhardt

1844–1923

There are five kinds of actresses: bad actresses, fair actresses, good actresses, great actresses—and then there is Sarah Bernhardt.

> —MARK TWAIN
>   In Arthur Gold and Robert Fitzdale,
>   *The Divine Sarah*

Sarah Bernhardt was the first theatrical superstar, an actress of such magnitude that she became a cultural icon, as notorious for her off-stage love affairs, unpredictable behavior, and outrageous eccentricities as she was for the intensity and passion of her acting. Bernhardt set the standard against which all the great actresses who followed her came to be measured, defining for all time the essence of the tempestuous, temperamental star: self-absorbed, self-promoting, and completely captivating. Few actors before or since have created such a durable sensation.

Sarah Bernhardt's reputation as a great romantic trage-dienne had its roots in a background as colorful and dramatic as any of the heroines—or heroes—she played. Born Rosine Bernard in Paris, Bernhardt was the daughter of a Dutch-born, Jewish courtesan. The identity of her father is uncertain, though she eventually took the surname of law student Edouard Bernhardt. Sarah was educated in convent and boarding schools well apart from her mother's fashionable Paris salon. She was sensitive, high-strung, and given to dramatic outbursts, and her childhood was marked by rebelliousness and bitter loneliness. Although she had been suspended three times from convent school for unruly behavior, she decided to become a nun. She was persuaded to try a career as an actress when her mother's lover, the Duc de Morny, secured a place for her in the prestigious conservatoire of the Comédie Française.

Bernhardt's stage debut in 1862 was not encouraging. The most powerful theater critic in Paris noted that she "is a tall attractive young woman with a slender waist and most pleasing face....She carries herself well and pronounces her words with perfect clarity. That is all that can be said for the moment." After critics panned her next two performances, the seventeen-year-old Bernhardt tried to poison herself by drinking liquid rouge. A violent quarrel with a respected actress in the company caused her dismissal, and she was forced to take small parts in lesser Paris theaters. As a contract player for the Odéon theater she played roles in works by George Sand, Shakespeare, Molière, and Racine. Her first notable success came in 1869, when she played a male page in *Le Passant*. The play was given a command performance before Napoleon III and the Empress Eugénie in the Tuilleries.

During the Franco-Prussian War (1870–1871), Bernhardt refused to abandon besieged Paris and opened a hospital in the Odéon. Following the armistice, she triumphed in an 1872 revival of Victor Hugo's *Ruy Blas*, directed by Hugo. Her success earned her a return to the Comédie Francaise, where she attained full stature as an actress with her superb portrayals in Racine's *Phèdre* and in Hugo's *Hernani*. Called the actress with "the golden voice," Bernhardt was praised for the poetic intensity of her readings and her passionate identification with the characters she played. English critic Lytton Strachey once wrote, "To hear the words of Phèdre spoken from the mouth of Bernhardt...is to come close to immortality, to plunge shuddering through infinite abysses, and to look, if only for a moment, upon eternal light." Throughout her career, Bernhardt acted with such intensity that she frequently fainted at the end of a performance.

Off stage, Bernhardt generated both adoration and controversy. She traveled with, and sometimes slept in, a coffin lined with letters from her lovers (said to exceed a thousand). Her entourage often included a menagerie of exotic pets. From 1874 to 1896 her sculptures were exhibited at the Salon, where, according to Arthur Gold and Robert Fitzdale, "they fetched prices high enough to exasperate professional artists and irritate her fellow actors." In 1877 she toured Paris in a hot-air balloon outfitted especially for her and used that experience as the basis for her only novel, *In the Clouds*. Hailed as a national treasure, Bernhardt became a must-see for tourists in Paris, like the *Mona Lisa*. Men fought duels for her, priests railed against her, and it is said that at least one woman killed herself after failing to get a ticket to a Bernhardt performance.

In 1880 Bernhardt embarked on tours of England and America, a move that established her worldwide reputation. She traveled throughout the United States in a private train, the Bernhardt Special, and was continually greeted by crowds eager for a look at her and hopeful of securing an autograph. During her American tour, Bernhardt premiered her most famous role, Marguerite, in *La Dame aux Camélias*. One critic wrote: "Only a beautiful, worldly woman, born and bred in Paris, only a master at transforming prose into poetry could combine restraint, feverish gaiety, and a tragic yearning for love with the infinite cynicism and careless insolence that was the product of a courtesan's life." Bernhardt returned home, however, to a hostile reception. The French felt that she had squandered her great talent abroad and shunned her. She won them back when she unexpectedly appeared on the stage of the Paris Opéra during a benefit performance commemorating the tenth anniversary of the departure of Prussian troops from France and gave an emotionally powerful spoken rendition of the "Marseillaise."

Bernhardt managed several theaters in Paris before leasing the Théâtre des Nations, renaming it the Théâtre Sarah Bernhardt. Here she revived some of her former successes and created a sensation when, in 1899, she appeared in the title role of *Hamlet*. In 1901 she played Napoleon's illegitimate son in *L'Aiglon*, which was written for her by Edmund Rostand. Although a knee injury sustained in 1905 led to the amputation of her right leg in 1915, Bernhardt continued to act on stage and in films, where she became one of the first stars of the fledgling medium. When she died in Paris, between six hundred thousand and a million fans lined the streets of her funeral procession.

More a comet than a star, Sarah Bernhardt dominated the world stage for over sixty years. The last great actress of the nineteenth century, few performers moved audiences as Bernhardt did, or succeeded in such a wide variety of roles. For many she was simply, as Oscar Wilde called her, "the Divine Sarah." And as one of her mourners remarked, "Immortals do not die."

71

Barbara Tuchman

1912–1989

The unrecorded past is none other than our old friend, the tree in the primeval forest which fell without being heard.

> —BARBARA TUCHMAN
> In "Can History Be Served Up Hot?"
> *New York Times*, March 8, 1964

Historian Barbara Tuchman performed a great public service by turning the past into bestselling books accessible to millions of readers. The winner of two Pulitzer prizes, she specialized in telling the story of history with the eye and understanding of a novelist, shaping the formless past into riveting and revealing drama.

Barbara Tuchman was born Barbara Wertheim in New York City, the daughter of an international banker and owner of the magazine *The Nation*. Her grandfather was businessman and diplomat Henry Morgenthau; her uncle was Franklin Delano Roosevelt's Secretary of the treasury. Barbara was educated at Radcliffe College, and, after her graduation in 1933, she took a job as a researcher and editorial assistant with the Institute of Pacific Relations. Her subsequent experience as a foreign correspondent in Tokyo for *The Nation* resulted in one of her earliest articles, a piece exploring the Japanese character, published in *Foreign Affairs* magazine when she was only twenty-three. In 1937 she covered the civil war in Spain, which produced her first book, *The Lost British Policy: Britain and Spain Since 1700*, published in 1938.

In 1940, Barbara Wertheim married Manhattan physician Lester R. Tuchman and, after a two-year stint as an editor for the Office of War Information, focused her attention on raising the couple's three children. In the early 1950s she embarked upon her career as a historian. "It was a struggle," she recalled. "I had three small children and no status whatsoever.... To come home, close a door and feel that it was your place to work, that was very difficult, particularly when you were—well, just a Park Avenue matron." However, Tuchman did not feel that her lack of academic credentials was a drawback. "I never took a Ph.D.," she once said. "It's what saved me, I think. If I had a doctoral degree, it would have stifled any writing capacity." She felt strongly that academic historians "who stuff in every item of research they have found, every shoe lace and telephone call of a biographical subject, are not doing the hard work of selecting and shaping a readable story." Tuchman approached the task of writing history as if she were a storyteller: "There should be a beginning, middle, and an end. Plus an element of suspense to keep the reader turning the pages."

Her first popular success was *The Zimmerman Telegram* (1958), a gripping and dramatic chronicle of Germany's attempt to incite Mexico to enter the war against the United States during World War I. In 1963 she became the first woman to receive the Pulitzer

Prize for general nonfiction with her book *The Guns of August*, an account of the opening weeks of World War I. Tuchman succeeded in untangling and then reweaving the complicated diplomatic maneuverings of the time into an epic story of the futility and calamity of war. Her interest in that period also produced *The Proud Tower: A Portrait of the World Before the War* (1966), which examined the cultural and political forces that led to the conflict. In all three books, Tuchman showed her remarkable ability to discover the telling detail, to trace the significant thread that brings the past alive, and to create memorable and rounded historical characters. She was awarded a second Pulitzer Prize for *Stilwell and the American Experience in China, 1911–45*, published in 1970. In it, the career of General Joseph W. Stilwell becomes the center and the emblem for a wider exploration of the relationship between the United States and China.

With her next historical work, *A Distant Mirror* (1978), Tuchman moved from the twentieth century to the tumultuous fourteenth. Following the career of Enguerrand de Coucy, a French knight, nobleman, and son-in-law of the English king Edward III, the book explores the politics, manners, and mores of a medieval century devastated by the Hundred Years War and the Black Death. *A Distant Mirror* was described as an "ambitious, absorbing historical panorama," and Tuchman was praised for her thorough scholarship. The following year, she became the first woman to be elected president of the American Academy and Institute of Arts and Letters. Her last book, *The March of Folly: From Troy to Vietnam* (1984), examined in depth the "folly" of four events in Western history: the episode of the Trojan horse; the corruption of the Renaissance popes, which led to the Reformation; England's treatment of her American colonies; and America's involvement in Vietnam. The book represented a departure for Tuchman, who said of it, "I've done what I always said I would never do, and that is to take a theory before I wrote a book. My other books were narratives, and I tried not to adopt a thesis except what emerged from the material. It's what I don't believe in when writing history, actually."

Tuchman has been criticized by academic historians for some of her theories and conclusions, and for her narrative selectivity. Yet she clearly achieved something different from what is usually done by the scholarly historian. As Jim Miller of

Newsweek observed, "Most academics lack the talent or inclination to write for a general audience. Into this vacuum has stepped Tuchman.... Her imaginative choice of topics and flair for words have enabled her to satisfy the popular hunger for real history spiced with drama, color, and a dash of uplifting seriousness."

Tuchman embraced the role of the historian, not as a collector of historical artifacts or esoteric data, but as a compelling teacher and synthesizer who linked the lessons of the past with the world of her audience. Few writers have mastered the art of historical narrative as expertly as Barbara Tuchman, or have left such a standard to follow.

72

Amelia Earhart

1897–1937

There are no heroines following the shining paths of
romantic adventure, as do the heroes of boys'
books....Of course girls have been reading the so-called
boys' books ever since there were such. But consider
what it means to do so. Instead of closing the covers
with shining eyes and the happy thought, "That might
happen to me someday!" the girls turning the final
page, can only sigh regretfully, "Oh, dear, that can
never happen to me—because I'm not a boy!"

—AMELIA EARHART

Amelia Earhart followed her own particular path of adventure by purposefully challenging and rejecting the gender roles of her time. The most famous woman aviator of the twentieth century, she achieved many firsts and opened up the field of aviation for women as pilots and engineers.

Born in Atchison, Kansas, Earhart was the older of the two daughters of Edwin Earhart, a lawyer and a railroad claim agent, and his wife, Amy. She was an active, outgoing child who wore bloomers instead of skirts and pursued boys' activities such as football. Because of Edwin Earhart's work and alcoholism, the family moved frequently. By the time Amelia was seventeen, she had attended six different high schools. In 1916, after graduating from high school in Chicago, Earhart enrolled at the Ogontz School, a small liberal arts college outside Philadelphia. Tall and lanky, she enjoyed sports, and the college's president once re-called that she "helped very much to impress the over-indulged girls with the beauty and comfort of simple dressing." At Ogontz, Earhart began keeping a notebook of newspaper clippings de-scribing women who had taken jobs previously restricted to men.

In 1917, while visiting her sister who was studying in Toronto, Earhart decided to remain in Canada to work for the war effort. She took a first aid course and joined the Voluntary Aid Detachment of a military hospital in Toronto, where she worked through the end of the war and during the ensuing Great Flu Epidemic of 1918. She then spent several months in random pursuits, including a course in engine mechanics. In 1919 she decided to try a career in medicine, and she entered Columbia University as a premedical student, but once again her schooling was interrupted; this time by a trip to Los Angeles to try to hold her parents' marriage together. She took her first airplane ride in Glendale and was captivated by what she termed the "breathtak-ing beauty" of the experience. After taking lessons from pioneer woman pilot Netta Snook, Earhart soloed for the first time in June 1921. A year later, on her twenty-fifth birthday, she bought her first plane, a Kinner Canary, in which she set a short-lived women's altitude record of fourteen thousand feet. In 1924 she moved to Boston with her newly divorced mother. There she taught English for a time to immigrant factory workers and eventually became a social worker at Denison House, a settlement house. She continued to fly and work with other local fliers and mechanics.

In April 1928, one year after Charles Lindbergh's landmark solo flight across the Atlantic, Earhart received a phone call from a group sponsoring a transatlantic flight that was to include "an American girl of the right image." At the suggestion of aviator-explorer Richard E. Byrd, a Bostonian, the group, led by publisher George P. Putnam, had selected Earhart to be one of the three crew members of the *Friendship*. Although her role was to keep the logbook, Earhart viewed the flight as "a shining adventure." The plane took off from Newfoundland on June 17 and landed in Wales twenty hours and forty minutes later. Thus, Amelia Earhart became the first woman transatlantic plane passenger. The immediate notoriety that followed the flight embarrassed the modest Earhart, who characterized herself on the flight as little more than a "sack of potatoes." Nevertheless, her achievement made her the inspiration of newly emancipated women of the 1920s, and her newfound fame firmly established her career. She lectured extensively on flying, became the aviation editor of *Cosmopolitan* magazine, participated in the first Women's Air Derby in 1929, and in 1931 was the first woman to pilot an autogiro (a precursor of the helicopter) carrying passengers. She was active in Zonta International, a service club of professional women, and was a founding member and president of the Ninety-Nines, an international organization of women pilots.

In 1931 Earhart married George Putnam, who became her manager and the publisher of her books, *The Fun of It* (1932) and the posthumous *Last Flight* (1937). In 1932 she became the first woman (and only the second person) to make a transatlantic solo flight and the first person to cross the Atlantic twice by air. With her solo flight, she set a new speed record and earned the first Distinguished Flying Cross awarded to a woman. In 1935 she was the first person to fly solo from Hawaii to California, the first woman to fly solo anywhere in the Pacific, and the first to solo over both the Atlantic and the Pacific. That same year she was appointed career counselor to women students and special adviser in aeronautics at Purdue University.

After receiving the gift of a Lockheed Electra from Purdue trustees, Earhart began to prepare for "just one more long flight," a twenty-seven-thousand-mile trip around the equator, the longest flight in aviation history. The most dangerous part of the flight would be across the Pacific from Lae, New Guinea, to the tiny island of Howland, 2,550 miles away. With primitive navigational instruments, finding the island in the middle of the Pacific would be a challenge. On June 1, 1937, Earhart took off from Miami, Florida, with her navigator, veteran pilot Fred Noonan. Their route took them to Brazil, across Africa to India, Burma, Thailand, Australia, and New Guinea. On July 2 they left Lae, New Guinea. Earhart recorded the final entry in her diary mailed back home before taking off: "Not more than a month ago I was on the other shore of the Pacific, looking westward. This evening I looked eastward over the Pacific. In those fast-moving days which have intervened, the whole width of the world has passed behind us—except this broad ocean. I shall be glad when we have the hazards of its navigation behind us." Radio contact between the plane and Coast Guard vessels was intermittent. Finally, after twenty-one hours of the expected eighteen-hour flight, the Coast Guard cutter *Itasca* received a final message from Earhart that she had approximately thirty minutes of fuel left and had not sighted land.

Amelia Earhart's disappearance in the Pacific prompted the largest naval search in history. No trace of fliers or plane was ever found. Since 1937 many theories and rumors have circulated to explain the Electra's disappearance, including the popular conjecture that Earhart was on a spy mission, and was captured and executed by the Japanese. Another theory is that she is still alive and in hiding. No conclusive proof has been found to disprove the most likely explanation: Her plane ran out of fuel and crashed in the Pacific. The mystery of her final flight has served to turn Amelia Earhart into a figure of myth and legend, obscuring her considerable contributions as an aviator and a forceful influence on women who have chosen to follow in her trailblazing footsteps.

73

Murasaki Shikibu

c. 978–1030

[The art of the novel] happens because the storyteller's own experiences of men and things, whether for good or ill—not only what he has passed through himself, but even events which he has only witnessed or been told of—has moved him to an emotion so passionate that he can no longer keep it shut up in his heart.

—MURASAKI SHIKIBU
The Tale of Genji

A lady of the eleventh-century Japanese court, Murasaki Shikibu is celebrated for what is widely regarded as the first great novel in world literature, *The Tale of Genji*. Drawing on the tradition of Chinese historical writing and Chinese and Japanese lyric poetry, Lady Murasaki produced something new and unique, a prose romance filled with believable characters in real situations—the essential ingredients for the novel form that would be perfected in the West in the eighteenth century. *The Tale of Genji* is, however, more than an historical artifact. It ranks as one of the supreme masterworks of prose fiction in Japanese and one of the greatest works of the imagination ever written.

Unfortunately, very little is known about the author of *The Tale of Genji*. Her father was a provincial governor and a not-very-prominent member of the ruling Fujiwara family. Her diary, which describes events at court from late 1008 to early 1010, records the fact that her father, who noticed her capacity for learning, lamented that she had not been born a boy. Although her family was not powerful, it was distinguished by literary achievement. Murasaki Shikibu's great-grandfather played a role in the compilation of the first imperial anthology of Japanese verse, and her father was a poet and a scholar of Chinese classics. Murasaki Shikibu was married around 998 to her cousin, a member of the Imperial guard; her only child, a daughter, was born in 999; and in 1011 she was widowed. Around the middle of the first decade of the eleventh century she entered the world of the Japanese court in the service of the Empress Akiko. There she remained until about 1013. What happened after her retirement from court and the details of her death are not known.

While a lady at court, it is believed that she began *Genji-Monogatari* (*The Tale of Genji*), most likely written over many years for oral performance at court. The literature of the period was dominated by women, and Murasaki Shikibu's literary talent was no doubt a major asset in her court service. Noblewomen of the time lived a cloistered and sedentary life hidden behind walls and screens. Even their names were rarely documented, since it was considered bad manners to record the names of well-born women except for imperial consorts and princesses of the blood. Instead, women were called by names derived from the titles of their fathers. Shikibu designates an office held by Lady Murasaki's father. The name Murasaki may have stemmed from the name of a character in the *Genji* or from the first half of her family name, *fuji*, which means "wisteria." The wisteria is a purple flower; murasaki means "purple." From her diary, it seems that Lady Murasaki had few specific duties to perform at court except as a companion. She had time to write, and possibly was encouraged to record the events of life at court, notably births of heirs. What emerges from her diary is a reflective and melancholy woman who largely shunned contact and correspondence with the other notable writers and poets of the period.

The Tale of Genji is a massive work that covers nearly seventy-five years and chronicles the career of the nobleman Genji, the illegitimate son of the emperor; and Kaoru, known to the world as Genji's son, although he is actually the son of Genji's best friend. What makes the novel unique is that instead of the expected tale of the marvelous, *The Tale of Genji* is filled with real characters in real situations. As Lady Murasaki writes in the book, "Anything whatsoever may become the subject of a novel, provided only that it happens in mundane life and not in some fairyland beyond our human ken." The novel follows the loves and intrigues of Genji and Kaoru in a style that is simultaneously exact and full of nuance, and filled with poetic intensity. The end result is a beautifully rendered evocation of time and place that invites comparison with other great novelists, such as Proust.

Murasaki Shikibu's masterpiece is the crowning achievement of a period in Japanese history notable for the predominance of literary women. It would take another eight hundred years before the distinctive voices of women would again be heard as clearly in fiction as was Murasaki Shikibu's in *The Tale of Genji*.

74

Jessie Redmon Fauset

1882–1961

Living as I have nearly all my life in a distinctly white neighborhood, and for the past four years as the only colored girl in a college community...I have *had* to let people know that we too possess some of the best, or else allow my own personality to be submerged.

—JESSIE REDMON FAUSET
In a letter written while a student
at Cornell University, 1905

Jessie Redmon Fauset, teacher, editor, novelist, and poet, was one of three influential women authors of the Harlem Renaissance, the vibrant period during the 1920s when African-American literary and artistic culture flourished and became more visible to white society. Fauset was the most prolific fiction writer of the era, publishing four full-length novels between 1924 and 1933. Her portraits of black women from middle- and upper-class families represent what has been called the "best foot forward" school of black writing.

Fauset's greatest influence upon the Renaissance was as the literary and then the managing editor of *The Crisis*, the magazine of the NAACP, whose editor was author, civil rights leader, and NAACP founder, W. E. B. Dubois. During Fauset's seven years at *The Crisis*, she encouraged, mentored, and published such young black writers as Langston Hughes, Walter White, and Countee Cullen, who would, in turn, breathe new and rich life into the genre of African-American literature. Langston Hughes, a central figure of the Harlem Renaissance, once said of Fauset that she "midwifed the so-called New Negro literature into being."

Jessie Redmon Fauset's background had a definite influence on her work. She was born in Philadelphia, the seventh child, and fifth daughter, of the Reverend Redmon Fauset and Anna Fauset. Hers was an upper-class, financially secure, though not wealthy, old Philadelphia family (known as an OP family in the black society of the period). Fauset attended an integrated public elementary school, and when she graduated from her virtually all-white high school, her father gave the commencement address. This was an unusual and progressive event, even in the somewhat enlightened culture of Philadelphia, and was probably more a tribute to Jessie Fauset's record of academic excellence than a result of her father's privileged OP social status.

After graduating Phi Beta Kappa from Cornell in 1905, Fauset was unable to find a teaching job in Philadelphia because of her race. In 1906 she moved to Washington, D.C., to teach French and Latin at M Street High School (renamed Dunbar in 1916), one of the best all-black high schools in the country. She began to write book reviews, stories, and poems for *The Crisis* in 1912, and in 1918 took a leave of absence from Dunbar to write a column for the magazine, "The Looking Glass." Fauset received a master's degree in French from the University of Pennsylvania in 1919, and shortly thereafter joined the staff of *The Crisis* as a full-time editor.

Fauset's desire to work at *The Crisis* was fueled by her literary ambitions, her involvement with the fledgling NAACP, and most of all, by her emotional attachment to W. E. B. Dubois. Fauset's relationship with Dubois had begun while she was in college. He had helped her obtain a summer teaching position at Fisk University, and the two began a correspondence that continued throughout their lives. "In her mind," writes David Levering Lewis in *When Harlem Was in Vogue*, "he took the place of the strong father who died while she was at Cornell, and of the grand physical passion she seems never to had—unless that passion was, in reality, Dubois himself." Fauset and Dubois developed a mutually admiring and supportive friendship during Fauset's years at *The Crisis*. Dubois encouraged her literary endeavors and praised her work highly, both privately and publicly. When he organized European meetings of the Pan-African Congress, Fauset made travel arrangements for him, did research, edited his speeches, and ran *The Crisis* in his absence.

In addition to fostering the work of young writers for *The Crisis*, Fauset developed and edited *The Brownie's Book*, a magazine for children. In 1921 she attended the second Pan-African Congress in London, Paris, and Brussels and wrote two valuable articles for *The Crisis* on the meetings. Her first novel, *There Is Confusion*, published in 1924, featured characters drawn from a genteel, patrician society similar to the one in which she had been raised. Some white reviewers and publishers doubted that such a world really existed in black America. But Fauset had not invented a "more white" black world, nor did she choose to cater to black stereotypes. She had simply and correctly written about what she knew. *There Is Confusion* proved to be a critical and commercial success. To celebrate, Fauset took a few months leave of absence from *The Crisis* to travel in Europe. There she studied at the Sorbonne and gathered material for a series of articles based on her travel experiences.

In 1926 Fauset resigned from *The Crisis*, for reasons that are not entirely clear. It may be that Dubois's long absences from the office left Fauset without the emotional and professional support she felt she needed. Lewis suggests that Fauset and Dubois clashed over the issue of what was and was not socially relevant African-American art, and that the friendship further soured after Dubois coldly refused to pay back $2,500 lent to him by Fauset and her sister in 1923.

Fauset returned to teaching after she gave up full-time work with *The Crisis*. She taught first in a Harlem junior high school and then at DeWitt Clinton High School in the Bronx. In 1929 she married businessman Herbert E. Harris and published her second novel, *Plum Bun*. This novel was followed by *The Chinaberry Tree* (1931) and *Comedy: American Style* (1933). Fauset also lectured on the value of young black writers and on the role of the black woman in American culture. She left DeWitt Clinton in 1944, and her only recorded teaching job afterward was a semester spent as a visiting professor at the Hampton Institute in Virginia. She died in Philadelphia at the home of her stepbrother, Earl Huff, on April 30, 1961.

During the years of the black nationalist movement in the 1960s, Fauset's novels were dismissed as unrealistic and not representative of the true black experience. However, Fauset's works created, according to Harlem Renaissance critic William Stanley Braithwaite, "an entirely new milieu in the treatment of race fiction." She provided black and white readers with a fuller and more sympathetic portrait of black middle-class life than any other writer of the Renaissance. What also cannot be dismissed are Fauset's important editorial contributions to African-American literature. "For honesty and precocity," writes Lewis, "[Fauset's influence] was probably unequaled."

75

Hillary Rodham Clinton

1947–

The question is whether being first lady will change
Hillary Clinton or whether she will change the
role....After all, a new generation of leaders brings with
it new assumptions about the roles that women—even
wives—should play. Hillary may eventually conclude that
she can use the first lady's bully pulpit however she
wishes, and then let her accomplishments carry the day.

—MARGARET CARLSON

266

When Margaret Carlson's profile of Hillary Rodham Clinton appeared in *Time*, Bill Clinton had just been elected president of the United States. At this writing, Hillary Clinton's career and achievements as first lady are very much works in progress. That is why she did not earn a higher ranking in this book. However, because she has so radically redefined the role of first wife, Hillary Clinton merits inclusion here as one of the most influential women of the twentieth century. As an accomplished lawyer and policymaker, she would be qualified to serve in a senior administrative post if she were not married to the president. Negotiating the delicate balance between career, family, and the public's expectations of her role, Hillary Clinton surely is a first lady for our times.

Born in Chicago, where her father, Hugh Rodham, owned a drapery business, Hillary was the oldest in a family of five children. She was an overachiever in school and was active with her Methodist church group. As her minister recalls, "She was serious, but she was also gregarious. She wasn't the cheerleader type, but she wasn't the shy bookworm, either." While attending Wellesley College, her political views shifted from the Republican conservatism of her parents to Democratic liberalism, in synch with the politics of many other young people of her generation in the 1960s. She majored in political science, worked for Eugene McCarthy's unsuccessful 1968 presidential campaign, and participated in demonstrations following the killing of Martin Luther King Jr. In 1969 she went on to Yale Law School, where she met Bill Clinton. As a fellow student recalled, "They were very strong personalities. They were both ambitious—they both had aspirations to make a mark on the world. And what is often the case with those types of couples is that they either work wonderfully or fail miserably; there's no in-between. And so we were all kind of holding our breath, wondering if it was going to work or not."

In 1972 Hillary Rodham and Bill Clinton worked on George McGovern's campaign in Texas. After they graduated from Yale the following year, Bill Clinton went back to Arkansas to teach law at the University of Arkansas and prepare for his first election campaign. Hillary, whose major interest in the law was children's legal rights, moved to Washington to work for Marian Wright Edelman's Children's Defense Fund. However, she was soon hired to assist the House Judiciary Committee in preparing impeachment proceedings against President Richard Nixon, a job that included listening to and transcribing Nixon's tapes and developing the legal procedures to follow in the inquiry. After Nixon's resignation in 1974, Hillary decided not to take a job with a prominent Washington law firm or return to the Children's Defense Fund. Instead, she chose a third option that shocked her friends: She followed Bill Clinton to Arkansas to teach law at the University of Arkansas. The couple married in 1975, and in 1976 they moved to Little Rock when Clinton was elected attorney general. In Little Rock, Hillary joined the Rose law firm, specializing in property law. She also continued her interest in children's rights, writing an important article, "Children Under the Law" for the *Harvard Educational Review*. In 1978 Hillary Rodham became Arkansas's first lady when Bill Clinton was elected governor. Two years later the couple's daughter, Chelsea, was born.

Following Bill Clinton's surprise reelection defeat in 1980, the first of several "Hillary transformations" occurred. Feeling that she might have cost her husband the election, she tried to eliminate what she perceived to be her negatives in the mind of the voters. She stopped using her own last name and became Hillary Clinton, and she dropped her casual appearance for a more stylish and sophisticated look. Bill Clinton was reelected in 1982 and would remain governor for the next ten years. During his years in office, Hillary chaired the commission to reform the state's educational system, Clinton's top priority. She also continued to serve as a board member of the Children's Defense Fund, in 1987 becoming the chairperson of its board of directors. In 1987 and 1991 she was named as one of the hundred most influential lawyers in the country by the *National Law Journal*.

During the 1992 presidential campaign, the "Hillary factor" emerged as a serious issue when Republicans tried to brand the Democrats as anti-family, and Hillary as an unfeminine careerist. She was tarred as a liberal "yuppie" and a radical feminist who argued in favor of children suing their parents. The charges were groundless and misleading, but once again Hillary adjusted her style to gain voters' approval. When the election was over, Hillary Rodham Clinton emerged as a major adviser and policymaker in the Clinton administration. When Bill Clinton appointed her to lead the group drafting health care reform, she assumed the most important policy role ever assigned to a first lady. Hillary Clinton has earned respect for her expertise and ability but continues to draw fire from those who are uncomfortable with a presidential spouse exercising so much power. One argument against her is that she was not elected along with her husband. Yet this argument is only partly valid since Bill and Hillary Clinton have clearly worked as a political team from the start of their public life together. There have also been other first ladies of great influence, most notably Eleanor Roosevelt. Hillary Rodham Clinton represents a generation of women for whom career and family are of equal importance. As first lady, she has legitimized the concept of career woman and has brought to that role talents and experience the nation can ill afford to waste.

76

Leni Riefenstahl

1902– 2003

Oh! I know very well what propaganda is. That consists
of recreating certain events in order to illustrate a
thesis, or, in the face of certain events, to let one thing
go in order to accentuate another. I found myself, me, at
the heart of a certain time and a certain place. My film
is composed of what stemmed from that.

> —LENI RIEFENSTAHL
> On her 1934 film, *Triumph of the Will*

Regarded by many as the greatest woman filmmaker of all time, Leni Riefenstahl must forever be marked by her association with Adolf Hitler and Nazism. She never joined the National Socialist Party, and she claims that her film chronicling the Nuremberg Rally of 1934, *Triumph of the Will*, considered the most brilliant and influential propaganda film ever made, is a straight-forward documentary. However, there is no question that her skill as a film director and editor helped deify Hitler and celebrate Nazism. Only a naif or a rank opportunist could have so disingenuously separated the medium from its message. Riefenstahl was both, and has paid the price of over fifty years of exile from her craft for her dance with the devil of Nazism.

The daughter of a businessman who owned a heating and ventilation firm in Berlin, Leni Riefenstahl grew up in comfortable middle-class circumstances. She was an athletic girl, who excelled at swimming and gymnastics, but her main passion was the theater, particularly dance. After studying fine art at the Berlin Academy, she received ballet training and danced in Max Reinhardt's theater company. By the age of twenty-four, she had performed in solo dance concerts throughout Europe. While convalescing from the knee injury that ended her dance career in 1924, Riefenstahl saw her first "mountain film," a German movie genre that featured adventure and romance set in the mountains and contained sentimental and idealistic themes. Enthralled by the locales and power of the film, Riefenstahl went to Switzerland to meet the leading director of the genre, Arnold Fanck. Fanck, who became Riefenstahl's mentor, cast her in several of his films, the first of which was *Peaks of Destiny* (1926).

In 1931 Leni Riefenstahl formed her own film company and cowrote, directed, and starred in *The Blue Light*. The film was a popular success and brought Riefenstahl to the attention of Adolf Hitler, who was just coming to power in Germany. In a major way, Riefenstahl's mountain film became a metaphor for her later life. As she once observed, "In *The Blue Light*, I played the role of a child of nature, who on the nights of the full moon, climbed to this blue light, the image of the ideal....When her dream is destroyed, Yunta dies. I spoke of that as my destiny." Riefenstahl, the idealistic artist, would shortly be swept up in the reality of Nazi Germany. When she returned to Berlin after filming, she attended her first National Socialist rally and admits she was moved by Hitler's power to captivate and electrify an audience. Soon afterward, Hitler invited her to make a film of the 1934 Nuremberg rally. Riefenstahl has maintained that she accepted the assignment with great reluctance and that she insisted on maintaining artistic control of the project in order to produce a straightforward recording of an historical event. But as film critic Richard Barson observed, "The film is a visual, sensual, kinetic, and cinematic marvel.... *Triumph of the Will*, like *Birth of a Nation*, embodies an overwhelming contradiction: it is cinematically dazzling and ideologically vicious." There is, for example, an early sequence in the film showing Hitler's plane descending from the clouds. Cinematically, the sequence is both straightforward and cleverly manipulative. The Nuremburg rally was, in fact, conceived and organized with filming in mind, which makes Riefenstahl a willing collaborator in a propagandistic exercise.

In 1936 Riefenstahl was commissioned by the International Olympic Committee to make the official film of the 1936 Olympic Games in Berlin. Again she insisted on complete artistic control over her project. The result was a two-part film, *Olympiad: Festival of the Nations* and *Olympiad: Festival of Beauty*, that is widely held to be the greatest documentary ever made about the Olympic Games. Riefenstahl defied the order of Propaganda Minister Josef Goebbels to delete the footage of black athlete Jesse Owens that dominates the first part. However, her almost absurdly lyrical footage of German athletes in training—all of them perfect Aryan specimens—suggests a certain affinity for Nazi ideology. A landmark in documentary filmmaking, *Olympiad* won the Grand Prize at the Venice International Film Festival in 1938.

The war halted much of Riefenstahl's film work, and when Germany surrendered she was interned by the French for nearly four years until she was cleared of Nazi involvement. In 1954 her uncompleted film, *Tiefland*, made in Spain during the war, was released to critical acclaim. A film about the slave trade, *Black Cargo*, shot in Ethiopia in 1956, was never finished. Her former association with the Nazi regime caused other film projects to fall through, and she began to work as a photographer and also served as a camerawoman for an African expedition. A book of her African photographs, *The Last of the Nuba* (1973), gave her a new reputation and was followed by *People of the Kau* (1976), *Coral*

Gardens (1978), and *Mein Afrika* (1982). In 1994 she published her memoirs.

Riefenstahl's masterpiece, *Triumph of the Will*, remains, despite the director's fervent disclaimers, an outstanding example of the filmmaker's unique ability to move mass audiences. Like Yunta in *The Blue Light*, Leni Riefenstahl reached ever upward for the "image of the ideal." What she created was, as one critic put it, "such a monument to warped beauty that it serves to make us cautious of beauty itself."

77

Margaret Bourke-White

1904–1971

A pioneer, she always seemed to be first: the first to do it, and then first in her field....She dared to become an industrial photographer and a photojournalist at a time when men thought they had exclusive rights to those titles, then rose with startling speed to the top of both professions.

—VICKI GOLDBERG
Margaret Bourke-White: A Biography

Margaret Bourke-White, who contributed significantly to the rise of photojournalism as an art form, was born in the Bronx, New York, and grew up in the small town of Bound Brook, New Jersey. She was the second of three children of Minnie Bourke White and Joseph White, a successful engineer-designer for the printing industry and an amateur inventor and photographer. Raised within the strict moral and intellectual structure of the Ethical Culture movement, Bourke-White was encouraged early on to set high standards for herself. She later wrote that her parents' emphasis on achievement, as well as their constant striving for perfection, gave her "perhaps the most valuable inheritance a child could receive." She was especially close to her father, who was probably the chief inspiration of her life and work. His death in 1922, while Margaret was attending Columbia University, was a terrible blow to her.

At Columbia, Bourke-White's main academic interest was in herpetology, but she began to gravitate toward photography after studying with Clarence White, a leader of the pictorial school of photography. While a student of herpetology at the University of Michigan from 1923 to 1925, Bourke-White took pictures for the yearbook. In 1925 she married Everett Chapman, a graduate student in engineering at the university. They divorced after a year. She finished her college education at Cornell University, where she made an impressive and painterly photographic study of the rural campus for the *Cornell Alumni News*.

Bourke-White soon abandoned her interest in nature for the allure of modern technology embodied in the machine esthetic, a stylistic concept celebrating the beauty of industrial architecture and feats of engineering popular with many artists of the 1920s and 1930s. In 1927, after her graduation, she moved to Cleveland to establish a career as a photographic specialist in architectural and industrial subjects. By 1929 she had mastered her medium, and her artistically rendered photographs of bridges, smoke-stacks, factories, and steel mill interiors were featured in magazines throughout the Midwest.

That same year she became one of the first photographers for the new magazine, *Fortune*, published by *Time* cofounder Henry Luce. She set up a studio on one of the uppermost floors of the unfinished Chrysler Building in New York City and spent half the year working for *Fortune* and the other half as a successful commercial freelance photographer in advertising. Her public persona grew along with her career: She gained fame as the young, talented, "little girl photographer" who took risks, such as perching herself on a gargoyle outside her studio to get better shots, and who produced better pictures than older, far more experienced male photographers.

In 1930 Bourke-White made the first of several trips to the Soviet Union for *Fortune*, becoming the first Western photographer allowed into the country for many years. Her photographic surveys of Russian industry yielded a 1931 book, *Eyes on Russia*. In the mid-thirties, Bourke-White began to shift her focus from industrial to human subjects after a *Fortune* assignment during which she photographed drought victims of the Dust Bowl. However, after joining the staff of Luce's new magazine, *Life*, in 1935, it was her architectural photograph of the Fort Peck Dam that was chosen as the weekly's first cover.

The next year, Bourke-White spent months traveling through the South with writer Erskine Caldwell to document the appalling conditions of sharecroppers. Their collaboration resulted in a historically significant 1937 book, *You Have Seen Their Faces*. Also in 1937, one of Bourke-White's most famous photos appeared in *Life*: Black victims of a devastating Ohio River flood in Louisville, Kentucky, are pictured standing in a breadline beneath a billboard of a smiling white family in a car. The billboard's headline reads: "World's Highest Standard of Living—There's no way like the American Way." "The irony," writes Goldberg, "was tailor-made for her camera."

Bourke-White married Erskine Caldwell and collaborated with him on two more books: *North of the Danube* (1939), which chronicled life in Czechoslovakia before the Nazi occupation, and *Say, Is This the U.S.A.* (1941), a survey of American life on the eve of the United States entrance into World War II. The couple were in Moscow when Germans attacked the city, and they covered the event for *Life*. Bourke-White, the only foreign photographer in the Soviet Union at the time, sent the magazine a series of spectacular photos, including a night shot of the Kremlin illuminated by the sparks of exploding bombs. Bourke-White and Caldwell divorced in 1942.

During the war, Bourke-White became the first army air

force woman photographer in action in North Africa and Italy. In 1945, she was attached to General George Patton's Third Army as it marched across Germany, and was one of the first photographers to enter the death camps. Among her many pictures of the camps was the classic, *The Living Dead of Buchenwald.* After the war, she was sent by *Life* to India, where she shot the famous photograph, *Gandhi at His Spinning Wheel.* From 1949 to 1953 she documented life in South Africa under apartheid, covered the Korean War, and worked in Japan.

By the mid-1950s Bourke-White's career had been curbed by the effects of Parkinson's disease. She completed her last photo essay for *Life* in 1957. Between 1959 and 1961 she underwent a series of delicate operations to slow the spread of the disease. Her autobiography, *Portrait of Myself,* was published in 1963. She died in Connecticut in 1971 at the age of sixty-seven.

During her career, Margaret Bourke-White produced some of the most significant artistic and journalistic photographs of the twentieth century. Her work influenced later photojournalists and her adventurous life made her the ideal of legions of women everywhere. She was, writes Goldberg, "a true American heroine, larger than life—perhaps even larger than *Life.*"

78

Frida Kahlo

1907–1954

A ribbon around a bomb.
—ANDRÉ BRETON
Describing Kahlo's art,
"Frida Kahlo de Rivera,"
Surrealism and Painting

The fierce intensity, unswerving honesty, and originality of Frida Kahlo's work has brought her recognition as Mexico's greatest woman artist. In the opinion of many, she is Mexico's greatest artist.

Kahlo's art is unique because she is so often the primary subject of her work. "I paint self-portraits," she once said, "because I am so often alone, because I am the person I know best." According to her biographer, Hayden Herrera, "For Kahlo, painting self-portraits was a form of both psychological surgery and denial. By projecting her pain onto an alternate Frida, she not only confronted and confirmed her embattled reality, she also exorcised pain." A major source of Kahlo's emotional pain was her adored husband, Marxist muralist Diego Rivera, who said of Kahlo that she was "the only example in the history of art of an artist who tore open her chest and heart to reveal the biological truth of her feelings."

Frida Kahlo was born in a cobalt-blue house named the "Blue House" in Coyoacán, a residential suburb of Mexico City. She was one of five children of Guillermo Kahlo, a professional photographer and amateur painter of Austro-Hungarian, Jewish ancestry, and Matilde Kahlo, a devoutly Catholic *mestiza*. When Kahlo entered the National Preparatory School in 1922, she claimed 1910 as the year of her birth. A bout with polio at the age of seven may have kept her back in school, and she probably did not want her classmates and her boyfriend to know that she was older than they were. However, it is also possible that she chose 1910 because the Mexican Revolution broke out that year. "Outspoken in her commitment to that long and bloody struggle," writes Herrera, "Frida expressed her ties to what she called *la raza*, or the people, not only in her art but in her dress, her behavior, and the decoration of her home." She became a dedicated Communist in the late 1920s, partly, but not exclusively, because of her association with Rivera, and social themes appear in some of her work, including *My Dress Hangs There*, a personal and sardonic view of capitalist New York during the Depression.

Kahlo was a high-spirited, rebellious teenager and a gifted writer and brilliant student, whose early ambition was to become a doctor. In 1925 the school bus in which she was riding collided with a trolley. The accident, Kahlo later recalled, "harmed everybody and me most of all." She eventually recovered from the most serious of the injuries she had received, but for the rest of her life suffered physically and emotionally from the effects of the accident, as well as from what may have been undiagnosed spina bifida, a congenital malformation of the spine.

While convalescing, Kahlo began painting because she was "bored as hell in bed." She also hoped painting would provide her with a way to make money at home. Although she enjoyed looking at art books and loved to draw, she had no formal art training apart from a brief apprenticeship with printer Fernando Fernández, who taught her drawing and thought she had great talent. Her first paintings show some originality, but she was clearly influenced by various styles: Cubism, Italian Renaissance painting, Art Nouveau, Oriental art, and the work of Mexican painter-teacher Adolfo Best Maugard, whose use of pre-Columbian design was popular in the 1920s.

Kahlo's first *Self-Portrait* (1926) hints at the work of the English Pre-Raphaelites and Modigliani, but the beginning of her signature style is there in the impassive expression, dark, watchful eyes framed by heavy eyebrows that join together in a V, and full, sensual lips framed by a slight mustache. Her style later became both more realistic and more surrealistic. Her face and body, superimposed upon landscapes, were also landscapes that featured objects of her pain and pleasure: Diego Rivera's face, a necklace of thorns, a skull in a circle on her forehead to represent thoughts about death, Kahlo's pet monkeys, a steel column inserted into her naked body to symbolize the steel corset she was forced to wear (*The Broken Column*, 1942).

In 1928 Kahlo showed her paintings to Diego Rivera, who was impressed with them, as well as with the painter. They married in 1929, but it was a stormy relationship, marked by Rivera's infidelities (although Kahlo also had affairs, most notably with sculptor Isamu Noguchi and exiled Russian revolutionary Leon Trotsky), their divorce, remarriage, second divorce, and Kahlo's despair at her inability to have a child. Her feelings about childbirth and children are recorded in such paintings as *My Birth* (1932), *Henry Ford Hospital* (she recovered from a miscarriage there in 1932), *My Nurse and I* (1937), and *Me and My Dolls* (1937). In *The Love Embrace of the Universe, the Earth (Mexico), Diego, Me, and Señor Xolotl* (1949), she holds a naked Diego in her arms like a newborn baby.

Kahlo's works were promoted by André Breton in 1938, but she did not receive a major independent exhibition in Mexico until 1953. At the time, she was extremely ill after suffering the amputation of her right leg. She continued to deteriorate, and on

July 13, 1954, died at the Blue House. Her cause of death was reported as pneumonia, although, given her depressions and suicide attempts, many of her friends believe that she killed herself.

"I paint my own reality," Kahlo once said. The two hundred works she produced "force us," writes Herrera, "to come face to face with Frida, both the legend and the reality, and through her to come face to face with unexplored parts of ourselves."

79

Gabriela Mistral

1889–1957

Gabriela Mistral was very Chilean and provincial, and yet she was universal. She represents one of the most original voices in Latin American poetry. Her work will always walk the edge between the ordinary places where she created her own myth as rural school teacher, and the place where she allowed herself the luxury of being the delirious woman of free fantasy.

—MARJORIE AGOSIN,
Gabriela Mistral, the Restless Soul

Born in a small Andean village in northern Chile's Elquia Valley, Gabriela Mistral began her career as a rural schoolteacher and went on to become a renowned diplomat, educator, author, and poet. For her poetry, she became the first Latin American to win the Nobel Prize in literature, the only Latin American woman ever to be so honored. Through her fluent and lyrical verse, Mistral attempted to speak for the voiceless, for women and children. Her epitaph—"What the soul does for the body so does the poet for her people"—aptly describes the contributions of this unique and multifaceted woman.

Mistral, whose real name was Lucila Godoy Alcayaga, was the daughter of Petronila Alcayaga, a schoolteacher of Basque descent, and Jeronimo Godoy Alcayaga Villanueva, a vagabond poet and schoolteacher of Indian and Jewish heritage. Mistral was a timid, imaginative child, given to daydreaming and fond of imaginative literature and folklore. At fifteen she began working as a teacher's assistant in a rural Chilean primary school, and in 1910 earned a certificate allowing her to teach in secondary schools throughout the country. She began writing melancholy verse after the tragic suicide of her fiancé in 1909, and several years later had produced a small body of poetry. In 1914, she entered *Sonetas de la Muerte* (Sonnets of Death) in a Santiago writing contest, and won first prize. She would later publish her works under the pseudonym Gabriela Mistral, chosen either from admiration of the poets Gabriel D'Annunzio and Frédéric Mistral, or as a combination derived from the Archangel Gabriel and the cold, dry "mistral" wind that blows across southern France.

Sonetos de la Muerte, considered one of Mistral's finest achievements, brought her instant fame as a poet. Her work as an educator also earned her a growing reputation. Her success as a teacher and director of rural schools brought her to the attention of José Vasconcelos, Mexico's minister of education, who in 1922, invited Mistral to collaborate with him on rural educational reform in his country. The same year, Mistral published her first major volume of poetry, *Desolación* (Desolation), in which she expresses with characteristic passion, intensity, and honesty her grief and anguish over the loss of her first love and a subsequent failed love affair.

In 1923, the Chilean government awarded Mistral the title,

"Teacher of the Nation." The following year, she began a new career as a diplomat for the Chilean Consular Corps. She served as Chilean consul in various European and Latin American cities and in Los Angeles, and represented her country at the League of Nations. *Ternura* (Tenderness), a collection of poetry for children, was published in 1924. Unlike *Desolación*, which reflects the poet's pain and obsession with death, *Ternura* is a celebration of the joys of birth and motherhood, and is considered to be a work of renewed hope and reconciliation. Mistral's other major poetic works include *Tala* (Feeling) and *Lagar* (Wine Press). She also wrote fables and contributed to various periodicals. She was named Nobel Laureate in 1945. Her later years were spent in the United States as the Chilean delegate to the United Nations. Several anthologies of her work were published the year of her death, including a collection of selected poems translated by Langston Hughes.

The constant during Mistral's career as both an educator and a diplomat was her poetry. As she described her writing method, "I write on my knees; the desk-table has never been any use to me—not in Chile, Paris, or Lisbon." For her, "Writing tends to cheer me; it always soothes my spirit and blesses me with the gift of an innocent, tender, childlike day. It is the sensation of having spent a few hours in my homeland, with my customs, free whims, my total freedom." The dominant themes of her poetry are love, death, childhood, maternity, religion, and a burning desire for justice. Her work also celebrates nature and her homeland. As critic Margot Arce de Vazquez writes, "No other poet, with the exception of [Pablo] Neruda in his songs to the Chilean land, has spoken with more emotion of the beauty of the American world and of the splendor of its nature." The intense lyrical intimacy and frank simplicity of Mistral's poetry particularly affirms children and the impoverished—those without a voice—in a way that reaches the universal by way of the personal. Mistral, the educator and diplomat, remained true to her earliest visions, creating matchless expressions of essential humanity that transcend a particular time and place.

80

Flannery O'Connor

1925–1964

I have found...that my subject in fiction is the action of grace in territory held largely by the devil. I have also found that what I write is read by an audience which puts little stock either in grace or the devil.

—Flannery O'Connor
"On Her Own Work,"
Mysteries and Manners

Flannery O'Connor is one of the most important fiction writers of post–World War II American literature. Her novels and short stories, filled with stark, brutal comedy, disturbing violence, and grotesque characters, explore the difficulty and necessity of spiritual belief and redemption in a world increasingly devoid of meaning and transcendence. A Catholic southerner, O'Connor labored with patience and determination to express her uncompromising moral vision, remaining unmoved by demands that her fiction should conform to another's standard. She once declared that she could "wait a hundred years for readers." It has not taken that long for her to be recognized as one of the most influential writers of the century.

Mary Flannery O'Connor was born in Savannah, Georgia, the only child of Edward Francis O'Connor and Regina Cline O'Connor. As a child she was precocious and independent, preferring the company of adults to other children, and loved reading and writing. She early cultivated an interest in the odd and different. Her passion was raising chickens, and she was particularly fond of the more peculiar-looking birds. The star of her collection was a chicken that could walk backward, and the Pathé News photographed O'Connor, age five, and her chicken for the newsreels. "Shortly after that she died, as now seems fitting," O'Connor later wrote. She also liked to say that this was the high point of her life, and the rest was anticlimactic. When O'Connor was twelve, her father became terminally ill with lupus erythemetosus, the same illness that would later afflict O'Connor. She and her mother moved to Regina O'Connor's family home in Milledgeville, Georgia, where Flannery attended Peabody High School and Georgia State College for Women, graduating in 1945. Her family was devoutly Catholic in the predominantly Protestant South, which no doubt contributed to the religious themes in O'Connor's work and cultivated in her the sense of being both a member of the Southern community but also somewhat apart and critically distant from it.

After her graduation, O'Connor went on to the Graduate School of Fine Arts at the University of Iowa, where she studied at the Writer's Workshop. She perfected her craft and in 1946 sold her first short story, "The Geranium," to *Accent* magazine. During her second year at Iowa she won the Rinehart-Iowa prize for fiction on the basis of the draft of what would become her first novel, *Wise Blood*. In 1948 she accepted an invitation to work at Yaddo, the prestigious retreat for writers and artists in Saratoga Springs, New York. *Wise Blood* tells the story of a profoundly religious backwoodsman who, after rejecting the fundamentalist faith in which he was raised, creates his own religion, the Church of Christ Without Christ, to attack that faith. His subsequent desperate search for salvation leads to violence and disaster. O'Connor's editor at Holt, Rinehart found the novel too bizarre and tried to redirect the author into more conventional channels. O'Connor resisted and changed publishers. In 1949 she moved to Redding Ridge, Connecticut, to live with friends and there finished her novel, while occasionally publishing chapters in literary quarterlies.

In December 1950, on her return to Georgia for Christmas, O'Connor was diagnosed with lupus, which, although incurable, was able to be controlled with medications developed since her father's death. It would be a year before O'Connor was again mobile. Once her illness had stabilized, she moved with her mother to Andalusia, a dairy farm near Milledgeville. The two women divided the household labor and O'Connor once again raised birds, adding to her flocks peacocks, a bird associated with her by her readers. O'Connor's return to the South, which she loved and where she felt she belonged, put her again in close touch with the scenes and the themes of her fiction. A steady flow of stories followed, all marked by a combination of the gothic and the grotesque, as well as by superb craftmanship. *Wise Blood* was published in 1953. In 1955 a collection of stories, *A Good Man Is Hard to Find and Other Stories*, was published. The title story, perhaps O'Connor's most famous, tells of the murder of a thoroughly unpleasant southern family; the killer, called the Misfit, becomes the unlikely divine agent of a victim's spiritual salvation. Some critics found O'Connor's work too harsh and lacking in compassion and complained that she was unsympathetic to Southern regional customs and character. O'Connor patiently persisted, unaffected by any obtuse objections and misinterpretations. Her second novel, *The Violent Bear It Away*, appeared in 1959.

In 1963 O'Connor's health declined, and after undergoing an operation, her lupus reactivated. She continued to write, producing two of her most admired stories, "Judgment Day" and "Parker's Back." She died in 1964 of kidney failure. The following year, her last collection of short stories, *Everything That Rises Must Converge*, was published. In 1969, *Mystery and Manners*, a collection of O'Connor's articles and unpublished essays, appeared to critical acclaim. Despite years of illness, Flannery O'Connor had produced a significant body of work that will stand as some of the most original and provocative writing of the twentieth century. She created, writes critic Josephine Hendin, "a remarkable art, unique in its time. Unlike any Southern writer before her, she wrote in praise of ice in the blood."

81

Katharine Graham

1917–2001

Katharine Graham came to national prominence during
the Watergate scandals, when the *Washington Post*...ran a
daring series of stories on political corruption which
ultimately led into the Nixon White House and which
caused President Nixon to resign from office. The
Watergate stories established Mrs. Graham as a
publisher of conscience and courage, and of legendary
power—she was the woman who brought down a
president.

—DEBORAH DAVIS
Katharine the Great

As the owner of the *Washington Post*, Katharine Graham became the most famous newspaper publisher and one of the most influential women in America. Contrary to all expectations, she emerged from the giant shadows cast by her famous father, notorious mother, and brilliant husband, successfully took on the man's world of publishing, and in the process earned the respect and admiration of presidents, Supreme Court justices, business leaders, and influential writers and the literati.

Graham's father, Eugene Meyer, was a prodigy. His father, a Jewish immigrant from France, had settled in California and achieved success in banking and retail. Eugene, educated at Yale, bought a seat on the New York Stock Exchange and retired as a multimillionaire in his twenties. He married socialite Agnes Ernst in 1910. Katharine, the couple's fourth child, grew up in considerable luxury but saw little of her parents. By the time of her birth her father had begun a twenty-year career of public service: He acted as an adviser to seven presidents and held several important political posts, including the governorship of the Federal Reserve Board. Katharine grew up in Washington, largely raised by family servants, ignored and neglected by her busy parents: "I thought I was the peasant walking around brilliant people." The Meyers were solid conservative Republicans, but while attending Vassar College, Katharine moved toward the Left. Seeking greater intellectual stimulation and student diversity, she transferred to the University of Chicago. After her graduation in 1938, Graham's father urged her to start her journalism career at the *Washington Post*, which he had bought five years earlier. Instead, she moved to San Francisco to work on the *News* as a reporter for twenty-five dollars a week. Seven months later, despite her ambivalent feelings toward her parents, she agreed to her father's offer of a four-dollar-a-week raise to come home to work for the *Post*.

In 1940, Katharine Meyer married lawyer Philip Graham, who, after serving in World War II, had assumed the position of publisher of the *Post*. In 1948 he and Katharine bought the paper from Eugene Meyer for $1 million. Katharine Graham then largely retired from journalism to raise her family and become her husband's hostess, watching his career from the sidelines.

Philip Graham played political kingmaker, helping to convince John F. Kennedy to take on Lyndon Johnson as his running mate, and in 1961 he acquired *Newsweek* magazine.

In 1963, Philip Graham, who was affected by bouts of manic-depression, committed suicide. Suddenly, with no preparation, Katharine Graham found herself in charge of the family publishing empire.

Katharine assumed the presidency of the Washington Post Company with reluctance and a certain degree of terror. She saw herself as an interim president until her son, Donny, was old enough to take over, but she quickly realized that a newspaper required hands-on management. The *Post*, in particular, had been suffering from a lack of leadership and a demoralized staff. At first patronized and intimidated by her male employees, as well as painfully shy (she reportedly needed to practice over and over again a "Merry Christmas" greeting to her staff), Graham slowly gained self-confidence and executive authority. Her goal was to remake the *Post* into a respected, world-class newspaper, and to achieve that end she brought in Ben Bradlee, known for his aggressive, investigative reporting style, as managing editor.

In 1971 Graham decided to publish the Pentagon Papers, the classified government study of United States involvement in Southeast Asia which first appeared in the *New York Times*. Graham's decision resulted in a restraining order from the Nixon administration against the *Post*. The Supreme Court ruled in the *Post*'s favor, enhancing the prestige of both the paper and its publisher. Graham gained further national prominence after the *Post* broke the story of the Watergate burglary in 1972. The *Post* was virtually alone in following the trail from a seemingly third-rate burglary to the Nixon White House. Graham encouraged and financed the Watergate investigation, threatening to go to jail rather than comply with a subpoena for her reporters' notes, and it has been argued that she, not Ben Bradlee, was the true hero in the *Post*'s standoff against a defensive, all-out White House attack designed to discredit the paper. Powerful friends in government warned Graham to stop pursuing the investigation, but she persisted, even after Post company stock dropped from thirty-eight to twenty-one dollars a share. By the time of the Watergate and Senate Judiciary Committee hearings that led to Richard

Nixon's resignation in 1974, the *Post* and Graham had been vindicated, and Katharine Graham was praised for her independence and courage.

The year before Nixon's resignation, Graham became the first woman to receive the John Peter Zenger award, given for distinguished service on behalf of freedom of the press and the people's right to know. In 1977 *U.S. News and World Report* voted her the "top leader and shaper of national life" among women. She passed the day-to-day management of the *Post* to her son, Donny, in 1979 and remained chair of the board until 1991. When Graham retired, she was one of only two female heads of *Fortune* 500 companies. She transformed the *Washington Post* into a respected and influential newspaper and managed a media empire with skill and determination. Columnist James Reston has called her role as publisher of the *Post* "one of the greatest achievements of journalism in this country."

82

Bessie Smith

1894–1937

Bessie Smith might have been a "blues queen" to the society at large, but within the tighter Negro community where the blues were part of a total way of life, and a major expression of an attitude toward life, she was a priestess, a celebrant who affirmed the values of the group and man's ability to deal with chaos.

—RALPH ELLISON
Shadow and Act

293

Queen, priestess, or empress of the blues—all of these are fitting titles for Bessie Smith, one of the most important figures in the history of American music. By successfully blending African and Western styles of music, she helped transform the folk tradition of the blues into an indigenous American art form with worldwide impact. There are few contemporary singers of pop, jazz, or the blues who have not been influenced by her. An electrifying performer, she expressively and emotionally verbalized actual life. As music critic Carl van Vechten summerizes: "This was no actress, no imitator of women's woes; there was no pretense. It was the real thing."

Bessie Smith was born into a large, poor family in Chattanooga, Tennessee. Her father was a Baptist preacher who died soon after she was born. When Bessie was nine, her mother died, and her oldest sister, Viola, became the head of the family. Bessie soon went to work singing on street corners for tips, accompanied by her younger brother on the guitar. Other than low-paying manual or domestic jobs, the only employment open to African Americans at the time was in the segregated music entertainment industry. The teenage Smith chose the latter as a means of escape from poverty. She won a job as a dancer in a minstrel show with the help of her older brother, Clarence, a comedian with the show. While touring with the troupe, Smith met blues legend Ma Rainey, who became a lifelong friend and whose influence on Smith's singing style is evident in her earliest recordings.

In 1913 Smith moved to Atlanta and became a headliner at a local club, but she also continued to tour rural areas, performing in dance halls, cabarets, and camp meetings with F. S. Walcott's Rabbit Foot Minstrels and with other traveling shows. In 1920 she formed her own musical troupe with herself as the star. Her rich contralto and commanding stage presence projected emotional depths never heard before. Her vocal power and her material, drawn from vernacular African-American oral tradition, struck a resonant chord with black audiences. As one music critic observed, "More than any other singer, she set the blues tradition in terms of style and quality. She not only gave a special musical aura to this tradition but her own singing and accompaniments of the many jazz artists who assisted her in her recordings placed her firmly in the broader jazz tradition."

Smith's early attempts to record met with resistance. In contrast to the lightweight, bourgeois Tin Pan Alley standard of the day, she sounded too rough and coarse, and her mannerisms were considered by many to be lower class. Finally, in 1923, she began recording blues numbers as well as popular tunes, selling 780,000 copies of her first record, "Downhearted Blues" backed by "Gulf Coast Blues," in six months. During the 1920s, she began to tour northern cities where she was a phenomenal success with African-American audiences, who lined up around city blocks to hear her sing. She was also one of the first black performers to attract a large white audience and the first black woman to broadcast her concerts live on local radio stations in Memphis and Atlanta.

Bessie Smith's recording sessions of the mid-twenties produced some of the finest work of her career. With such talented musicians as pianist Fletcher Henderson, cornetist Joe Smith, saxophonist Coleman Hawkins, and trumpeter Louis Armstrong, among others, Smith used her impressive range and skill to turn her voice into another instrument with remarkable results in such songs as "Weeping Willow Blues," "The Bye Bye Blues," and "St. Louis Blues." Her material from 1925 to 1930 emphasized the daily plight of African Americans, as she viewed it, and concentrates on such themes as poverty, bootlegging, unemployment, injustice, drinking, gambling, and love gone wrong. "Rent House Blues" tells the story of an eviction; "Woman's Trouble Blues" depicts an unjust incarceration of a young black woman. After seeing the devastating effects of a flood along the Ohio River, Smith wrote her biggest selling blues number of the decade, "Backwater Blues," told from the point of view of a woman victim of the flood. Each topical issue is filtered through Smith's experience as an African-American woman, reaching though common and personal experience to universal themes. Always candid on the subject of sex, Smith recorded songs with risqué double entendres, such as "Kitchen Man" and the popular "Empty Bed Blues."

Bessie Smith's was married twice, the first time to Earl Love, who died shortly after their marriage. In 1922 she married Jack Gee, a night watchman. They eventually separated after a stormy and violent seven-year relationship. She had numerous lovers, including musicians Sidney Bechet; Porter Grainger, who wrote one of Smith's most enduring songs, "T'aint Nobody's Business If I Do"; and former Chicago bootlegger Richard Morgan. Smith had female lovers as well and was open about her bisexuality. She was a familiar figure in the late-night club world of the cities she visited and at parties where, as she put it, "the funk was flying." To avoid the Jim Crow difficulty of finding accommodations in the South, Smith traveled in her own Pullman coach.

During the Depression Smith's fortunes fell—as they did for all black performers. Venues closed and the record industry collapsed. Columbia terminated her contract in 1931. A final recording session, arranged by record producer John Hammond in 1933, produced the classic Depression-era song, "Nobody Knows You When You're Down and Out." Smith continued to perform on tour until her death due to an automobile accident in September, 1937. In an article for *Downbeat* magazine, John Hammond stated, on the basis of hearsay, that she bled to death because an all-white hospital refused to admit her. Edward Albee dramatized the story in his 1961 play *The Death of Bessie Smith*. This rumor, however, simply wasn't true. After the accident she was taken to a black hospital in Clarksdale, Mississippi, where she died from the massive injuries she had suffered.

Bessie Smith was a great original whose life epitomized the excesses of the Roaring Twenties, and she produced a body of work that is a landmark of American music. She sang the experience of African Americans with the deep emotion and empathy of a woman who, despite her fame, was traveling the same hard road. James Baldwin summarized the titanic appeal of Bessie's blues: "'It's a long, old road' as Bessie Smith puts it, 'but it's got to find an end.' And so, she wearily, doggedly informs us, 'I picked up my bag, baby, and I tried it again.' Her songs end on a very bitter and revealing note. 'You can't trust nobody, you might as well be alone / Found my long-lost friend, and I might as well stayed at home!' Still she was driven to find that long-lost friend, to grasp again, with fearful hope, the unwilling, uncaring, human hand."

83

Joan Ganz Cooney

1929–

We started out thinking that *Sesame Street* might teach simple things. We learned you do so much more.

— JOAN GANZ COONEY
Interview in *Changing Times*, July 1989

On November 10, 1969, *Sesame Street*, an entirely new concept in children's educational programming, premiered on American public television. Produced by the newly formed Children's Television Workshop (CTW), *Sesame Street* was created by CTW cofounder Joan Ganz Cooney, who had sought to fill the "vast wasteland" of 1960s children's television with a program that would educate preschoolers, particularly those from disadvantaged homes, in basic number, language, and reasoning skills, while also providing, in Cooney's words, "an increased awareness of self and the world." Borrowing from the slick, quick-cutting tactics of network commercials, *Sesame Street* used humor, music, and the visual power of television to instruct as well as to entertain. The show's innovative technique, together with its urban setting and culturally diverse cast supplemented by a cuddly and comical assortment of Jim Henson muppets, attracted huge audiences from the first. Almost thirty years later, Cooney's brainchild remains one of the most popular and influential educational programs on television, beloved by children and adults alike.

Joan Ganz Cooney's creation of the Children's Television Workshop grew out of her long-held belief that mass media could and should be used as an agent of social change. After graduating in 1951 from the University of Arizona, where she majored in education, Cooney began her career as a reporter for the *Arizona Republic*. In 1954 she moved to New York and worked as a television publicity writer, first for NBC and later for the CBS dramatic anthology series *The United States Steel Hour*. In 1962 she began producing public affairs documentaries for the New York educational station, WNDT, and in 1966 won an Emmy for her three-hour documentary, *Poverty, Anti-Poverty, and the Poor*.

In 1966, at the suggestion of Lloyd Morrisett, then vice-president of the Carnegie Corporation, Cooney prepared a study on the possible exploitation of public television for preschool education. Her report made clear the potential educational value of a television "classroom without walls" for young children, the majority of whom were already watching television an average of sixty hours a week. Citing the National Education Association's recommendation that all children should be given the opportunity to enter public school at age four, Cooney also stressed the cost-saving benefits of such an enterprise. In 1968, on the strength of her report, the Children's Television Workshop was founded with funding from several foundations and the federal government, which had been seeking a way to augment its costly Project Head Start program for disadvantaged preschoolers.

After setting up a curriculum with considerable input from early childhood experts and lengthy research into the viewing habits of children at nurseries and day-care centers, Cooney and her staff produced five *Sesame Street* pilots, which were tested over a VHF channel in Philadelphia and in New York City day-care centers. *Sesame Street* began its first regular season in 1969 to rave reviews. In the early 1970s, studies carried out by the Educational Testing Service and similar groups showed that *Sesame Street* was indeed having a positive impact on the cognitive skills of preschoolers.

The success of *Sesame Street* led CTW to produce other highly regarded educational programs that focused on the building of specific skills, such as reading (*The Electric Company*), science (*3–2–1 Contact*), mathematics (*Square One*), and geography (*Where in the World is Carmen Sandiego?*). Critics have argued that the CTW technique of entertaining while teaching leads children to expect school to provide them with a similar entertaining format. Others have suggested that if television can teach, then schools should let it do part of the job. For Joan Ganz Cooney, the medium and the message are inextricably linked. As she once told an interviewer, "If I were a teacher, I'd see what kids were watching and try to relate it to school. Instead, they never see that progress is what matters, not the machine."

84

Cleopatra

69 B.C.—30 B.C.

> Rome, who had never condescended to fear any nation
> or people, did, in her time fear two human beings; one
> was Hannibal, and the other was a woman.
>
> —W. W. TARN,
> *Cambridge Ancient History*

The woman Rome feared was Cleopatra, the seventh Egyptian
queen of that name and the last pharaoh of the Greek-founded
Ptolemaic empire. Her fame rests largely upon her status as one

of the great romantic heroines of all time and upon her almost legendary cachet as history's complete seductress. Although alluring, she apparently was not the great beauty characterized in fiction and film. As her biographer, Julia Samson, writes, "It was the gleam of her personality which attracted people." She was seductive, but there is no evidence to support claims that she was promiscuous or that she had any lovers other than Julius Caesar and Marc Antony. As the ruler of a once-great country that had fallen under the sway of the rising Roman empire, Cleopatra's choice of lovers was undoubtedly the result of royal ambition as well as personal desire. Because of both desire and ambition, the "Queen of Kings" was destined to play an influential role in determining the fate of Imperial Rome.

Cleopatra was descended from Ptolemy I Soter, a general of Alexander the Great, who secured Egypt for himself after Alexander's death in 323 B.C. Her childhood was marked by the struggles of her father, Auletes, and her older sisters for the Egyptian throne. Auletes won the struggle with financial help from Rome and its ruling triumvirate—Pompey, Julius Caesar, and Crassus—and with military aid from a young Roman cavalry officer, Marc Antony. Auletes died in 52 B.C., and under the terms of his will, Cleopatra was proclaimed his successor, with her ten-year-old half-brother and husband, Ptolemy XIII. Cleopatra's assumption of power was threatened by a regency council set up to support Ptolemy against her, and she was eventually forced to flee Alexandria and go to Ashkelon, a city on the north coast of Gaza that remained loyal to her. There she gathered forces to defeat Ptolemy, whose own army stood ready for action nearly opposite Ashkelon, at Pelusium.

At this juncture, in 48 B.C., Julius Caesar arrived in Alexandria. The last surviving member of the triumvirate, Caesar was anxious to reassure the Romans, who supported the joint rule of Cleopatra and Ptolemy, and were wary of any political instability in Egypt that might lead to an uprising against Rome. Egypt was also rich and owed Caesar money he needed for his wars. He sent for Cleopatra, who, according to the Greek historian Plutarch, was smuggled ashore past Ptolemy's men in a carpet tied with a leather thong. Caesar crushed a new revolt led by Ptolemy, who drowned while fleeing capture after his defeat. Caesar restored Cleopatra to the throne with her twelve-year-old brother and new husband, who became Ptolemy XIV. Caesar and Cleopatra had a son, Caesarion, and remained lovers until Caesar's murder in 44 B.C.

After Caesar's death, Cleopatra worried, with good reason, that the inevitable power struggle for Rome represented a threat to her son's life, and possibly to her throne and life as well. Brutus and Cassius, the architects of Caesar's murder, fled Rome and began to prepare for war against Antony and Octavian, Caesar's great-nephew and heir. Cleopatra sent Roman legions to help Dolobella, a loyal friend of Caesar's, who was battling Cassius in Syria. Dolabella was defeated, which weakened Cleopatra's military strength and turned the greedy Cassius's attention toward Egypt. When Cassius asked Cleopatra for financial support, she refused, and in 42 B.C. led her fleet out of Alexandria to support Antony and Octavian at Philippi. A storm destroyed her ships and forced her back to Egypt. Then came two decisive battles at Philippi, which resulted in the deaths of Brutus and Cassius and the division of the Roman world among the ruling coalition of Marc Antony, Octavian, and Lepidus.

Marc Antony, who planned a campaign to acquire Parthia (Persia), needed Egypt for its gateway position to the East, for financial support, and for its plentiful grain supply. He sent an invitation to Cleopatra to meet him in Tarsus, on the southeast coast of Asia Minor (Turkey). She arrived in sumptuous splendor, according to Plutarch, on a barge with a poop deck of gold, reclining "under a pavilion of cloth of gold of tissue, appareled and attired like the goddess Venus." We tend to visualize Cleopatra's barge in Hollywood terms as a luxurious, floating boudoir, but it must be remembered that Cleopatra was pharaoh of a rich country and would have wanted to impress Antony with her wealth and majesty as well as with her seductive self. The two forged a heady alliance of love and ambition. In 36 B.C., Marc Antony married Cleopatra, although four years earlier he had made a politically advantageous marriage to Octavian's sister, Octavia. Cleopatra encouraged Antony's Parthian campaign, which, if successful, would have increased her own empire. Their goal was "a partnership in ruling the kingdoms of the East, which could then be handed on to her children," Samson observes. "It was this partnership of Cleopatra's strength behind Antony that Rome was to fear."

Antony's attempt to annex Parthia was a dismal failure despite Cleopatra's support. It shook her faith in Antony as a military strategist, but it did not weaken her devotion to him. When Antony launched an offensive against Armenia, Cleopatra traveled with him as far as the Euphrates, then left him to cement their alliances with the rulers of Syria and Judea. Antony's victory in Armenia enabled him to return to Alexandria as a conqueror. There he staged a strange and flamboyant theatrical display, the "Donations," during which he declared Cleopatra the "Queen of Kings," Caesarion the "King of Kings," and bestowed kingdoms, including the unconquered Parthia, on his three children by Cleopatra. In Rome, Antony's dual position—as monarch in Asia with Cleopatra and as Roman ruler—was viewed with hostility, especially by Octavian who deeply resented Antony's neglect of his noble wife and whose ambition to rule alone was by now evident. The fragile accord between Antony and Octavian snapped, and each prepared for war.

In 31 B.C., Antony and Cleopatra's forces clashed with Octavian's at Actium. The battle might have had a different outcome if Antony had heeded Cleopatra's advice to attack Octavian's small fleet as it approached Actium. But Antony favored a land battle, which proved disastrous and resulted in his defeat. Antony fell on his sword and, mortally wounded, died in Cleopatra's arms. Cleopatra, who had taken refuge in her tomb, thwarted Octavian's attempts to take her alive by poisoning herself with an asp smuggled to her in a basket of figs. The ruthless Octavian, soon to become the Emperor Augustus, killed Caesarion and then took Cleopatra and Antony's children back to Rome to be raised by Octavia as loyal Roman citizens.

Cleopatra's greatness has been obscured over the centuries by the popular portrait of her as an Aphrodite figure romantically and inextricably linked with the two outstanding Romans of her day. While that portrait is historically accurate and poetically compelling, Cleopatra also stands on her own as a capable, politically savvy, and courageous ruler who was one of only two women in history (the other was the Celtic queen, Boudicca) to challenge—and very nearly defeat—the might of Rome.

85

Madame C. J. Walker
(Sarah Breedlove)

1867–1919

It is given to few persons to transform a people in a generation. Yet this was done by the late Madam C. J. Walker...[She] made and deserved a fortune and gave much of it away, generously.

—W. E. B. Du Bois
From Walker's obituary in
The Crisis magazine

Hair-care entrepreneur Madam C. J. Walker was an early twentieth-century phenomenon. The child of former slaves, she raised herself up from poverty to become a successful businesswoman and America's first black, self-made female millionaire. Walker acquired her fortune by creating and marketing an innovative line of beauty products and techniques to African-American women. Her Walker Method, or Walker System, of hair care set a new standard of beauty for black women, and the outstanding success of her company—by 1919, the largest and most lucrative black-owned enterprise in the United States—helped to define the role of African Americans in business.

Walker was born Sarah Breedlove on a cotton plantation in Delta, Louisiana, to sharecroppers Owen and Minerva Breedlove. After her parents' death from yellow fever in 1874, Walker and her older sister, Louvenia, took in washing to support themselves. Four years later, a second yellow fever epidemic devastated the area, and the sisters were forced to move to Vicksburg, Mississippi, to find work. At fourteen, Walker married Moses McWilliams, a Vicksburg laborer. Six years later, McWilliams was killed in an accident, and Walker moved to St. Louis, where she supported herself and her daughter, A'Lelia, by working as a laundress and part-time door-to-door sales agent for the Poro Company, a manufacturer of hair products.

In 1915 Walker set out to devise her own hair preparation formulas. Unwilling to compete with the St. Louis–based Poro Company, she moved to Denver, where her older brother, Alex, lived, to start her new business. She worked as a cook and laundress and spent her evenings developing hair products, which she tested on herself and her nieces. She eventually came up with three satisfactory preparations and began selling them door to door, giving free demonstrations of her hair-care system to potential customers. Walker's regimen consisted of a shampoo, followed by the application of her Wonderful Hair Grower, a medicated pomade to combat dandruff and prevent hair loss. She completed her treatment by applying a light oil to the customer's hair, and then straightening it with a heated metal comb. Because of her hair-straightening technique, Walker would later come under fire for attempting to make black women look more white, a charge she strenuously denied. Walker's great-great-grand-daughter and biographer, A'Lelia Perry Bundles, has written that Walker "sought to create a look that was truly Afro-American," by urging black women to emphasize their individual good points "without trying to imitate whites."

Walker's hair products became popular in Denver and were even more successful when she started selling them through the mail. In 1906 she married Charles Joseph Walker, a sales agent for a black-owned newspaper, whom she had met in St. Louis. C.J. Walker helped his wife expand her mail-order business and became involved in all aspects of her rapidly growing company. (The couple would divorce in 1912 over disagreements about control and expansion of the company.) To identify her marital status and give her products an added cachet, Walker began calling herself Madam. In the fall of 1906, Walker embarked on a sales tour to nine states, where she lectured on her Walker Method and demonstrated her technique in African-American clubs, churches, and homes. The tour was a financial success and enabled her to organize a second office in Pittsburgh, which was managed by her daughter. In 1910 Walker transferred both offices to Indianapolis and built a factory there. Six years later, she moved her base of operations to Harlem, in New York City.

The Madam C. J. Walker Manufacturing Company, of which Walker was sole owner and president, eventually provided employment for some three thousand African Americans. Many were "Walker agents," primarily women,who were trained at the beauty colleges and schools founded by Walker and then sent throughout the United States and the Caribbean to demonstrate the Walker Method and sell the company's products. Dressed in the Walker uniform—white shirtwaists tucked into long black skirts—and carrying black satchels containing hair preparations and hairdressing apparatus, Walker agents became familiar figures in African-American communities. A number of agents went on to open their own Walker-based hair salons. An equally familiar figure was the company's founder, whose portrait appeared on tin containers of her Wonderful Hair Grower and some sixteen other products, as well as in newspaper and magazine advertisements.

To motivate her agents, Walker sponsored sales conventions and formed Walker Clubs, whose members were required to perform community service and were awarded cash prizes according to their efforts. Walker herself was involved in a number of philanthropies. She made sizable contributions to the programs of the NAACP, the National Conference on Lynching, homes for the aged in St. Louis and Indianapolis, and the Indianapolis YMCA. In addition, she sponsored scholarships for young women at the Tuskegee Institute, contributed to the Palmer Memorial Institute, a private secondary school for African Americans in North Carolina, and led a fundraising effort on behalf of noted educator Mary McLeod Bethune's Daytona Educational Industrial Training School.

In 1917 Walker built Villa Lewaro, a country home designed by African-American architect Vertner Tandy, at Irvington-on-Hudson, New York. In 1919, despite her failing health, Walker was active in the ultimately unsuccessful efforts of civil rights groups to secure guarantees of equality for African Americans and self-determination for black Africans in the Treaty of Versailles. In the spring of 1919, Walker became ill while in St. Louis to launch a new line of products. She was taken to Villa Lewaro, where she died of kidney disease brought on by hypertension. She left an estate worth $2 million, two-thirds of which went to charities, educational institutions, and African-American civic organizations. Among the many tributes to her after her death was one from Mary McLeod Bethune, who called Walker's life "the clearest demonstration I know of Negro woman's ability recorded in history. She has gone, but her work...shall live as an inspiration to not only her race but to the world."

Sandra Day O'Connor

1930–

Ruth Bader Ginsburg

1933–

My hope is that ten years from now, after I've been across the street at work for a while, they'll all be glad they gave me that wonderful vote.

—SANDRA DAY O'CONNOR
After her unanimous confirmation
to the Supreme Court, 1981

Having experienced discrimination, she devoted the next twenty years of her career to fighting it and making this country a better place for our wives, our mothers, our sisters, and our daughters.

—PRESIDENT BILL CLINTON
On Ruth Bader Ginsburg's
nomination to the Supreme Court, 1993

In 1981 to fulfill a campaign pledge, President Ronald Reagan nominated Sandra Day O'Connor as the first woman justice to sit on the U.S. Supreme Court. Twelve years later, President Bill Clinton, in his first opportunity to name a replacement to the Court, nominated Ruth Bader Ginsburg. Two ideologically different presidents, both with a commitment to reflecting diversity on the Supreme Court, brought forward two women to serve in the highest judicial capacity in the nation. O'Connor broke new ground; Ginsburg raised the expectation that the future presence of women on the Court would be a norm rather than an exception.

Sandra Day O'Connor was born in El Paso, Texas, and grew up on a ranch on the Arizona–New Mexico border. She was educated at home by her mother and was later sent to live with her grandmother in El Paso, Texas, where she attended school. She entered Stanford University at sixteen and earned her undergraduate and law degrees in five years. On graduation, she was rejected by law firms in San Francisco and Los Angeles because she was a woman. She married law school classmate John Jay O'Connor, and they both worked as lawyers in Frankfurt, Germany, for three years. In 1957 they moved to Phoenix, Arizona, and O'Connor halted her career for four years to raise their three sons. She went back to work, joking, "I decided I should go back to paid employment to get a little peace and quiet in my life." She served first as an assistant attorney general in Arizona and then as a state senator. She was appointed to the Arizona Court of Appeals, where she earned a strong reputation as an advocate for women, the poor, and the mentally ill. In 1981 President Reagan selected O'Connor as his nominee because of her experience in all three branches of government and for her reputation for taking difficult positions on issues in which she believed strongly.

Born in Flatbush, Brooklyn, Ruth Bader Ginsburg was the younger daughter of orthodox Jewish immigrants. Her older sister, Marilyn, died at the age of eight, and Ruth grew up an only child. Her father was a furrier. Her mother, who wished that she could have gone on to college, refused to teach Ruth how to cook to encourage her to choose a career over homemaking. As a child, Ginsburg was acutely aware of anti-Semitism and once related to an interviewer her memories of seeing signs in restaurants which read, "No dogs or Jews allowed." She attended Brooklyn's James Madison High School and Cornell University, where she met her future husband, Martin Ginsburg. Both went on to Harvard Law School. At Harvard, Justice Ginsburg has recalled, she was invited to a professor's home with nine other female law students and asked why they were taking up men's spots at the school. When Martin Ginsburg was offered a job in New York City, Ruth Ginsburg transferred to Columbia Law School where she became a member of the law review and graduated first in her class. Because she was a woman and a mother, she had difficulty obtaining a position with a law firm. She turned to teaching, and in 1971 became Harvard Law School's first tenured woman professor. She also organized and led the American Civil Liberties Union's Women's Rights Project, arguing six cases concerning women's rights before the Supreme Court and winning five of them. One admirer has stated that Ginsburg "created the intellectual foundations for the present law of sex discrimination." Another has claimed that Ginsburg "is to the women's movement what former Supreme Court Justice Thurgood Marshall was to the movement for the rights of African Americans." In 1980 Ginsburg was appointed by President Carter to the U.S. Court of Appeals for the District of Columbia. Nominated for the Supreme Court by President Clinton in 1993, she was confirmed by a vote of ninety-six to three and became the first Jewish justice to sit on the Court in twenty-four years.

O'Connor's history on the Court since 1981 has earned her a reputation consistent with her pledge when confirmed "to do equal right to the poor and to the rich." She has avoided the tag of consistently voting with either conservative or liberal justices. In one case, she wrote the opinion that a state nursing school could not restrict a male nursing student from entering and warned that it was important not to make "inaccurate assumptions about the proper roles of men and women." In the notorious American–flag-burning case, she was on the minority side that did not feel that flag burning was protected by the First Amendment. Both sides in the debate over abortion have lobbied hard to claim her support. In the early 1990s she emerged as the leading figure of a centrist bloc of justices who, in 1992, upheld most of the provisions of *Roe v. Wade.*

Justice Ginsburg has yet to establish a similar history on the Court. President Clinton marked her as a consensus-building moderate, and Ginsburg has praised conservative Chief Justice Reinquist for deciding on facts and law despite unpopular decisions. When she appeared before the Senate Judiciary Committee as it considered her nomination, she stated her belief that the courts had a role to play on social issues when the political process failed. Her response to the tinder-box issue of abortion was that the right of a woman to have an abortion was based on the equal protection clause of the Fourteenth Amendment of the Constitution.

During the course of their careers, both O'Connor and Ginsburg have shown their determination to serve justice and to overcome prejudice and restrictions based on gender. But both have also proven that women are neither monolithic in attitude nor uniform in experience. O'Connor and Ginsburg each bring to the Court perspectives as varied and as richly influenced by past experience as those of their male colleagues. If they are in any way representational, it not as "the first woman" or "the second," but as a concept of diversity that has finally become a reality.

88

Diane Arbus

1923–1971

> Most people go through life dreading they'll have a traumatic experience. Freaks were born with their trauma. They've already passed their test in life.
>
> —DIANE ARBUS
> Quoted by Patricia Bosworth
> in *Diane Arbus*

Diane Arbus is renowned for her extraordinary, disconcerting photographic studies of ordinary people and especially of people who were once disparagingly called "freaks": giants, midgets, dwarfs, sideshow fat ladies, nudists, and transvestites. Arbus's complete acceptance of what she saw gave her access to the unapproachable and set her work apart from the few photographers who had previously documented nontraditional members of society. Her pictures earned her an international reputation and brought new dimensions to the art of documentary photographic portraiture.

Arbus was born in New York City, the second of three children of David and Gertrude Nemerov. Her father was the owner of Russeks Fifth Avenue, a fashionable women's clothing and fur store founded in the 1890s by his father-in-law, a Polish immigrant. In 1940 Diane graduated from the progressive Fieldston School in the Bronx, but she did not go on to college. Instead, she briefly studied fashion drawing, and at eighteen married Allan Arbus, a paste-up designer in the Russeks advertising department. After receiving a camera from her husband shortly after their marriage, Arbus took a short course with the celebrated photographer Berenice Abbott. Arbus and her husband studied the work of major photographers, then embarked upon a successful career in fashion photography. She set up the shots, while he handled the technical side.

Diane Arbus hated working in such a competitive field and quit in 1957. Resolved to focus on her own work, she began to take pictures on the streets of New York, but her shyness made it difficult for her to approach people. A two-year course with Austrian-born documentary photographer Lisette Model helped her to identify her subject, described by her daughter, Doon, as "the forbidden." Arbus separated from her husband in 1960 and moved with her two daughters into her own apartment. The couple remained friends, however, and Allan Arbus continued to refine Diane's skills in the technical craft of photography. They divorced in 1969.

Arbus was fascinated by her subjects, whom she saw, writes Catherine Lord in *Notable American Women*, as "unprotected by the invisibility of normality," whether by birth (in the case of giants and dwarfs) or by choice (in the case of transvestites, prostitutes, and nudists). Working with these people also revealed to her the flaw in the concept of one's public persona, the gap between, as she stated in a 1972 *Aperture* monograph, "what you want people to know about you and what you can't help people knowing about you." Genuinely curious about her subjects, she disarmed them into posing for her, making friends with them in the process.

Arbus won two Guggenheim Fellowships, in 1963 and 1966, and between 1965 and 1971, taught at the Parsons School of Design, Cooper Union, and Hampshire College. From 1970 to 1971, she taught privately. She also produced photographs for such magazines as *Esquire* and *Harper's Bazaar*. Throughout the 1960s, her reputation grew steadily among photographers, and she gained many new fans and imitators after a 1967 exhibition at the Museum of Modern Art. Her last subjects were the mentally retarded, described by Arbus as "enveloped in innocence." In 1971 the forty-eight-year-old Arbus committed suicide. Her death made her a cult figure, and a posthumous exhibition at the Museum of Modern Art in 1972 drew large crowds. That same year, Diane Arbus became the first American photographer to be included in the Venice Biennale.

Diane Arbus's work has been regarded as both shocking and intriguing, voyeuristic and compassionate. How the viewer sees her portraits may ultimately depend on how he or she views the subjects of them. To Arbus, they were nothing less than "aristocrats."

89

The tomb of Empress Wu Chao and her husband Emperor Gao Zong

Wu Chao

625–705(?)

China's only woman ruler, the Empress Wu was a
remarkably skilled and able politician, but her
murderous and illicit methods of maintaining power
gave her a bad repute.

—JOHN FAIRBANKS
China: A New History

Empress Wu ranks here as the only woman in Chinese history to rule exclusively in her own name. Her fifty-year rule during the early years of China's historically significant T'ang dynasty was a period of peace and prosperity marked by major reforms. At the same time, she held on to her power with a ruthless determination. Called the "most indomitable of Chinese women," Empress Wu has been admired for her achievements and simultaneously criticized for her excessive violence and favoritism.

Born and raised in Shansi province, Wu Chao was the beautiful daughter of a general who had served the first T'ang emperor, Kao Tsu, in the wars to establish his dynasty. At thirteen she was summoned to the palace of the Emperor T'ai Tsung as a junior concubine. Legend has it that the ascent of a woman to the throne had been foretold to the emperor, and that when a fortune-teller first saw Wu Chao, he declared she would be empress. After T'ai Tsung's death in 649, all his concubines dutifully followed tradition and entered a convent, where they were expected to spend the rest of their lives. Wu, however, was recalled from the convent by T'ai Tsung's heir, Kao Tsung. As Kao Tsung's favorite wife and the mother of his four sons, the ambitious Wu easily supplanted the childless empress. She dominated the weak and ailing emperor, who allowed her to administer the government, and took steps to appoint officials loyal to her and to eliminate all other concubines and opposition, including members of her own and the imperial family.

In 660, after Kao Tsung was further weakened by the first in a series of paralytic strokes, Wu Chao cemented her control over the government and, with the aid of military leaders she had appointed, successfully concluded China's war with Korea. During the inevitable power struggle that followed Kao Tsung's death in 683, Wu Chao's authority was threatened by the new emperor, her son Chung, and his wife, Wei. Wu Chao continued to govern with the loyal support of the army. She eventually exiled Chung, maintaining control through her second son, Jui. Although she defied tradition by usurping the throne in 690, there was no revolt, and for the next fifteen years she reigned supreme.

During Wu's reign, the T'ang Empire was unified, and the military aristocracy was replaced by a scholarly meritocratic bureaucracy, in which positions were filled through examination rather than by the traditional method of inheritance. Wu Chao's reign was also distinguished by high cultural achievement in art and architecture. In her later years the empress fell under the influence of a series of favorites, whose power over her led to their deaths and her downfall. She recalled her son Chung to be her heir in 698, and seven years later was persuaded to retire to her summer palace where she died at the age of eighty. That Wu Chao achieved such power and ruled so successfully in a society that asserted that men alone should rule is a testament to her considerable ruthlessness, determination, cunning, and skill. Her remarkable achievement has justly earned her a reputation as one of the strongest leaders in Chinese history.

90

Billie Holiday

1915–1959

With few exceptions, every major pop singer in the
United States during her generation has been touched
in some way by her genius. It is Billie Holiday...who
was and still remains the greatest single musical
influence on me.

—FRANK SINATRA

Regarded by most jazz critics as the greatest jazz singer ever
recorded, Billie Holiday revolutionized vocal performing, taking
it from the accompaniment position of the big band "girl singer"
to center stage and the main attraction. Her highly emotional

renditions and skill in improvisation are the hallmarks of the great jazz soloist. Vocal artists as far-ranging in style as Sarah Vaughn, Lena Horne, Carmen McRae, and Frank Sinatra have been influenced by her. Others continue to be judged by her standard.

Born Eleanora Fagan to teenagers Sadie Fagan and Clarence Holiday, who married when she was about three years old, Billie grew up in Baltimore raised by her mother and other relatives. She took the name "Billie" in honor of her screen idol, Billie Dove. Her father, who never lived with the family, was a guitarist with the Fletcher Henderson orchestra. Before she was ten, Holiday began working for the proprietress of a local brothel, performing menial chores and errands. It was here that she first heard the recordings of Bessie Smith and Louis Armstrong, who would become major influences on her singing career. As she said, "I always wanted Bessie's sound and Pop's feeling." In 1927, after completing a fifth-grade education, she joined her mother in New York City and worked as a maid and possibly as a prostitute. She sought work as a dancer in Harlem nightclubs, and in one club she was also encouraged to sing. Accompanied solely by a piano, she began to perform at various New York clubs for a few dollars a night plus tips.

Holiday's style was unique from the start. Instead of the high-volume dramatics of Smith and Armstrong, she offered subtlety and nuance, and was given the nickname Lady for the dignity of her bearing and her delivery. In 1933 Holiday was discovered by jazz enthusiast and record producer John Hammond, who arranged her first recordings within twenty-four hours after producing Bessie Smith's final album. Hammond recalled that Holiday "was not a blues singer, but she sang popular songs in a manner that made them completely her own. She had an uncanny ear, an excellent memory for lyrics, and she sang with an exquisite sense of phrasing." In 1935 she appeared in Duke Ellington's short film, *Symphony in Black*, and made her stage debut at the Apollo Theater in Harlem. She began to tour with the Count Basie and Artie Shaw bands, becoming one of the first black performers in Shaw's otherwise all-white band.

While on tour throughout the country, Holiday experienced both racial prejudice and the sexism of the male-dominated jazz world. Jazz was still considered disreputable both inside and outside the musical community, and it carried the strong association of the brothel and the speakeasy. Women performers had to earn the respect of the male players, and performing, particularly in the South with a white band such as Shaw's, was dangerous. Holiday survived the stigma attached to the genre and responded to discrimination with forthright determination, maintaining a fierce pride in being black and a performer. During Harlem jam sessions, she met many notable jazz musicians, including saxophonist Lester Young, with whom she formed a close and lasting friendship. It was Young who gave her the enduring nickname Lady Day. As one observer of Holiday's recording sessions with Young recalled, "To hear her sing along with Lester Young, while he was playing a chorus, was something to make your toes curl. No words; she just scatted along with his tenor sax as though she was another horn."

From 1937 to 1941 Holiday performed regularly at Café Society in Greenwich Village, a club opened for the purpose of providing entertainment to integrated audiences. There, Holiday adopted as her closing number "Strange Fruit," a song about lynching, in which hanging bodies are described as "strange fruit," the "bitter crops" of Southern racial politics. Because of the unusual directness of its powerful message, Columbia Records refused to let Holiday record the song, but she was able to release it on the independent Commodore label. On the Decca label, Holiday recorded her most famous songs, "Lover Man" and her own compositions, "God Bless the Child" and "Don't Explain." In 1947 Holiday entered a clinic to try to kick a drug addiction that had escalated after her 1941 marriage to nightclub manager Jimmy Monroe, whom she divorced in 1949. Three weeks after her discharge, she was arrested for narcotics possession and served nine and one-half months at Alderton, the federal reformatory for women in West Virginia. Upon her release, her cabaret license in New York City was revoked, and Holiday could no longer perform in local clubs. Instead, she toured outside New York and in Europe.

During the 1950s, Holiday continued to perform, and she recorded over a hundred songs for the Verve label. Although these were standards and remakes of her earlier numbers, they showed her great ability to reinterpret past renditions. She married her manager, Louis McKay, in 1956, and both were arrested the same year; Holiday for narcotics possession and McKay on a weapons offense. She continued to record and perform although her health and her voice had become increasingly debilitated by drugs and alcohol. In 1959 she was admitted to Metropolitan Hospital in New York, a victim of drug and alcohol abuse, and was arrested in her hospital bed for narcotics possession. She died of liver failure in July 1959.

Holiday's life was a sad litany of neglect, divorce, arrests, and addiction, interspersed by remarkable vocal and musical achievements. She was a unique performer whose accomplishments were earned at great personal cost. As jazz performer Anita Day observed, Billie Holiday remains "the one true genius among jazz singers.... Only somebody who'd gone through the things she did and survived, could sing from the soul the way she did."

91

Helen Gurley Brown

1922– 2012

How would I most like to use my influence?...I want to
convince women that so much is *possible*, not on a grand
scale, but just by doing a little every day. And pretty
soon you get further, you make more money, people are
listening to you more, and you have more friends, it just
all falls into place. I want to inspire and encourage.

—HELEN GURLEY BROWN
From an interview with Roy Newquist
for his 1967 book *Conversations*

In 1965, when American women were barely beginning the struggle of defining themselves within a newly revived women's movement, and single "girls" were starting to take up positions on the barricades of the sexual revolution, forty-three-year-old Helen Gurley Brown became editor-in-chief of the ailing housewife-oriented magazine *Cosmopolitan*. Brown, a former advertising account executive and copywriter, had no editing experience. She had, however, written a 1962 runaway bestseller, *Sex and the Single Girl*, a guide offering advice on, as she put it, "how to stay single in superlative style." Brown changed the format of *Cosmopolitan*, moving its appeal away from the housewife toward the new single career woman between the ages of eighteen and thirty-four. That "*Cosmo* girl," said Brown, "looks as good as she can, works as hard as she can, and the smarter she is, the better off she is." Under Brown's editorship, *Cosmopolitan* became—and remains—one of the most successful magazines in the world. Clearly, when *Cosmo* began to burble about the joys of love, lust, and loot, women were more than ready to listen.

Helen Gurley Brown was born in Green Forest, Arkansas, one of two daughters born to school teachers Cleo and Ira Gurley. After her father was elected to the state legislature, the family divided their time between Green Forest and Little Rock. Ira Gurley died when Helen was ten, and the family moved to Los Angeles where Cleo Gurley intended to resume her teaching career. She had to abandon her plans, however, when Helen's sister, Mary, came down with polio. Like many others who grew up during the Depression, Brown developed a nagging sense of insecurity and of being underprivileged, which manifested itself in a drive to excel. In high school she wrote for school publications, became president of the Scholarship Society, and graduated in 1939 as valedictorian.

A lack of finances forced Brown to return to Los Angeles after only one semester at a Texas college. From 1940 to 1941, she studied shorthand and typing at Woodbury Business College and worked part time answering fan mail at a local radio station. She later described herself during this time as a "mouseburger." "I was a little tyke of eighteen—flat-chested, pale, acne-skinned, terrified, and convinced of one thing only: Working in an office was practically the most gruesome thing that could happen to a woman."

In 1948, after working at eighteen different secretarial jobs, Brown secured a position as an executive secretary to Don Belding, chairman of the board of the advertising agency, Foot, Cone & Belding. While at the agency, Brown decided that she wanted to become a copywriter. Impressed by the liveliness of her letters to him during his business trips, Belding gave her the chance to fulfill her ambition. In 1957 she won the first of three Frances Holmes Advertising Copywriters awards, and in 1958, she joined Kenyon & Eckhardt as an account executive and copywriter, becoming the highest paid woman in advertising on the West Coast. The following year, she married film producer David Brown, who had been an editor at *Liberty* magazine and *Cosmopolitan*.

With the publication of *Sex and the Single Girl*, whose concept and title had been suggested by David Brown, Helen Gurley Brown became the acknowledged standard-bearer for single women. "Nobody was championing them," she later told Newquist. "Volumes had been written about this creature, but they all treated the single girl like a scarlet-fever victim, a misfit, and...you can't really categorize one-third of the female population as misfits." Brown followed up the success of *Sex and the Single Girl* with the equally popular *Sex and the Office* (1964), and in 1970 published *Sex and the New Single Girl*, a sequel to her first book. Brown also wrote a syndicated column, "Woman Alone," in which she answered fan mail generated by *Sex and the Single Girl* and dispersed advice on fashion, grooming, careers, and men. The column led to a 1966 book, *Helen Gurley Brown's Outrageous Opinions*, and a TV celebrity interview show, *Outrageous Opinions*, hosted by Brown.

In 1964 the Browns created a format for a women's magazine to be called *Femme*. After being rejected by several publishers because of the enormous expense required to launch such a magazine, the format was brought by Bernard Geis, Helen Gurley Brown's publisher, to Richard Deems, the president of the Hearst Corporation. Deems felt the format could be superimposed onto the foundering *Cosmopolitan* and named Helen Gurley Brown editor-in-chief of the magazine. With *Cosmopolitan*'s steady rise in circulation came condemnation of its new format. Critics charged that Brown had turned the magazine into a women's version of *Playboy*, and feminist leader Betty Friedan castigated *Cosmopolitan* for debasing women: "Instead of urging women to live a broader life, it is an immature teenage-level sexual fantasy. It is the idea that woman is nothing but a sex object." Given the magazine's notorious 1972 centerfold featuring a strategically naked Burt Reynolds, its ubiquitous covers of sexily-clad models, and the narcissistic promises of its yearly "Bedside Astrologer," such criticisms seem fairly justified. But Brown, who once stated that she considered herself a feminist, was the first to give unmarried young women a feeling of inclusion in a society that wrote them off as deviants. *Cosmopolitan's* considerable influence lies in its ability to tell its readers, some twelve million of them, exactly what they perceive they need to hear.

92

Julia Morgan

1872–1957

This great Californian, who designed not only San
Simeon, but more than seven hundred other buildings
in her long career...deserves in American architecture
at least as high a place as Mary Cassatt in American
painting or Edith Wharton in American letters.

—ALLAN TEMKO,
architecture critic

Julia Morgan, the prolific and innovative architect, whose
success helped pave the way for women in architecture, was born
in San Francisco and grew up in Oakland, the second child in a
family of two girls and three boys. Her family was a wealthy one,
owing to the considerable inheritance of her mother, Eliza
Parmalee Morgan, the daughter of a millionaire New York cotton

broker. Her father, Bill Morgan, tried his hand at a number of business enterprises without much success. Julia and her younger sister, Emma, were early encouraged by their mother to achieve, and both were excellent students. Morgan was a small, shy, frail-looking child, who nevertheless possessed an iron will. She circumvented her parents' protectiveness after her recovery from a severe mastoid infection and defied their attempts to impose proper feminine behavior upon her by stealing forbidden work-outs on her brothers' gym equipment and performing daring athletic feats in the family barn.

Morgan's interest in architecture was stimulated by architect Pierre Le Brun, her mother's cousin and the designer of the Metropolitan Life Insurance Tower in New York. After her graduation from Oakland High School, Morgan became the first woman student admitted to the College of Engineering at the University of California at Berkeley. Although the college's curriculum included courses taught in architecture schools, Morgan felt she needed to learn more about architectural decoration and the creation and manipulation of space. After graduating with a B.S. degree in civil engineering in 1894, Morgan studied and worked with architect Bernard Maybeck, who taught descriptive geometry at the university and also offered informal classes in architecture at his home.

Maybeck urged Morgan to apply to the prestigious École des Beaux-Arts in Paris, and in 1898, after her third attempt to pass the entrance exam, she became the first woman student to be admitted to the school's architectural section. During her three years there, Morgan was awarded four medals for outstanding work in design and drawing, and in 1901 became the first woman to graduate from the school. She returned to California in 1902 and obtained her architect's license, becoming the first woman in the state to do so. She then went to work for architect John Galen Howard, who boasted that in Morgan he had, "the best and most talented designer, whom I have to pay almost nothing, as it is a woman," Despite her status as an important member of Howard's staff and the chance to work on two important University of California projects—a Greek theater and the building housing the school of mining—Morgan grew increasingly dissatisfied by the lack of recognition from her male colleagues and decided to open her own architecture office.

Morgan's decision to set up her own business was fueled in part by encouragement from philanthropist Phoebe Apperson Hearst, who had befriended Morgan in Paris and had provided the financing for Howard's University of California projects. Mrs. Hearst, the mother of newspaper magnate William Randolph Hearst and an active supporter of feminist causes, was impressed by Morgan's talent and steered her toward some of her early commissions. These included the design of two buildings on Mrs. Hearst's estate and a Mission-style bell tower for Mills College, Mrs. Hearst's alma mater. Morgan also designed several informal redwood-shingled homes with tasteful, unostentatious outer detailing and inner space tailored to the client's needs.

In 1906 Morgan was asked to rebuild the luxurious Fairmont Hotel, which had been severely damaged during the San Francisco earthquake. Her work on the hotel established her reputation and led to numerous other commissions. Over the next decade she designed houses, stores, churches, offices, and educational buildings, including the Berkeley Baptist Seminary and a library, gymnasium, and social building for Mills College. From 1908 to 1910 she worked on St. John's Presbyterian Church, a rambling, shingled building that is a Berkeley architectural landmark. She also designed residence halls throughout California for the YWCA, as well as the organization's Asilomar Conference Center in Pacific Grove.

After World War I, Morgan began her work for William Randolph Hearst, who had taken control of the Hearst fortune following his mother's death from influenza. For almost twenty years, in addition to her regular practice, Morgan built a castle and guest houses on the Hearst family ranch, and designed Hearst newspaper facilities and mansions in California and Mexico. Building San Simeon was a challenging task, which required incorporating architectural sections of castles and monasteries bought by Hearst in Europe. It also required dealing with Hearst's whims regarding the placement of design elements. Although Morgan and Hearst frequently differed, they developed a strong relationship based upon mutual admiration.

One of Morgan's non-Hearst commissions, as well as one of her most famous, was the 1929 construction of the Berkeley City Club, a handsome women's club-hotel, whose detailing reflected elements of Hearst's castle at San Simeon. During the 1930s,

Morgan continued to maintain personal control over every aspect of her numerous commissions, despite the debilitating effects of a botched mastoid operation, which left one side of her face permanently paralyzed and profoundly affected her speech and balance. She collaborated with her old mentor, Bernard Maybeck, on a design for the new campus of Principia College in Illinois and designed YWCAs in Salt Lake City and Honolulu. In 1937 she stopped working for Hearst, whose publishing empire had fallen into financial difficulty. During World War II she was forced to reduce her practice due to a shortage of labor and materials. She retired in 1946 and traveled extensively until her death from a stroke in 1957.

Quiet, modest, and completely dedicated to her work, Julia Morgan's social life revolved around her family, with whom she was very close. She ran her office in the atelier style, making it a learning place for those who worked for her. She was not active in the feminist movement, but she employed many women architects and drafters, and gave financial support to women students.

Morgan was a creatively eclectic and original architect, who worked in a variety of motifs, although her favorite style was Spanish Revival. Her early work demonstrated a unique talent for taking architectural traditions of the American West, such as Spanish and Native American, and integrating them with the sophisticated Beaux-Arts style in which she had been trained. She was the first architect of her era to use structure as a means of architectural expression, and she is recognized by architectural scholars as one of the leading form-givers of her region, perfectly embodying the concept of architect as artist. She was, as the citation that accompanied her 1929 honorary Berkeley degree stated, an architect "in whose works harmony and admirable proportions bring pleasure to the eye and peace to the mind."

93

Rosa Bonheur

1822–1899

I don't know what Rosalie will be, but I have a
conviction that she will be no ordinary woman.

—RAYMOND BONHEUR
On his seven-year-old daughter, Rosa Bonheur
Quoted in Theodore Stanton,
Reminiscences of Rosa Bonheur

Rosa Bonheur lived up to her father's conviction, achieving recognition as one of the foremost woman artists of the nineteenth century. Denied training because of her sex, she nevertheless perfected her art, producing informed and sympathetic paintings of animals and winning international acclaim for the distinctive power of her work.

Born in Bordeaux, France, Rosa Bonheur was the oldest child of painter Raymond Oscar-Marie and Sophie Marquis Bonheur. As a young child, Rosa loved animals and frequently played in the horse stables. She was allowed to draw on the white walls of her room, and she quickly filled them with remarkable studies of animals. The Bonheurs relocated to Paris when Rosa was seven. Four years later her mother died, and the family was split apart. Bonheur's brothers were enrolled in boarding school and her sister was sent to live with family friends in Bordeaux. Rosa refused to be apprenticed to a seamstress and begged her father to send her to the same boarding school as her brothers. Raymond Bonheur obtained a scholarship for his daughter in exchange for his services as a drawing instructor, but the arrangement ended when Rosa was expelled from the school for her rebellious behavior.

Rosa Bonheur wanted to become an artist, but she was initially discouraged in her ambition by her father, who knew from experience the financial difficulties faced by artists, especially women. Nevertheless, he gave in to his determined daughter and began teaching her drawing, painting, sculpture, and engraving in his studio. He encouraged her to develop her unique talent for painting from nature and sent her on excursions to the Louvre where she would spend the day copying paintings.

Rosa Bonheur exhibited her work for the first time in the Paris Salon of 1841. Her exhibit included bronze sculptures of rabbits, sheep, and goats, and a painting, *Rabbits Nibbling Carrots*, a characteristic depiction of animals rendered with scrupulous realism. Three animal paintings made in 1842 drew great critical and public acclaim, and from then on Bonheur exhibited her works annually. In 1848 she was chosen by her fellow artists as a member of the hanging committee of the Fine Arts Society, and the following year she succeeded her father as director of l'Ecole

Impériale de Dessin, where her sister, Juliette, was an instructor. In 1849 she produced *Plowing in the Nivernais*, which was bought for the Louvre. In 1855 she completed her most famous work, *The Horse Fair*, a huge canvas that became so popular that Queen Victoria requested a private viewing.

To make her paintings as realistic as possible, Bonheur cut up animal parts she obtained from butcher shops and visited slaughterhouses, dressed as a man. In general, Bonheur preferred to wear men's clothes, a preference she shared with her contemporary, author George Sand, whom she greatly admired. In 1852 Bonheur won police permission to wear male dress.

Bonheur deliberately avoided marriage, and in 1853 bought a chateau near Fountainbleau where she lived with her friend Nathalie Micas for forty years. At the chateau, Bonheur assembled a menagerie of horses, sheep, gazelles, bulls, monkeys, and a lion, all of which would become favorite subjects for her paintings. In 1865 Bonheur became the first woman ever to receive the medal of the French Legion of Honor. Fascinated by the American Wild West, Bonheur painted showman Buffalo Bill Cody when he visited the Paris Exposition in 1889. She also won international awards, and was visited by royalty and by leading figures in society.

What is striking about Bonheur's work is its unexpectedness. Her choice of subject was an unusual one for a woman artist of her era. The lively strength and grace of her canvasses leave behind the notion that watercolors and miniatures were the only metier of nineteenth-century woman artists. An individualist, Bonheur painted what she loved with a control and passion.

The highest praise offered to Rosa Bonheur in her lifetime was that she painted "like a man." Because of Bonheur's influence and the stylistic barriers she broke, art and the role of the artist were wrestled from the exclusive province of only one sex.

94

Mary Pickford

1893–1979

I do not know who first called Mary Pickford "America's Sweetheart," but, whoever he was, he put in two words the most remarkable personal achievement of its kind in the history of motion pictures.

—CECIL B. DeMILLE
From the Foreword to Mary Pickford's autobiography, *Sunshine and Shadow*

Cecil B. DeMille's tribute to Mary Pickford was more than just a generous contribution to an old friend's autobiography: It was the truth. When sixteen-year-old Pickford abandoned her eleven-year stage career in 1909 to appear in movies, she became the first movie star and began a twenty-year reign as the world's most beloved female film actress. Her stardom unleashed a juggernaut of celebrity adoration that has profoundly affected American culture and shows no signs of diminishing.

Mary Pickford's appeal as a silent-screen heroine would not be well understood by the vast majority of today's moviegoers. Her screen image—childlike, sweet, demure, with a touch of mischievousness, and a great deal of spunk—belongs to a completely different era. In an age that prided itself on its innocence, "Little Mary," was acclaimed as the feminine ideal. As pundit Alistair Cooke once put it, "She was the girl every young man wanted to have—as his sister."

Although Mary Pickford primarily played children or young girls, off screen she was an enterprising adult who knew how to negotiate a contract. On her own initiative, her salary jumped from $40 a week in 1914 to an unprecedented $10,000 a week less than two years later. Producer Sam Goldwyn once stated, "It took longer to make one of Mary's contracts than it did to make one of her pictures." Financial security was all-important to Pickford, who had been her family's primary breadwinner since the age of six.

Mary Pickford was born Gladys Louise Smith in Toronto, Canada, the eldest child of John and Charlotte Smith. Pickford was five when her father, a laborer, was killed in a work-related accident and her mother was left destitute with three children to support. To make ends meet, Charlotte Smith took in sewing and rented a spare room to lodgers, one of whom was the stage manager of a Toronto theater company. He hired Pickford and her sister, Lottie, for roles in a play entitled *The Silver King*. Other roles in stock company productions followed for "Baby Gladys Smith," as she was billed, and, except for six months of schooling, Pickford spent her childhood either performing in Toronto or on the road. Her mother, sister, and brother, Jack, usually accompanied Pickford on road tours, and the whole family appeared on stage together in a famous play of the time, *The Fatal Wedding*.

Pickford became extremely close to her mother during her childhood and teen years, but in many ways, the relationship was one of equals rather than of mother and daughter. Pickford had taken on the adult responsibility of family provider early in life, and while this strengthened her bond with her mother, it also robbed her of a real childhood. For Pickford, the need to make money was a constant, overriding concern. When work in stock companies dried up, the fourteen-year-old Pickford traveled to New York alone and approached famed producer David Belasco for a job. He changed her name to Mary Pickford and gave her a part in his Broadway production of *The Warrens of Virginia*.

After the play's run, work again became scarce and funds low, and Charlotte Smith convinced her daughter to try acting in movies. Although Pickford felt that films were inferior to the theater, she agreed to apply for a job at Biograph Studios, headed by D. W. Griffith. The director, known as much for his blunt, often volatile personality as he was for his genius, informed Pickford that "You're too little and too fat, but I may give you a chance." Despite this inauspicious beginning, Pickford went to work for Griffith, and except for a stint at the Independent Motion Picture Company, remained at Biograph as the Biograph Girl until 1912.

After appearing in another Belasco Broadway production, *A Good Little Devil*, Pickford joined Adolph Zukor's Famous Players film company (later to become Paramount Pictures); Pickford called this period "the happiest years of my life." While at Famous Players, she starred in such signature films as *Tess of the Storm Country, Poor Little Rich Girl, Rebecca of Sunnybrook Farm*, and *A Little Princess*. In 1918 she became the first female movie star to head her own independent movie company when she and her mother formed the Mary Pickford Film Corporation. A year later, Pickford joined Charlie Chaplin, Douglas Fairbanks, and D. W. Griffith to form United Artists.

Pickford's popularity continued to soar, as did her salary. By 1920 "the girl with the golden curls" was a multimillionaire. Her best-known movies from the years 1919 to 1929 include *The Taming of the Shrew, Pollyanna, Little Lord Fauntleroy*, and her first talkie, *Coquette*, for which she won an Oscar. After making *Secrets* with Leslie Howard in 1933, Pickford retired from the screen to concentrate on producing, writing, and charity work. In 1953 she and Chaplin sold United Artists. Her last public appearance was at the 1976 Academy Awards where she received a special Oscar for her services to the film industry.

Mary Pickford was married three times. Her first marriage to handsome, alcoholic Biograph actor Owen Moore lasted five years. In 1920 she married swashbuckling movie star Douglas Fairbanks, whose wedding present to her was Pickfair, a mansion in Beverly Hills. The two were lionized as Hollywood's fairy-tale couple, and during their travels in the United States, Europe, and Russia they were constantly mobbed by crowds of adoring fans. The fairy tale ended with their divorce in 1936, and soon afterward, both remarried. Pickford's third marriage, to actor-bandleader Buddy Rogers, was her happiest and lasted until her death in 1979. Pickford's fortune at her death was estimated to be $50 million.

Mary Pickford's influence on the film industry was considerable. Her combination of childlike charm and hard-headed business acumen made her a singular presence on and off the screen. As Cecil B. DeMille wrote in his foreword to *Sunshine and Shadow*, "There have been hundreds of stars, there have been scores of fine actresses in motion pictures. There has been only one Mary Pickford."

95

Maria Callas

1923–1977 *53*

She was not just a singer, but a complete artist. It's foolish to discuss her as a voice. She must be viewed totally—as a complex of music, drama, and movement. There is no one like her today. She was an aesthetic phenomenon.

—ANTONIO VOTTO, conductor
Quoted in Ariana Stassinopoulos,
Maria Callas

Soprano Maria Callas, the last legendary, truly larger-than-life diva, reigned as the *prima donna assoluta* of opera for twenty years, adulated even after her voice had lost its power. She was responsible for the reintroduction of the largely forgotten bel canto operas of such nineteenth-century composers as Bellini, Donizetti, and Rossini, whose works had been considered too difficult and too musically uninteresting to merit revival. Callas not only showed that the operas could be sung, she transformed them from mere displays of vocal virtuosity into intensely felt works of dramatic art. She brought theater to opera and opened up a whole new repertory for future singers.

Maria Callas was born Maria Kalogeropoulas in New York City, a few months after her parents and five-year-old sister arrived from Greece. Soon afterward, her parents changed their last name to Callas. Maria's childhood was unhappy, marred by interminable parental squabbles and her jealousy of her attractive sister, Jackie, who was her parents' favorite. Callas, short, squat, nearsighted, and shy, felt that her only asset was her remarkable voice.

At thirteen, accompanied by her mother and her sister, Callas moved to Athens, where she won a scholarship to the Athens Conservatory. There she studied with soprano Elvira de Hidalgo, who later described her as "square and fat, but she put such force, such sentiment, such wonderful interpretation into all she sang. She would want to sing the most difficult coloraturas, scales, and trills. Even as a child her willpower was terrific." Callas was fourteen when she sang the role of Santuzza in the Mascagni opera *Cavalleria Rusticana*, at the conservatory, and four years later she made her official debut with the newly founded Athens Opera.

In 1947 Callas gave her first important operatic performance, singing the title role in Ponchielli's *La Gioconda* at the Arena in Verona, Italy. The opera's conductor, Tullio Serafin, would become one of Callas's most important mentors. From Verona, Callas went on to perform in Venice and other cities, scoring dramatic and vocal triumphs in such roles as *Isolde, Turandot, Aida,* and especially as Bellini's *Norma*. In 1949 she married her manager, Giovanni Battista Meneghini, and during their ten years together was known professionally as Maria Meneghini Callas.

The 1950s and early 1960s represented the height of Callas's performing career. She appeared at the major opera houses—Milan's La Scala, London's Covent Garden, New York's Metropolitan—and secured numerous other international engagements. Among her most acclaimed roles were Bellini's *Norma*, Violetta in Verdi's *La Traviata*, Puccini's *Tosca*, Lucia in Donizetti's *Lucia di Lammermoor*, and Cherubini's *Medea*. Some of her best performances were directed by filmmakers Luchino Visconti and Franco Zeffirelli, and conducted by Leonard Bernstein, who once summed up Callas's magnetic on-stage presence in two words: "pure electricity."

Her electrifying presence won Callas a host of adoring admirers, although critical reaction to her performances was usually mixed because of the often uneven technical quality of her voice. She was sometimes said to have three voices: at the top, it could be shrill, with high notes that were little more than shrieks; the middle register might have a beautiful covered or velvety sound; in the lowest register, it was imposing, if edgy. But her technical defects, which could be attributed to her minimal training, ultimately served to make her a more original and versatile performer, one whose burning emotional intensity and powerful musicianship made her, according to *New York Times* music critic Harold Schonberg, "the artist who lived her roles and made them come to life."

Callas's offstage life was equally dramatic. She fell out with colleagues she perceived had slighted her. A perfectionist, she summarily broke contracts when she felt she would be performing below her best. Such behavior led to several highly publicized altercations with managers, most notably Rudolf Bing of the Metropolitan, and earned her a reputation as a temperamental, mercurial *prima donna*. Callas also achieved "jet set" notoriety through her friendship with famous partygiver Elsa Maxwell and her affair with Greek shipping magnate Aristotle Onassis, for whom she left her husband in 1959. She retired from the stage in 1965. The affair with Onassis, who would not marry her and insisted that she abort their child, ended with his marriage to Jackie Kennedy in 1968.

In the late 1960s, Callas starred as a nonsinging Medea in Pier Paolo Pasolini's film version of the Euripedes play. In 1971 she gave a highly successful series of master classes at the Julliard

School in New York. Endeavoring to stage a comeback, Callas made extensive worldwide concert tours from 1973 to 1974 with tenor Giuseppe di Stefano. She was greeted, as usual, with almost hysterical adulation, and her interpretations remained unexcelled, even though there was not much left of her voice. The concerts were Callas's last public appearances. In the last few years of her life, unable to sing, emotionally spent, and physically fragile, Callas retreated to her Paris apartment, where she died of a heart attack at the age of fifty-three. "She exerted an influence on opera that was unique," wrote Schonberg after her death. "She looked on opera as theater as well as voice, and she was the one who put it all together."

96

Katharine Hepburn

1907– *2003*

[To teenagers] The Woman of the Year had become a
kind of guru. She had demystified old age, something
the young feared and did not like to be reminded might
some day befall them.

To those past fifty she remained one of the last
international figures who had been where they had been
and survived it with them....She had seen it all....She
represented continuum. She had come to symbolize
qualities that they had been taught as children to
recognize as heroic—integrity, strength, fearlessness,
dedication to friends and family and to ideals; not an
easy mark for cheats or deceivers.

—ANNE EDWARDS
A Remarkable Woman

The most distinguished, durable, independent, and individualistic actress in film history was born in Hartford, Connecticut,
the second of six children born to Dr. Thomas Hepburn and
Katharine Houghton Hepburn. The Hepburns were liberal
intellectuals, whose circle of friends included feminist Emmeline
Pankhurst, anarchist Emma Goldman, and novelist Sinclair
Lewis. Hepburn's mother scandalized conservative Hartford by
working for such controversial causes as birth control and women's suffrage and often brought her children along to political
meetings and demonstrations. In addition to political and intellectual consciousness raising, the Hepburns stressed the importance of sports, at which young Kate excelled.

In 1920, tragedy marred Hepburn's "most wonderful childhood," as she later termed it, when, on Easter Sunday, her older
brother, Tom, accidentally hanged himself in the attic. Hepburn,
who found the body, was devastated by the loss of her adored
brother and became moody and withdrawn. To lift her spirits,
her parents encouraged her interest in play-acting. At the same
time, they withdrew their headstrong daughter from public
school and provided her with a private tutor. At sixteen, she
arrived at Bryn Mawr College with an excellent education behind
her as well as great athletic prowess, but with few social skills. She
was an angular, awkward adolescent, who hid her profound
shyness beneath a haughty demeanor. "I was never a member of
the feminine club," she later recalled. "I never knew what other
girls were talking about." Hepburn took drama courses, appeared in college productions, and decided upon graduation to
pursue a career as an actress, to the dismay of her parents.

Hepburn's early New York stage appearances were dismal
failures. Her acting was artificial and extreme; she spoke her
lines too quickly in a voice that was high and tinny, and she
suffered from stage fright. There was also a brief, disastrous
marriage to Philadelphia socialite Ludlow Ogden Smith. The
breakthrough in Hepburn's career came in 1932, when she was
cast as the queen of the Amazons in a Broadway play, *The Warrior's
Husband.* Her beauty, athletic grace, and powerful presence
captivated audiences, and her success gave her much-needed
confidence. By playing an unconventional, emancipated, spirited
character, Hepburn also found her essence as an actress.

Hepburn's success in *The Warrior's Husband* led to a screen test at RKO Studios in Hollywood and a leading role opposite John Barrymore in *A Bill of Divorcement*, directed by George Cukor. Her performance as a sophisticated, judgmental young woman who meets her father, a former mental patient, for the first time, was hailed by the *New York Times* as "one of the finest characterizations seen on the screen." Although Katharine Hepburn was now a star, she clung to her privacy and refused to play the Hollywood game of endless self-promotion.

During the 1930s, Hepburn's most memorable roles included playing an aviator in *Christopher Strong*; an understudy who becomes a star in *Morning Glory*, a role that resulted in her first Academy Award; Jo in *Little Women*; a social-climbing small-town girl in *Alice Adams*; an aspiring actress in *Stage Door*; and a dithery but resourceful young woman who woos and wins shy paleontologist Cary Grant in the classic screwball comedy *Bringing Up Baby*.

By 1938, however, Hepburn's several flops weighed more heavily with audiences and studio executives than did her hits, and she was declared box office poison. To revive her flagging career, she joined forces with playwright Philip Barry and the Theater Guild in 1939 to produce Barry's *Philadelphia Story*. Hepburn scored a triumph as icy socialite Tracy Lord in both the stage and MGM movie versions of the play. As an added bonus, MGM offered her a lucrative long-term contract, which gave her the choice of leading man and director, story approval, and time off for stage work.

For her next project, *Woman of the Year*, Hepburn chose Spencer Tracy to play opposite her. The two fell in love but could not marry because Tracy, although separated from his wife, was a devout Catholic for whom divorce was unthinkable. Their twenty-five-year affair became a respected "open secret" in Hollywood. As a popular screen team, Hepburn and Tracy appeared together in such film favorites as *Adam's Rib*, *Pat and Mike*, *Desk Set*, and *Guess Who's Coming to Dinner*, completed a few weeks before Tracy's death.

In the 1950s, Hepburn's best screen work without Tracy was in *The African Queen*, *Summertime*, *The Rainmaker*, and *Suddenly, Last Summer*. She also appeared on stage in a number of Shakespeare's plays. In 1962 she took on the challenging role of morphine addict Mary Tyrone in the film version of Eugene

O'Neill's *Long Day's Journey Into Night*. The movie justly earned Hepburn a record ninth Academy Award nomination and praise from film critic Pauline Kael, who described her as "our greatest tragedienne." Hepburn won Oscars for her performances in *Guess Who's Coming to Dinner*, *The Lion in Winter*, and *On Golden Pond*. In 1970 she starred in her only Broadway musical, *Coco*, based on the life of fashion designer Coco Chanel.

Following a long standing ovation after her last performance of *Coco*, Hepburn told the audience, "Well—I love you and you love me and that's that." For over sixty years, the public has loved Katharine Hepburn the actress and Katharine Hepburn the woman. Her originality, vitality, and integrity on and off screen have, so far, been unmatched in the celebrity stratosphere.

97

Billie Jean King

1943–

Ever since that day when I was eleven years old and I wasn't allowed in the [tennis team] photo because I wasn't wearing a tennis skirt, I knew I wanted to change the sport.

—BILLIE JEAN KING
    Quoted in Marshall and Sue Burchard,
    Sports Hero: Billie Jean King

In 1973, a combined live and television audience of sixty million watched twenty-nine-year-old tennis star Billie Jean King demolish fifty-five-year-old tennis professional Bobby Riggs in three straight sets at the Houston Astrodome. King's prize was $100,000—the largest purse ever paid for a single tennis match at that time. Riggs, trading on his reputation as something of a prize boar among male chauvinist pigs, had boasted that a woman player, no matter how powerful, would never be able to beat a man, no matter how far past his prime. His defeat by King in what was billed as the "Battle of the Sexes" relegated him to the status of cultural oddity. For King, who would go on to win her sixth Wimbledon and fourth U.S. Open singles titles, it was one more victory in her fight for the equality of the sexes in sports, as well as another achievement in an already outstanding career.

Billie Jean King was born and raised in Long Beach, California. Her father, Bill Moffitt, was a firefighter; her mother, Betty, was an Avon cosmetics representative. Both parents were athletic, and, as a child, King played football and softball. Her skill at softball was such that whenever the fire department held a picnic, the men invited her to play on their softball game. Distressed at being dubbed a "tomboy" by other children, Billie Jean gave up softball at age eleven to concentrate on the more "ladylike" sport of tennis. She learned to play the game on the Long Beach public courts and received free lessons from coach Clyde Walker.

Six months after she started taking lessons, Billie Jean played in her first tournament at the Los Angeles Tennis Club. Despite her aggressiveness on the court, especially at the net, she did not win any tournaments until she was fifteen, when she won the Southern California girls fifteen-and-under championship. As a result, she was invited to play in the national championship for girls fifteen and under, where she advanced to the quarterfinals. In 1960 Billie Jean reached the finals of the national championship tournament, but lost to seventeen-year-old Karen Hantze. A year later, she teamed up with Hantze to win the women's doubles championship at Wimbledon. They were the youngest pair ever to win the event. In 1962 she and Hantze repeated their win and also helped the American women's team to victory in the Whightman Cup tournament.

In 1965 Billie Jean married Larry King, who became her agent, business manager, lawyer, and adviser. In 1966 she defeated Maria Bueno of Brazil to win her first Wimbledon singles championship. By 1975 she had won a record twenty Wimbledon titles: six singles, ten doubles, and four mixed doubles. In 1971, after joining the newly organized Virginia Slims tour, she became the first woman athlete to win $100,000 in a single year. She was named top woman athlete of the year in 1973, and in 1974 she won her fourth U.S. Open title, defeating Australian Evonne Goolagong.

King has been perhaps the single most influential figure in the successful fight for recognition and pay parity for women athletes. She was a founder and president of the Women's Tennis Association, a labor union for players; a founder of two leagues for professional women athletes, including the Women's Professional Softball League; and publisher, with her husband, of *WomenSport*, a magazine that reported the progress of women athletes in a variety of sports. In addition, King and her husband founded a string of tennis camps and shops across the country, and in 1976 created World Team Tennis, a league for professionals. In her role as coach for World Team Tennis, King became the first woman to coach male professional athletes. She is the author of *Tennis to Win* (1970) and an autobiography, *Billie Jean*, written with Kim Chapin and published in 1974.

Billie Jean King was inducted into the Women's Sports Foundation Hall of Fame in 1980 and into the International Tennis Hall of Fame in 1987. She is frequently seen as a TV commentator during tennis tournaments and has continued her involvement with World Team Tennis, hoping to bring more fans to a sport that has already greatly benefited from her participation in it.

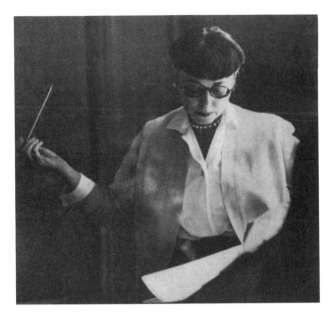

98

Edith Head

1897–1981

Clothes are symbols that provide identification—
especially in a film.

—EDITH HEAD
Edith Head's Hollywood

Edith Head was one of Hollywood's greatest fashion designers, as well as filmland's most famous costumer. She triumphed in a field dominated by men in the 1930s and 1940s, and in 1938 became the first woman to head the design department of a major motion picture studio. In her capacity as Paramount's chief designer, Head was enormously influential in shaping the public's view of Hollywood and its stars.

Edith Head was born Edith Claire Posener in San Bernardino, California, to Max and Anna Posener. When her parents divorced and her mother remarried, Edith took her stepfather's surname of Spare. An excellent student, Edith went on to earn a bachelor's degree from UCLA and a master's degree from Stanford University, where she specialized in languages. She was then hired by the Hollywood School for Girls to teach French, Spanish, and art, a subject she knew little about. To keep pace with her students, she took night courses at the Otis Art Institute and at Chounard, a prestigious Los Angeles art school. During this period, she married Charles Head, a traveling salesman for a metals company. The marriage faltered because of Charles Head's frequent absences from home and his drinking problem. The couple led separate lives but did not divorce until 1938.

In 1923 Edith Head answered a classified ad in the *Los Angeles Times* for a sketch artist at the Famous Players-Lasky (later Paramount) movie studio. Head's specialty was drawing seascapes, and she knew nothing about drawing the human form or costume design, but she desperately needed a summer job. She borrowed costume designs from a number of her Chounard classmates and showed her bulging portfolio to Paramount's chief designer, Howard Greer, who hired her. "It never occurred to me that it was quite dishonest," Head later recalled. "And all the students thought it was fun, too, just like a dare to see if I could get the job." Ever-resourceful, Head quickly learned to sketch costume designs and was soon given her own assignments.

After Howard Greer left Paramount in 1927, Head worked with Travis Banton, who had made a name for himself in 1920 by designing Mary Pickford's gown for her wedding to Douglas Fairbanks. From Banton, she learned the fine art of dressing such "glamour girls" as Carole Lombard, Marlene Dietrich, and Dorothy Lamour, whose Head—designed sarong would become a long-lived fashion trend. Head's first screen credit was for 1933's *She Done Him Wrong*, and the ostrich-feather boa she designed for the film's star, Mae West, became a trademark look for the actress. Head also designed costumes for such classic 1930s films as *Duck Soup, The Lives of a Bengal Lancer, Ruggles of Red Gap,* and *Beau*

Geste. In 1940 Head married Bill Ihnen, a highly acclaimed art director at Paramount. The marriage was a happy one, lasting until Ihnen's death in 1979.

In the 1940s, Head produced costumes for a number of notable films, including *The Lady Eve, Holiday Inn, For Whom the Bell Tolls, Double Indemnity, Going My Way, Hail the Conquering Hero, The Lost Weekend,* and *Notorious.* She also outfitted Bob Hope, Bing Crosby, and Dorothy Lamour for the *Road* comedies. During World War II, Head used her fashion influence with American women to urge them to adapt their wardrobes to "reflect a spirit of sacrifice." To make sacrifice seem desirable, she advised women that cotton and synthetic fabrics, rather than silk and furs, were fashion-forward choices. She also touted her own favorite work uniform, the clean, classic suit, which became a signature style frequently seen in her films. She closed out the decade by winning her first two Academy Awards, for *The Heiress* and *Samson and Delilah.* The following year she won a third Oscar for *All About Eve.*

Head designed some of the most memorable screenwear of her career during the 1950s. The advent of the glamorous New Look in fashion and the wide use of color in moviemaking, plus the competing force of television, resulted in greater lavishness on the big screen. Head, who had become Paramount's sole designer, was free to fully express her creativity. The fashions she designed for such films as *Sunset Boulevard, A Place in the Sun, The Greatest Show on Earth, Roman Holiday, Rear Window, and To Catch a Thief* became almost as famous as the stars who wore them.

Head continued at Paramount until 1967, when she moved to Universal Studios. There she designed costumes for some of the most popular movies of the late 1960s and 1970s, including Butch Cassidy and the Sundance Kid, Airport, and The Sting, for which she netted her eighth and final Oscar. Head's last design effort was for the Steve Martin comedy *Dead Men Don't Wear Plaid,* released the year after her death and dedicated to her.

In addition to her work in films, Head designed privately for friends like Joan Crawford and Elizabeth Taylor, created gowns for the public appearances of stars at Academy Awards ceremonies, and designed Vogue patterns. She also designed uniforms for Pan Am employees and United Nations workers. She was the author of a bestselling how-to book on fashion, *The Dress*

Doctor (1956), and published an autobiography, *Fashion as a Career* (1966).

During her fifty-eight-year career, Head worked on more than a thousand films and received thirty-five Oscar nominations. Her designs were co-opted by retailers and copied by scores of American women. She once said of her profession that "a designer is only as good as the star who wears her clothes." In an industry that has profoundly influenced twentieth-century culture, Head's designs came to represent the essence of Hollywood glamour.

99

Elsie de Wolfe

1865–1950

*A woman's environment will speak for her life, whether
she likes it or not. A house is a dead giveaway.*

—ELSIE DE WOLFE
The House in Good Taste

Given the intellectual weightiness and outstanding achievements of most of the women profiled in this book, Elsie de Wolfe, the first woman interior decorator, may seem a somewhat frivolous choice for inclusion. Yet de Wolfe not only dominated her profession during her career, but her innovations have continued to influence American interior design some forty years after her death.

The daughter of a Canadian doctor, at seventeen Elsie de Wolfe, was presented at the court of Queen Victoria through the influence of her mother's cousin, the Queen's chaplain. She went on to become a London and New York socialite of markedly good taste, and a popular actress, who appeared opposite John Drew and was understudied by his niece, Ethel Barrymore. The always forthright de Wolfe had no illusions about her greatness as an actress, however, once stating "I was no Sarah Bernhardt."

De Wolfe retired from the stage in 1905 and began her decorating career, working out of her New York townhouse on Irving Place. She had rented the townhouse in the early 1890s with her companion, Elizabeth Marbury, a powerful literary agent, who represented such authors as George Bernard Shaw and Oscar Wilde. The most famous lesbian couple in New York, de Wolfe and Marbury established a well-known salon in their house, mixing old money and new talent, from the Astors to the aforementioned Bernhardt. The couple also owned a home in the Paris suburb of Versailles.

De Wolfe's first commission was to decorate the Colony Club, the first elite social club for women in New York, which had been designed by de Wolfe's friend, architect Stanford White. De Wolfe's design featured one of her trademarks, an interior garden room with walls covered in latticework. The job was a notable success, and de Wolfe began receiving commissions to decorate the homes of the wealthy. She once said of her sometimes tasteless clients, whose conspicuous consumption was legendary, "There is often a lot of pig's ear left in these silk purses." She replaced the standard Victorian look of dark walls, hanging lamps, heavy velvet curtains, and potted palms with cream-colored walls, mirrors, table lamps, delicate eighteenth-century antiques, and, especially, brightly-colored chintz sofas, chairs, and curtains. Another de Wolfe innovation was to conceal electrical cords by placing them inside walls. Summing up her philosophy, she said, "I believe in plenty of optimism and white paint."

After she decorated publisher Condé Nast's Park Avenue penthouse, de Wolfe's work was featured in such Nast publications as *Vogue*, *Vanity Fair*, and *House & Garden*. Her taste was soon widely imitated throughout the country. She wrote many magazine articles on interior decorating, several of which were compiled into a bestselling book, *The House in Good Taste*, published in

1913. She also started the trend of wearing short white gloves, a fashion that was not abandoned by women until the watershed years of the 1960s. In 1924 she became the first woman of note to dye her graying hair blue.

In 1926 de Wolfe married Sir Charles Mendl, an attaché at the British embassy in Paris. She then became an international hostess, throwing lavish parties at the couple's homes in Beverly Hills, New York, and Versailles. When she was seventy, she was voted the best-dressed woman in the world by Paris dressmakers. Although confined to a wheelchair because of arthritis and a heart condition, de Wolfe continued to host parties into her eighties. She died at her Versailles home, the Villa Trianon, at the age of eighty-five.

"The Chintz Lady," as de Wolfe became known, was the first designer to bring the interior of American homes out of the nineteenth century into the twentieth. With her ladylike little white gloves and her motto, "Never Complain, Never Explain," embroidered on a silk pillow, de Wolfe was the perfect exemplar of what came to be considered feminine good taste.

100

Lucille Ball

1911–1989

Lucille Ball is one of the greatest performing artists
America has produced and probably the most familiar
by virtue of the reach of television....

Lucy Ricardo is a brilliant creation....[She] rebels
the way most people rebel—without intending to
abandon what is most comfortable about her life....A
blend of incompetence and cunning, she inspires
laughter with her subversion of the conventional and her
exaggerated way with the commonplace. In sum, Lucy
Ricardo defies the imperatives that mold lesser souls—
reason and judgment, propriety and the prudent
course—and proclaims that one dogged individual can
prevail on her own illogical terms.

—KATHLEEN BRADY
Lucille: The Life of Lucille Ball

355

Few would argue that television has become, for better or worse, the most influential medium in history. Thus, it seems fitting to include here the most influential woman in the medium. For nearly twenty-five years, Lucille Ball dominated the tube, progressing from inspired clown to spirited doyenne of television comedy to highly effective production executive.

Lucille Ball was born in Celeron, outside Jamestown, New York, the daughter of Désirée "De De" Hunt, a pianist, and Henry Ball, a telephone lineman, who died when she was three. Lucille showed an early interest in theater and left home at the age of fifteen to pursue an acting career in New York City. She enrolled in John Murray Anderson's drama school, where she was repeatedly told that she had no talent and should return home. Undaunted, Ball tried to get into Broadway chorus lines, but failed. She found work as a waitress and a soda jerk in a Broadway drugstore, and then became a hat model in Hattie Carnegie's salon and a model for commercial photographers. Her break came in 1933, when she won national attention as the Chesterfield Cigarette Girl and was invited to Hollywood to appear as a chorus girl in the Samuel Goldwyn movie *Roman Scandals*.

For the next two years, Ball played unbilled and bit parts in two dozen movies and two-reelers, appearing with such comedians as Leon Errol and the Three Stooges. She then moved to RKO where she began to win featured and leading roles including the part of a cynical young actress in *Stage Door* (1939), a temperamental movie star in *The Affairs of Annabel* (1938), a rejected lover in *Five Came Back* (1939), a gold-digging stripper in *Dance, Girl, Dance* (1940), and a tough-talking secretary-turned-detective in *The Dark Corner* (1943). In 1940 she married Cuban drummer and bandleader Desi Arnaz, whom she had met while the two were filming the college comedy *Too Many Girls*. During the forties she also won favorable reviews for a twenty-two-week tour in the title role of Elmer Rice's play *Dream Girl*.

From 1947 to 1950, Ball played the precursor to her Lucy Ricardo character, the harebrained wife of a Midwestern banker, in the radio comedy *My Favorite Wife*. In 1950 Ball and Arnaz tried to sell a television show entitled *I Love Lucy* to CBS. Network executives were enthusiastic about the concept, but they contended that the public would not accept the Cuban-born Arnaz as

Ball's on-screen husband. To prove the network wrong, Ball and Arnaz embarked on a nationwide tour with a twenty-minute husband-and-wife act, and early in 1951 produced a thirty-minute pilot with $5,000 of their own money. CBS was won over, and *I Love Lucy* made its prime-time debut on October 15, 1951.

An immediate hit, *I Love Lucy* eventually won two hundred awards, including five Emmys. It was one of the first shows to be filmed rather than performed live, making it possible to have high-quality prints of each episode available for endless reruns rather than the poor-quality kinescopes of live shows. The change from kinescope to film resulted in the shift of television production from New York to Hollywood. *I Love Lucy* was also the first show to be filmed before a live audience. Desi Arnaz obtained the rerun rights for the series, which he later sold to CBS. The deal allowed Arnaz and Ball's production company, Desilu, to buy the RKO studio.

Ball and Arnaz's collaboration ended with their divorce in 1960. That same year, Ball starred in the Broadway musical *Wildcat*. In 1962 she bought Arnaz's share of Desilu and headed the production company—one of the largest and most successful in Hollywood—until 1967. With her second husband, Gary Morton, a former nightclub comedian, Ball also founded and headed Lucille Ball Productions. From 1962 to 1974, she continued her reign as the queen of situation comedy in two series, *The Lucy Show* and *Here's Lucy*, which costarred her children, Lucie Arnaz and Desi Arnaz Jr. Her later movies include *The Facts of Life* (1961), *Critic's Choice* (1963), *Yours, Mine, and Ours* (1968), and *Mame* (1973). She played a spunky bag lady in a 1985 television movie, *Stone Pillow*, and attempted a comeback in 1986, playing a grandmother in the short-lived situation comedy, *Life With Lucy*.

Although all three of Lucille Ball's highly rated series are television rerun staples both in the United States and around the world, her first sitcom remains the funniest. With *I Love Lucy*, Ball not only became the first and only actress to raise slapstick comedy to a high art, she helped to firmly establish the sitcom as a major entertainment form for future generations of viewers.

HONORABLE MENTIONS

Berenice Abbott (1898–1991) American photographer

Christina Ama Aidoo (1942–   ) Ghanian author

Maya Angelou (1928–   ) African-American poet, autobiographer

Ella Baker (1903–1986) African-American civil rights leader; voting
    rights campaigner

Clara Barton (1821–1912) Founder, American Red Cross

Boudicca (d. A.D. 61) British queen of the Iceni and warrior

Julia Margaret Cameron (1815–1879) English pioneer photographer

St. Catherine of Siena (1347–1380) Italian mystic and diplomat

Bessie Coleman (1893–1926) First licensed African-American pilot

Dorothy Day (1897–1980) Founder, Catholic Worker Movement

Isadora Duncan (1878–1927) Modern dance pioneer

Mary Baker Eddy (1821–1910) Founder of Christian Science

Eleanor of Aquitaine (1122–1204) French and English queen

Rosalind Franklin (1920–1958) British biologist, researcher of DNA

Anna Freud (1895–1982) Psychoanalyst

Margaret Fuller (1810–1850) American feminist writer

Sophie Germain (1776–1831) French mathematician

Althea Gibson (1927–   ) African-American tennis champion; first
    African American to play in the U.S. Open

Lillian Gish (1896–1993) American movie actress

Lorraine Hansberry (1930–1965) African-American playwright

Hatshepsut (fl. 1400s B.C.) Queen of ancient Egypt

Lillian Hellman (1905–1984) American playwright, social critic

Octavia Hill (1838–1912) British housing reformer; did much to
    establish and preserve London's "green belt" of parks and
    playgrounds

Dorothy Crowfoot Hodgkin (1910–1994) English Nobel chemist

Lois Mailou Jones (1905–   ) African-American Impressionist
    painter

Florence Kelley (1859–1932) American social worker and reformer; director, National Consumer's League

Mary Kingsley (1862–1900) British explorer of Africa

Sofia Kovaleskaia (1850–1891) Russian mathematician

Maggie Kuhn (1905–1995) Founder of the Gray Panthers

Doris Lessing (1919–   ) British novelist

Juliette Gordon Low (1860–1927) Founder of the American Girl Scouts

Lise Meitner (1878–1968) Austrian nuclear physicist

Maria Mitchell (1818–1889) American astronomer

Marianne Moore (1887–1972) American poet

Grandma Moses (1860–1961) American primitivist painter

Lucretia Mott (1793–1880) American women's rights pioneer

Lillian Ngoyi (1911–1980) South African anti-apartheid activist

Emmy Noether (1882–1935) German mathematician, physicist

Christine de Pisan (1364–1430) Italian intellectual, feminist

Sylvia Plath (1932–1963) American poet

Jeanette Rankin (1880–1973) Pacifist, antiwar activist, first woman member of Congress

Sally Ride (1951–   ) First U.S. woman astronaut

Wilma Rudolph (1940–   ) African-American track-and-field athlete, first woman runner to win three gold medals at a single Olympic games

George Sand (1804–1876) French novelist

Augusta Savage (1900–1962) African-American sculptor

Gertrude Stein (1874–1946) American expatriot author

Ellen Stewart (1920–   ) African-American theater producer; founder of La MaMa experimental theater

Lucy Stone (1818–1893) American women's rights campaigner

St. Theresa of Avila (1515–1582) Spanish Carmelite nun and mystic; leader in the counter-reformation

Tz'u Hsi (1835–1908) Dowager empress of China; ended practice of footbinding

Eudora Welty (1909–   ) American author

Phillis Wheatley (1753–1784) African-American poet, slave

Emma Hart Willard (1787–1870) American educator, founder, Troy Female Seminary

ACKNOWLEDGMENTS

I shall be forever grateful to the professionals and friends who provided guidance and much-needed support during the preparation of this book. They are: the women's studies chairs and professors who so graciously responded to my survey; Evelyn Baker; Daniel Dougherty, associate professor of computer science, Wesleyan University; Elizabeth Milroy, assistant professor, art history, and assistant professor, women's studies program, Wesleyan University; Anne Monopoli; John D. Pothier, director of institutional research, Wesleyan University; Edmund A. Rubacha, reference librarian, Olin Library, Wesleyan University; Jack Ryff, the National Science Foundation; Margaret Ryff; Ellen Widmer, professor, Asian languages and literature, and professor, women's studies program, Wesleyan University; and Krishna Winston, chair, German studies, and professor, German studies, Wesleyan University. I am also indebted to my patient and helpful editors Eileen Schlesinger Cotton and James Ellison; my able assistants, Tiffany Holcombe, Seth Levin, and Alyssa Whitehead; and my husband, Daniel Burt.

Photo credits. Library of Congress (for Margaret Sanger and Gabriela Mistral); American Museum of Natural History; Jane Addams Memorial Collection, The University Library, The University of Illinois at Chicago; National Portrait Gallery, Washington, D.C.; National Portrait Gallery, London; *Life*; Schomburg Center for Research in Black Culture; *Mother Jones* magazine (for photo of Mother Jones); Carol Shookoff (for Florence Nightingale); the Peter Deri collection (for Melanie Klein); University of New Mexico; New York Public Library, Picture Collection; *Modern Maturity*; collection of Roget Viollet; Nickolas Muray (for Martha Graham); *New York Times*; David Miklos (for Barbara McClintock); *Newsweek*; UNESCO; Jack Mitchell; Music Division, New York Public Library for the Performing Arts, Aster, Lenox, and Tilden Foundations (for Nadia Boulanger); Association for the Study of Negro Life and History; Anne Frank Foundation; Harmon Foundation; *U.S. News and World Report*; Time Inc.; *Fortune; People*; Richard Strauss, Collection of the Supreme Court of the United States (for Ruth Bader Ginsburg); Dr. T. J. Suen, New Canaan, Conn. (for tomb of Wu Chao); Special Collections, California Polytechnic State University (for Julia Morgan); Metropolitan Opera Guild; and *Vanity Fair*.

360

SELECTED BIBLIOGRAPHY

Jane Addams

Addams, Jane. *Twenty Years at Hull House*. New York: New American Library, 1981.

————. *The Second Twenty Years at Hull House*. New York: Macmillan, 1930.

Marian Anderson

Anderson, Marian. *My Lord, What a Morning*. New York: Viking Press, 1956.

Susan B. Anthony and Elizabeth Cady Stanton

Barry, Kathleen. *Susan B. Anthony: A Biography*. New York: New York University Press, 1988.

Griffith, Elizabeth. *In Her Own Right: The Life of Elizabeth Cady Stanton*. New York: Oxford University Press, 1984.

Diane Arbus

Bosworth, Patricia. *Diane Arbus: A Biography*. New York: Alfred A. Knopf, 1984.

Hannah Arendt

Young-Breuhl, Elisabeth. *Hannah Arendt: For Love of the World*. New Haven and London: Oxford University Press, 1982.

Jane Austen

Halpern, John. *The Life of Jane Austen*. Baltimore: Johns Hopkins University Press, 1984.

Honan, Park. *Jane Austen: Her Life*. New York: St. Martin's Press, 1988.

Lucille Ball

Brady, Kathleen. *Lucille: The Life of Lucille Ball*. New York: Hyperion, 1994.

Simone de Beauvoir

Bair, Deidre. *Simone de Beauvoir. A Biography*. New York: Summit Books, 1990.

Beauvoir, Simone de. *All Said and Done*. New York: G.P. Putnam's Sons, 1974.

————. *Force of Circumstance: The Autobiography of Simone de Beauvoir*. New York: Paragon House, 1992.

Sarah Bernhardt

Gold, Arthur, and Robert Fitzdale. *The Divine Sarah: A Life of Sarah Bernhardt*. New York: Alfred A. Knopf, 1991.

Mary McLeod Bethune

Holt, Rackham. *Mary McLeod Bethune: A Biography*. New York: Doubleday, 1964.

Elizabeth Blackwell

Blackwell, Elizabeth. *Pioneer Work in Opening the Medical Profession to Women: Autobiographical Sketches*. New York: Schocken Books, 1977.

Rosa Bonheur

Stanton, Theodore. *Reminiscences of Rosa Bonheur*. New York: Hacker Art Books, 1976.

Nadia Boulanger

Rosenstiel, Leonie. *Nadia Boulanger. A Life in Music*. New York: W.W. Norton, 1982.

Margaret Bourke-White

Goldberg, Vicki. *Margaret Bourke-White: A Biography*. New York: Harper & Row, 1986.

Charlotte and Emily Brontë

Gordon, Lyndall. *Charlotte Brontë: A Passionate Life*. New York: W.W. Norton, 1995.

Winnifrith, Tom, and Edward Chitham. *Charlotte and Emily Brontë*. London: Macmillan Ltd., 1989.

Gwendolyn Brooks

Kent, George E. *A Life of Gwendolyn Brooks*. Lexington: University Press of Kentucky, 1989.

Maria Callas

Scott, Michael. *Maria Meneghini Callas*. Boston: Northeastern University Press, 1992.

Rachel Carson

Brooks, Paul. *The House of Life: Rachel Carson at Work*. Boston: Houghton-Mifflin, 1973.

Mary Cassatt

Mathews, Nancy Mowll. *Mary Cassatt: A Life*. New York: Villard Books, 1994.

Witzling, Mara Rose. *Mary Cassatt: A Private World*. New York: Universe Books, 1991.

Catherine the Great

Alexander, John T. *Catherine the Great: Life and Legend*. New York: Oxford University Press, 1989.

Troyat, Henri. *Catherine the Great*. New York: E. P. Dutton, 1980.

Hillary Rodham Clinton

Radcliffe, Donnie. *Hillary Rodham Clinton: A First Lady for Our Time*. New York: Warner Books, 1993.

Marie Curie

Curie, Eve. *Madame Curie: A Biography by Eve Curie*. New York: Doubleday, 1938.

Quinn, Susan. *Marie Curie: A Life*. New York: Simon & Schuster, 1995.

Elsie de Wolfe

Campbell, Nina. *Elsie de Wolfe: A Decorative Life*. New York: Clarkson Potter, 1992.

Smith, Jane S. *Elsie de Wolfe: A Life in the High Style*. New York: Atheneum, 1982.

Emily Dickinson

Benfey, Christopher E. G. *Emily Dickinson: Lives of a Poet*. New York: G. Braziller, 1986.

Farr, Judith. *The Passion of Emily Dickinson*. Cambridge: Harvard University Press, 1992.

Dorothea Dix

Wilson, Dorothy Clarke. *Stranger and Traveler: The Story of Dorothea Dix, American Reformer*. Boston: Little, Brown, 1975.

Amelia Earhart

Lovell, Mary S. *The Sound of Wings: The Life of Amelia Earhart*. New York: St. Martin's Press, 1989.

George Eliot

Haight, Gordon S. *George Eliot: A Biography*. New York: Oxford University Press, 1968.

Queen Elizabeth I

Johnson, Paul. *Elizabeth I: A Biography*. New York: Holt, Rinehart and Winston, 1974.

Somerset, Anne. *Elizabeth I*. New York: Alfred A. Knopf, 1991.

Jessie Redmon Fauset

Sylvander, Carolyn Wedin. *Jessie Redmon Fauset: Black American Writer*. Troy, N. Y.: Whitston, 1981.

Anne Frank

Frank, Anne. *The Diary of a Young Girl: A Definitive Edition*. Eds., Otto H. Frank and Mirjam Pressler. New York: Doubleday, 1995.

Betty Friedan

Friedan, Betty. *The Feminine Mystique*. New York: W. W. Norton, 1963.

Indira Gandhi

Gupte, Pranay. *Mother India: A Political Biography of Indira Gandhi*. New York; Scribner's, 1992.

Jayakar, Pupul. *Indira Gandhi. An Intimate Biography*. New York: Pantheon Books, 1992.

Emma Goldman

Goldman, Emma. *Living My Life*. New York: Dover Publications, 1970.

Jane Goodall

Goodall, Jane. *In the Shadow of Man*. Boston: Houghton-Mifflin, 1971.

————. *Through a Window: My Thirty Years With the Chimpanzees*. Boston: Houghton-Mifflin, 1990.

Katharine Graham

Davis, Deborah. *Katharine the Great: Katharine Graham and the Washington Post.* New York: Harcourt, Brace, Jovanovich, 1979.

Felsenthal, Carol. *Power, Privilege, and the Post.* New York: G. P. Putnam's Sons, 1993.

Martha Graham

De Mille, Agnes. *Martha: The Life and Work of Martha Graham.* New York: Random House, 1991.

Sarah and Angelina Grimké

Lerner, Gerda. *The Grimké Sisters From South Carolina: Rebels Against Slavery.* Boston: Houghton-Mifflin, 1967.

Edith Head

Head, Edith, and Paddy Calistro. *Edith Head's Hollywood.* New York: E. P. Dutton, 1983.

Katharine Hepburn

Edwards, Anne. *A Remarkable Woman: A Biography of Katharine Hepburn.* New York: Random House, 1986.

Billie Holiday

Chilton, John. *Billie's Blues: Billie Holiday's Story, 1933–1959.* New York: Stein and Day, 1975.

White, John. *Billie Holiday: Her Life and Times.* New York: Universe Books, 1987.

Karen Horney

Quinn, Susan. *A Mind of Her Own: The Life of Karen Horney.* New York: Summit Books, 1987.

Zora Neale Hurston

Hemenway, Robert E. *Zora Neale Hurston: A Literary Biography.* Urbana: University of Illinois Press, 1977.

Queen Isabella

Liss, Peggy. *Isabella the Queen: Life and Times.* New York: Oxford University Press, 1992.

Joan of Arc

Lucie-Smith, Edward. *Joan of Arc.* London: Penguin Books, 1976.

Mother Jones

Fetherling, Dale. *Mother Jones: The Miner's Angel.* Carbondale and Edwardsville: Southern Illinois University Press, 1974.

Frida Kahlo

Herrera, Hayden. *Frida Kahlo: The Paintings.* New York: Harper Collins, 1991

Helen Keller and Anne Sullivan

Keller, Helen. *The Story of My Life.* New York: Doubleday, 1954.

————. *Teacher: Anne Sullivan Macy. A Tribute by the Foster Child of Her Mind.* New York: Doubleday, 1955.

Lash, Joseph P. *Helen and Teacher. The Story of Helen Keller and Anne Sullivan Macy*. New York: Delacorte Press, 1980.

Melanie Klein

Grosskurth, Phyllis. *Melanie Klein: Her World and Her Work*. New York: Alfred A. Knopf, 1986.

Elisabeth Kübler-Ross

Gill, Derek L. T. *Quest: The Life of Elisabeth Kübler-Ross*. New York: Harper & Row, 1980.

Dorothea Lange

Meltzer, Norman. *Dorothea Lange: A Photographic Life*. New York: Farrar, Strauss & Giroux, 1978.

Rosa Luxemburg

Nettl, J. P. *Rosa Luxemburg*. Abridged ed. New York: Schocken Books, 1989.

The Virgin Mary

Warner, Marina. *Alone of All Her Sex: The Myth and Cult of the Virgin Mary*. New York: Vintage Books, 1983.

Barbara McClintock

Keller, Evelyn Fox. *A Feeling for the Organism*. New York: W. H. Freeman & Co., 1983.

Margaret Mead

Howard, Jane. *Margaret Mead. A Life*. New York: Simon & Schuster, 1984.

Golda Meir

Martin, Ralph G. *Golda: Golda Meir, the Romantic Years*. New York: Scribner's, 1988.

Meir, Golda. *My Life*. New York: G. P. Putnam's Sons, 1975.

Gabriela Mistral

de Vazquez, Margot Arce. *Gabriela Mistral. The Poet and Her Works*. New York: New York University Press, 1964.

Maria Montessori

Kramer, Rita. *Maria Montessori. A Biography*. New York: G. P. Putnam's Sons, 1976.

Louise Nevelson

Lisle, Laurie. *Louise Nevelson: A Passionate Life*. New York: Summit Books, 1990.

Florence Nightingale

Woodham-Smith, Cecil. *Florence Nightingale*. New York: Atheneum, 1983.

Georgia O'Keeffe

O'Keeffe, Georgia. *Georgia O'Keeffe*. New York: Viking Press, 1976.

Emmeline Pankhurst

Mitchell, David J. *The Fighting Pankhursts: A Study in Tenacity*. New York: Macmillan, 1967.

Frances Perkins

Martin, George. *Madam Secretary, Frances Perkins*. Boston: Houghton-Mifflin, 1976.

Mary Pickford

Eyman, Scott. *Mary Pickford. America's Sweeheart*. New York: Donald I. Fine, 1990.

Leni Riefenstahl

Riefenstahl, Leni. *Leni Riefenstahl. A Memoir*. New York: St. Martin's Press, 1993.

Eleanor Roosevelt

Goodwin, Doris Kearns. *No Ordinary Time. Franklin and Eleanor Roosevelt: The Home Front in World War II*. New York: Simon & Schuster, 1994.

Lash, Joseph P. *Eleanor and Franklin*. New York: New American Library, 1973.

————. *Eleanor: The Years Alone*. New York: W. W. Norton, 1972.

Margaret Sanger

Chesler, Ellen. *Woman of Valor. Margaret Sanger and the Birth Control Movement in America*. New York: Simon & Schuster, 1992.

Harriet Beecher Stowe

Hedrick, Joan D. *Harriet Beecher Stowe: A Life*. New York: Oxford University Press, 1994.

Dorothy Thompson

Kurth, Peter. *American Cassandra: The Life of Dorothy Thompson*. Boston: Little, Brown, 1990.

Harriet Tubman

Bradford, Sarah. *Harriet Tubman: The Moses of Her People*. New York: Citadel Press, 1961, 1974.

Queen Victoria

Weintraub, Stanley. *Victoria: An Intimate Biography*. New York: E. P. Dutton, 1987.

Madame C. J. Walker

Bundles, A'Lelia Perry. *Madame C. J. Walker: Entrepreneur*. New York: Chelsea House, 1993.

Ida Wells-Barnett

Thompson, Mildred I. *Ida B. Wells: An Exploratory Study of an American Black Woman, 1893–1930*. New York: Carlson Publishing, 1990.

Wells-Barnett, Ida B. *The Memphis Diary of Ida B. Wells*. Boston: Beacon Press, 1995.

Mary Wollstonecraft

Larch, Jennifer. *Mary Wollstonecraft: The Making of a Radical Feminist*. Great Britain: Berg Publishers, 1990.

Sustein, Emily A. *A Different Face: The Life of Mary Wollstonecraft*. New York: Harper & Row, 1975.

Virginia Woolf

Bell, Quentin. *Virginia Woolf: A Biography*. New York: Harcourt, Brace, Jovanovich, 1972.

Wu Chao
Fitzgerald, C. P. *The Empress Wu*. London: The Cresset Press, 1968.

Babe Didrikson Zaharias
Johnson, William O. *"Whatta-Gal": The Babe Didrikson Story*. Boston: Little, Brown, 1977.

General Reading

Barlow, William. *"Looking Up at Down": The Emergence of Blues Culture*. Philadelphia: Temple University Press, 1989.

Bernstein, Irving. *A Caring Society. The New Deal, the Worker, and the Great Depression: A History of the American Worker, 1933–1941*. Boston: Houghton-Mifflin, 1985.

Lewis, David L. *When Harlem Was in Vogue*. New York: Alfred A. Knopf, 1981.

Palmer, Edward L. *Television and America's Children: A Crisis of Neglect*. New York: Oxford University Press, 1988.

Rubinstein, Charlotte Streifer. *American Women Artists: From Indian Times to the Present*. New York: Avon Books, 1982.

INDEX